FAMILY LAW

IN A
NUTSHELL

THIRD EDITION

By

HARRY D. KRAUSE

Max L. Rowe Professor of Law
University of Illinois

ST. PAUL, MINN.
WEST PUBLISHING CO.
1995

Dedication

Benjamin

Joseph

To

Aiesha

Elizabeth

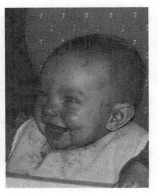

PREFACE

This book presents a thoroughly updated view of the revolution in family law that began in the 1960s. Many new developments and significant refinements of ongoing trends have asked for inclusion. Whole new subjects have sprung up that, a short twenty-five years ago, did not exist in any measurable form. Indeed, the very definition and the boundaries of "family law" have become blurred. Family law now draws from constitutional law, and extends into criminal law, conflict of laws, and the laws of contracts, torts, property, inheritance, even taxation—to name just a few. Moreover, state law no longer provides all the answers, because an important federal presence has made itself felt, legislatively and judicially.

While preserving the completeness of the underlying information, this edition captures and distills highlights of the exciting new decade that has passed since the second edition was published in 1986. Care has been taken to be as comprehensive as is compatible with compactness. Numerous current references to instructive decisions supply detail and provide further references to the reader who wants to pursue matters in more depth and breadth. 93,496 purchasers of the two previous editions have demonstrated the need for and value of this approach.

PREFACE

Law students reviewing course work, lawyers desiring a summary "update" on movement in their field of practice, social workers, marriage counselors, mediators and paralegals involved with family law will find here a comprehensive guide. In addition, mental health professionals and sociologists may want to know more about a subject matter that furnishes the background for so much of their work. Any intelligent reader who has found family law a "closed book" because technical texts are too technical and popular writings too often too inaccurate, will find here an understandable and accurate description of law that not only concerns all of us individually but that is basic to a fuller understanding of our changing society.

My thanks are due to Mary Palumbo, my student-assistant, who patiently and expertly helped with the often less than glamorous tasks of retrieving library materials, proof-reading and producing WESTLAW citations from newspaper clippings, as well as to my secretary, Carrie May, for her always capable and reliable assistance. Eva, my wife and the grandmother of the four dedicatees of this volume, carefully read the galleys and made useful suggestions. Last but certainly not least, I wish to thank colleagues at other institutions who have read previous editions of this book and who have provided helpful comments.

HARRY D. KRAUSE

Champaign, Illinois
July, 1995

OUTLINE

PART III. SPOUSAL RIGHTS AND OBLIGATIONS IN THE ONGOING MARRIAGE

PART IV. CREATION OF THE PARENT AND CHILD RELATIONSHIP

PART VI. TERMINATION OF MARITAL STATUS

Page

OUTLINE

*

TABLE OF CASES

References are to Pages

TABLE OF CASES

XXXI

TABLE OF CASES

TABLE OF CASES

TABLE OF CASES

TABLE OF CASES

TABLE OF CASES

FAMILY LAW

IN A
NUTSHELL

*

PART I

PERSPECTIVES

CHAPTER 1
SOURCES AND APPLICATIONS
OF FAMILY LAW

§ 1.1 Family Law in Modern America

Three unprecedented decades have brought fundamental change to our family life and law. Much of what was presaged in the rhetoric of the 1960's, then rejected by the "silent majority," was assimilated into our culture and laws in the 1970's. The "moral majority" of the 1980's slowed the clock, but the 1990's may seal the doom of the traditional *patriarchal* family that, in one variation or another, made society function throughout history. Revised social conventions and reformed legal structures that allow the indispensable social mission of the family—child rearing—to be fulfilled on the basis of the marital partners' equality in law and fact must be discovered, encouraged, provided.

Let's look at the facts: The Census Bureau reports that, in the years from 1970 to 1993, the percentage of men between 25 and 29 years of age

1

who had never married rose from 19% to 48%, that of women from 10% to 33%. In 1970, 13% of households were headed by single mothers, but by 1993 that statistic had risen to 28%. About one half of single mother families live in poverty, compared with only about 8% of two-parent families. These shifts notwithstanding, American marriage rates remain near record levels. So do the rates of divorce and remarriage. What the statistics do not tell is how greatly the realities of marriage have changed. Today, 60% of married women with children under 6 years of age and 75% of married mothers with children younger than 18 are in the labor force, whereas in 1960, only 19% of married mothers with children under 6 were in the labor force. With the help of modern contraceptive medicine, many potential parents, including married couples, are deciding not to parent children. By 1992, abortion had become the alternative to childbirth in one of four pregnancies. Non-marital births have increased relentlessly, reaching 28% of all births by 1990, and a quarter of all unmarried women become mothers, an increase of 60% in ten years. The family's procreative and child-rearing function is in doubt.

Let's look at the law: In the last 30 years, non-marital children have obtained equal rights. Despite the failure of the federal E.R.A., women have all but accomplished the same. A new emphasis on children's rights all the way up to the U.S. Supreme Court has wreaked havoc with age-encrusted notions of parental prerogatives. Abortion remains legal and is likely to remain so, even while an ever more contentious backlash has led to multiple murders, and federal legislation now limits the right to demonstrate. At the other end of the spectrum, new ways for pregnancy to begin range from artificial insemination and "surrogate motherhood" to *in vitro* fertilization and embryo transplants, and have spawned ethical and legal questions without precedent and, so far, without satisfactory answers.

The treatment in separate property states of marital property on divorce has moved from judicial discretion without rules to detailed rules with some level of predictability of outcome. Joint custody has swept through the courts, but is being rethought. Grandparents have rights to visit their grandchildren, and parents may be punished for refusing access. Domestic violence has the attention of a nation overdosed on O.J. Simpson's trial. Husbands are prosecuted for spousal rape—with many definitional uncertainties—and in a reversal of the "unwritten law" that excused a husband for killing his unfaithful wife, wives have been excused for "terminating" abusive husbands. Real and imagined sex abuse is everywhere.

The Supreme Court emphasizes that marriage is a "fundamental human right", but new personal lifestyles and increasing opportunity for women to have full careers are reducing the importance of that right—even as same-sex partners, still excluded, may soon succeed in their quest for legal marriage. Heterosexual and same-sex cohabitation *without* marriage (still criminal on many states' books as fornication, adultery or sodomy) may produce legally binding partnerships.

Disillusionment with law and lawyers has given rise to a search for non-adversary alternatives. "Mediation" has come to the fore, but it is wishful thinking to conclude that no-fault divorce implies non-adversary settlements. The reality remains that where important rights are at stake there must be rules and those who are trained to interpret the rules. We shall continue to need law and lawyers, even as both strive to become more "user-friendly".

§ 1.2 Sources of Family Law

Family law springs from five sources: *First*, of course, there is the states' comprehensive common, statutory and constitutional law regulating sexual behavior and ordering family relationships. It should be emphasized that there is no family law in a national, unified sense. Instead, more than 50 more or less sovereign jurisdictions have their own say on the subject. *Second*, there is the United States Constitution by means of which, especially in the last two decades, our courts have made unprecedented incursions into family law, often upsetting centuries-old state laws that traditionalists had thought immune to federal challenge. (An important incidental effect of these incursions has been to make the resulting law nationally uniform.) *Third*, there is the vast complex of state and federal social and tax legislation. Providing and withholding benefits on the basis of marital status or dependency, tax law and laws regulating welfare and entitlements indirectly but vitally affect, sometimes govern, many aspects of family behavior. *Fourth*, an increasing volume of federal law and interest, ranging from child support enforcement to interstate custody disputes, has quite specifically injected federal authority into family law. *Fifth*, regulation occurs on the local level, including zoning ordinances that restrict a large proportion of our living space to "one family residential" uses (*Moore*, *Boraas*). Despite all this, it may fairly be said that family law continues to remain primarily in the hands of the states, less perhaps because of the Tenth Amendment and more because of tradition-bound reluctance to enact express federal legislation in this area.

§ 1.3 State Sources

Many basic rules of state family law are accepted generally. On many specific issues, however, the full range of state statutes extends from one logical extreme to the other, and sometimes to illogical extremes. Even within one jurisdiction, the law is not always ascertained easily. Its origin is an uncertain admixture of old English common law tempered with flashes of modern thought through statutes that are directed at selected subjects. In several states, state constitutions have played a role in reshaping family law. For instance, about one-third of state constitutions contain women's equal rights amendments. In addition, some state equal protection clauses or the right of privacy have been construed more broadly than their federal counterparts.

No state has undertaken a comprehensive review of all of its positions on the family and fashioned a comprehensive, modern family code. Since 1892, some help has been provided by the National Conference of Commissioners on Uniform State Laws who, although so far refraining from proposing a uniform national family code, have drafted and proposed uniform acts on numerous family law subjects. Their acts include the "Marriage and Divorce Act" ("UMDA"), the "Parentage Act" that superseded the withdrawn "Paternity Act", the widely enacted "Reciprocal Enforcement of Support Act" ("URESA"), superseded in 1992 by the "Interstate Family Support Act", the "Abortion Act", the "Child Custody Jurisdiction Act", the "Marital Property Act", the "Premarital Agreements Act", the 1994 "Adoption Act" (superseding a withdrawn prior version), the "Probate Code" (revised in 1993 on the issue of marital property rights), the (long withdrawn) "Marriage Evasion Act", the "Disposition of Community Property Rights at Death Act", the "Blood Test Act" and others with incidental effects on family law. In 1995, an "Interstate Visitation Act" was under consideration. While the Commissioners have had some measure of success, they have not reached the stature, nor have they sought the role of a national law reform commission. Regrettably, that role remains unfilled, even in the informal sense of a think tank—in this day of think tanks on so many subjects of much lesser social impact. In the late 1980's, the American Law Institute began to work on its "Principles of the Law of Family Dissolution", not so much a Restatement as a "Prestatement", and a tentative, partial draft on marital property was narrowly approved on the ALI floor in May, 1995.

§ 1.4 Federal Constitution

The infusion into family law of federal constitutional interpretation is a national source that supersedes state regulation and thus tends toward uniformity. The Tenth Amendment holds that "the powers not delegated to the United States by the Constitution, nor prohibited by it to the States, are reserved to the States respectively, or to the people". This had long been thought to put family law under the exclusive jurisdiction of the states. The traditional view was expressed by the late Justice Black: "The power of the States over marriage and divorce is complete except as limited by specific constitutional provisions" (dissenting in *Boddie*), and "the power to make rules to establish, protect and strengthen family life * * * is committed by the Constitution of the United States and the people of Louisiana to the legislature of that State. Absent a specific constitutional guarantee, it is for that legislature, not the life-tenured judges of this Court, to select from among possible laws" (*Labine*).

Justice Black's view is of the past, perhaps because so many state legislatures failed for so long to "select from among possible laws", if Justice Black meant "possible" in terms of a livable, modern family law. Yet Justice Black's conviction still echoes uncertainly in current constitutional adjudication. With Justices Burger, Douglas, Stewart, Blackmun and Powell concurring, Justice Rehnquist said in 1975: "[R]egulation of domestic relations [is] an area that has long been regarded as a virtually exclusive province of the States" (*Sosna*). Dissenting with Justices Burger, White and O'Connor he said in 1982: "[T]he majority invites further federal court intrusion into every facet of state family law. If ever there were an area in which federal courts should heed the admonition of Justice Holmes that 'a page of history is worth a volume of logic,' it is in the area of domestic relations. This area has been left to the States from time immemorial, and not without good reason "(*Santosky*). Justice Powell concurred in *Zablocki* (1978): "I write separately because the majority's rationale sweeps too broadly in an area which traditionally has been subject to pervasive state regulation." Justice Blackmun said in *McCarty* (1981): "This Court repeatedly has recognized that '[t]he whole subject of the domestic relations of husband and wife * * * belongs to the laws of the States and not to the laws of the United States.' * * * Thus, '[s]tate family and family-property law must do major damage' to 'clear and substantial' federal interests before the Supremacy Clause will demand that state law be overridden."

Notwithstanding these pronouncements, the last time the U.S. Supreme Court resisted a serious invitation to enter family law arguably dates back to 1961 (*Poe*). In 1965, the Court actively stepped into the void with its historic decision on the right of family privacy in *Griswold*. The enormous power of the Equal Protection Clause was brought to bear on family law with *Loving* in 1967 and *Levy* in 1968 (§§ 2.1, 11.8). This was soon followed by pronouncements on individual sexual rights in *Eisenstadt* (1972), *Wade* (1973) and many other cases (§ 2.4). While the Due Process Clause had long been in the picture, its important presence was reaffirmed in *Boddie* (1971), *Stanley* (1972), *Little* (1981), *Santosky* (1982) and elsewhere.

By now, great inroads have been made into the states' formerly all but unfettered autonomy by a rapidly growing body of U.S. Supreme Court, state supreme court and lower court decisions that subject state family laws to federal and state constitutions. The federal constitutional provisions do not speak expressly of the family, nor to subjects such as marriage, divorce, illegitimacy, birth control, abortion, adoption, neglect and dependency or termination of parental rights. Concern may be raised about long-term implications for our federal-state structure, but in terms of substantive results achieved, the U.S. Supreme Court's involvement must, in the main, be welcomed. It *was* time for the Court to clarify that the marriage contract does not supersede the Constitution.

Rooted in substantive, ideological differences, the Supreme Court's sharp divisions increasingly are being played out to the tunes of "tradition" and "framers' intent" vs. the logic and worth as precedent of the Court's newer interpretations of the Equal Protection and Due Process Clauses. In 1986 the majority invoked (1) the "ancient roots" of the prohibition on homosexual conduct, (2) the common law when the Bill of Rights was ratified, (3) the fact that most states continued to criminalize sodomy until recently and about one-half still do, as well as (4) "the presumed belief of a majority of the electorate in Georgia that homosexual sodomy is immoral and unacceptable (*Bowers*)." This renewed emphasis on the past, also at play in *Michael H.* (§§ 11.5, 7), seems at odds with landmark civil rights cases that override the fact that, in terms of long tradition, the majority of the electorate in many states had not believed in racial integration (*e.g. Loving*).

§ 1.5 Federal Courts

Relying on century-old U.S. Supreme Court *dictum* (*Barber*) many federal courts have practiced voluntary abstinence from litigation relating to the family, even where all objective grounds for federal jurisdiction (diversity of citizenship, amount in controversy) are fulfilled (*Solomon, Cole, Crouch*). Some had taken a less serious view of this "exception" and argued that "if there is anything at all to the rule that diversity jurisdiction does not extend to domestic relations matters it narrows down to the possibility, though not the certainty, that a diversity court may not grant a divorce." (Dissent in *Solomon*). In 1992, however, the U.S. Supreme

Court reaffirmed and redefined the exception: "We conclude * * * that the domestic relations exception, as articulated by this Court since *Barber*, divests the federal courts of power to issue divorce, alimony, and child custody decrees" (*Ankenbrandt*). On the opposite end of the scale, federal legislation on child support enforcement specifically invests the federal courts with limited jurisdiction.

§ 1.6   Social Legislation

Many welfare laws are indirectly a source of family law and family behavior. After fifty years of pervasive federal interest, welfare laws are largely a national, thus unified, source. As increasing interdependence of the members of our complex society has brought increased dependence on laws and government, a coordinated approach to dealing with social problems related to the family has become a necessity, albeit one that remains inadequately fulfilled.

Legislation dealing both with the family and with social welfare has been the product of intuitive (moral-religious-political) value judgments. Religious tradition has predominated and is currently reasserting itself in the family sphere. In the social welfare arena, the guiding force has been modern liberalism, recast from the "charity"-mold and "altruism," past the "welfare rights" and "entitlements" philosophy of the 1970's, to a variant of not altogether "benign neglect" in the 1980's. After 1994's Republican victory in Congress, Speaker Gingrich's "Contract With America" will bring an end to "welfare as [President Clinton] knew it", to paraphrase the latter's unimplemented 1992 campaign promise. *But whatever the outcome of the sharpening debate, the harsh reality remains that our economy offers scant opportunity to those without adaptability and marketable skills.* Here lies much of the problem.

Of course, many of the social assistance laws under attack are deserving targets. In terms of their effect on the family, important policy issues have been ignored or shrugged off. To illustrate, we need look no further than the negative effect on family stability of the Aid to Families with Dependent Children (AFDC) program that long required fathers to absent themselves in order to make their families eligible for assistance. Other problems are less visible, such as the complex relationships between spousal, parental and relative responsibility laws and Supplemental Security Income (SSI), Medicaid and social security insurance. Further tensions involve laws regarding women's rights, and the continuing discussion regarding public day care in relation to freeing women for work as well as in terms of the quality of child rearing, public provision of means of birth control and abortion, maternity care and parental leave. The enactment in 1993 of P.L. 103–3 providing unpaid, limited parental leave was a small step forward.

Often neglected in the discussion of "social" legislation, the tax laws (income, inheritance and gift taxes and especially the deduction and tax credit framework) are an important factor in that they grant or deny benefits or impose burdens on the basis of marital status or family-related dependency. The 1993 tax reform that substantially increased the "virtue tax" by penalizing marriage of middle- and upper-income working couples represented a step backward (§ 28.8).

Conversely, family law may affect welfare facts. For instance, the enactment of liberal divorce legislation and the concomitant relaxation of economic ties that used to survive divorce have left their mark on dependency statistics, and so has the reversal of centuries-old tradition on abortion. The obvious (though opposite) effect on welfare burdens of either change in the law typically was not an operative or even a conscious factor in the legislator's—judicial or elected—mind.

§ 1.7 Federal Legislation

While this trend may be reversed if the "back to the states" welfare reforms proposed in 1995 become law, federal legislation has injected itself into family law ever more deeply, directly or "by purchase." The Parental Kidnapping Prevention Act of 1980 (§ 18.22) illustrates "direct" involvement. The "purchase" method provides funds to the states on condition that they enact laws that follow federal specifications. Examples are the AFDC program, Medicaid, and the child support enforcement legislation of 1975 (§§ 16.4, 5). On a few occasions, Washington also has made efforts to influence state law, as by having the Department of Health and Human Services draft a "Model Act for Adoption of

Children with Special Needs'' (§ 12.1), or by way of a Congressional Resolution admonishing the states to adopt laws granting visitation rights to grandparents (§ 18.17).

§ 1.8 International Treaties

Numerous multilateral international conventions deal with matters of family law, including, for instance, international adoptions, the recognition of foreign divorces, and the international enforcement of maintenance obligations. In traditional deference to state autonomy in these matters, the United States typically has refrained from acceding to such agreements. One recent exception is the 1980 Hague Convention on Civil Aspects of International Child Abduction. Ratification of that treaty may be explained by the great interest Congress has shown in parental violation of custody orders, which it expressed in the federal Parental Kidnapping Prevention Act of 1980 (§ 18.22). In time, the 1993 Hague Treaty on Transnational Adoptions may become another exception. Also in 1993, the Senate was asked to, but did not, consider the 1989 U.N. Convention on the Rights of the Child (139 Cong. Rec. S. 1640), but in 1995 the U.S. signed the Convention. Ratification is not likely; existing laws would require too many reservations.

§ 1.9 Cultural Diversity and Family Law

This introduction would be incomplete if issue were not taken briefly with the body of writing that perceives unfairness in the unitary "white middle class" family law that applies in the United States to so many diverse cultural and ethnic groups. Indeed, some of the traditional, majoritarian values find only faint acceptance in minority cultures. A striking example is the complex of regulation involving illegitimacy. In the white population, illegitimacy ran to 22 percent of births in 1991 (2.3% in 1960) and may still be perceived not to be the norm. In the black population, however, illegitimacy in 1991 ran to 68 percent of births (21.6% in 1960), and thus can no longer be considered exceptional. In actual impact, however, white illegitimate births constituted 58 percent of the 1991 total, compared with 44 percent in 1970. (Statistical Abstract of the U.S. 1994, 114th ed. 1994, Table 100). When figures speak that loudly, it seems obvious that family law must be adapted to existing social circumstances. And in the specific case of illegitimacy, it was. Traditional law had all but denied a legal relationship between child and father. The pragmatic solution that has been implemented by law provides nonmarital children full legal status vis-à-vis their fathers. Aside from valuable intangibles, identification of the father opens the door to child support enforcement and provides eligibility for numerous social benefits. Only thirty years ago, the prevailing notion was that children of unmarried mothers have no fathers and that society must assume the cost of child support.

Just where is the socially fair balance point between majority law and individual freedom? Arguably, that point lies where special regulation and allowance for individual behavior seriously conflict with the rights of others. The test of self-sufficiency may be a useful criterion. If the behavior in question produces dependency on the taxpayer or does harm to children, the majority culture properly may question its propriety. Beyond that, society is well advised to stay out of the family process (*cf. Moore, Yoder, Wyman, Lassiter, Santosky*).

§ 1.10 Poverty and Family Law

Family law may be criticized more fairly in terms of unequal availability of remedies to the poor and the well-off (*cf. Boddie, Zablocki*). If the required formality of a simple divorce involves hundreds of dollars in legal work, it is effectively priced out of the reach of many low-income couples. One solution would be to provide the needed resources. A more intelligent approach may be to question and rewrite laws that unnecessarily require recourse to expensive procedures. One example is consensual divorce with no significant financial implications and no dispute over child custody. Abortion is another example of unequal availability to well-off and poor. Abortion has been freely available since 1973 (*Wade*), but not "for free". Congressional legislation made Medicaid funds unavailable for abortions, except where the woman's life was at stake. That attitude was criticized not only in terms of the likely dependency of resulting children on public funds, but even more harshly as governmental action that denies poor women the exercise of a choice that the U.S. Supreme Court has firmly protected from *Wade* to *Casey*. The Supreme Court upheld the legislation denying abortions under Medicaid (*Harris*). Numerous state courts, however, have held under state constitutions that abortion is to be available under the Medicaid program, in specified circumstances (*e.g., Committee*).

CHAPTER 2

THE NEW FAMILY AND THE NEW CONSTITUTIONAL LAW

§ 2.1 State Interest vs. Constitutional Rights

The issue of federal vs. state legislative competence in the context of family law has been referred to above in terms of the 10th Amendment's reservation of legislative powers to the states and federal reluctance to pierce that barrier (§§ 1.2–1.6). The 10th Amendment, however, is not the principal framework in which the important state-federal conflict has been played out. Since the 1960's, that conflict has centered on the issue of state regulation vs. individual rights, with the United States Constitution generally taking the side of the individual. A parallel suggests itself to the triumphant march, on the side of the individual, of constitutional law into the field of criminal procedure that began a few years earlier.

Indicating the seriousness with which the State traditionally has professed to regard the contract of marriage, Justice Field said in 1888 that "(m)arriage, as creating the most important relation in life, as having more to do with the morals and civilization of a people than any other institution, has always been subject to the control of the legislature" (*Maynard*).

An early preview of the current conflict between governmental interest in marriage regulation and the individual's constitutionally guaranteed rights involved the U.S. Supreme Court's rejection in 1878 of the Mormons' claim that the First Amendment (freedom of religion) exempted their practice of polygamy from the bigamy law of the Territory of Utah (*Reynolds*, § 3.3).   More recent cases have been more impressed with the importance of the marriage relationship to the individual's "right to happiness."   In 1942, Justice Douglas held that marriage and procreation "involves one of the basic civil rights of man", in a case involving an Oklahoma sterilization statute that was arbitrarily applied to some classes of criminals, but not to others (*Skinner*).   Fifteen years earlier, Justice Holmes had upheld a state sterilization statute applicable to mental defectives with the famous words "three generations of imbeciles are enough".   Holmes exhorted, "we have seen more than once that the public welfare may call upon the best citizens for their lives. It would be strange if it could not call upon those who already sap the strength of the State for these lesser sacrifices * * * in order to prevent our being swamped with incompetence" (*Buck*). This decision has not been overturned, but it does not stand without challenge, doubt and limitation, especially when federal funds and authority enter the field (*Relf*). On the state level, the basic thrust of *Buck* was reaffirmed by the Supreme Courts of North Carolina (*Moore,* 1976) and Nebraska (*Cavitt,* 1968). However, although a number of states retain applicable statutes, compulsory sterilization is not discussed in polite company (*cf. Grady*).

The conflict between State and individual returned to the U.S. Supreme Court in a better case and climate in 1967. Virginia's interest in marriage regulation (specifically, the anti-miscegenation statute) was held to be in direct conflict with the individual's fundamental right to marry. Since the regulation was not based on a rational state interest—Virginia's interest in maintaining white supremacy being entirely unacceptable—the individual's right prevailed (*Loving*). Although the decision heavily relied on the fact that the statute sought to maintain the very sort of discrimination (racial) against which the Fourteenth Amendment was enacted, the case has become an important precedent for situations not involving race. A broad interpretation of the "right to marry" was confirmed in *Zablocki* where the U.S. Supreme Court struck down a Wisconsin statute that denied marriage licenses to persons in default on support obligations and in *Turner*, where prisoners were held to have the right to marry. So far, the Court has not discovered a right to *re*marriage which would be another way of saying that there is a right to divorce (*cf. Boddie, Sosna*).

The last thirty years have seen the enormous power of the "rational relationship test" applied vigorously to outdated family law—with impressive results. In *Loving* and in other cases, ranging from illegitimacy to women's rights, constitutional attack on traditional family law or, as some have perceived it, on marriage and the family itself, has come mainly through the Equal Protection and Due Process Clauses. While specific applications will be discussed in their substantive contexts, a few words here will aid in understanding the operation of the Constitution in specific family law settings.

Not coincidentally, the touchstone of equal protection is "rationality." Family law is subjected to the question whether a given regulation accords with permissible legislative purposes. That, of course, is precisely the question the *legislatures* should ask. If they did, there would be much less call for judicial intervention. Instead, time and again, our judges have subjected traditional family law to the seemingly simple question whether it is "rational." Time and again, it has turned out that a judge and the U.S. Supreme Court did not think so. But blind "rationality" does not always equal good sense, and unmitigated equal protection analysis has not brought unmitigated benefit. In family law, as perhaps nowhere else, the accumulated experience of our culture has a weight and standing of its own. Perhaps, in this intimate sphere, the rational dictates of equal protection should tread over tradition more lightly than elsewhere. It is worth noting that an older U.S. Supreme Court based *Reynolds* on the perception that "polygamy has always been odious". In 1976, the U.S. Supreme Court affirmed a lower court that had supported its holding with a host of biblical citations (*Commonwealth*) and in *Bowers*, Justice White continued this theme in 1986:

"Even if the conduct at issue here is not a fundamental right, respondent asserts that there must be a rational basis for the law and that there is none in this case other than the presumed belief of a majority of the electorate in Georgia that homosexual sodomy is immoral and unacceptable. This is said to be an inadequate rationale to support the law. The law, however, is constantly based on notions of morality, and if all laws representing essentially moral choices are to be invalidated under the Due Process Clause, the courts will be very busy indeed. Even respondent makes no such claim, but insists that majority sentiments about the morality of homosexuality should be declared inadequate. We do not agree, and are unpersuaded that the sodomy laws of some 25 States should be invalidated on this basis."

In 1989, Justice Scalia elaborated in *Michael H.*: "What counts is whether the States in fact award substantive parental rights to the natural father of a child conceived within and born into an extant marital union that wishes to embrace the child. We are not aware of a single case, old or new, that has done so. This is not the stuff of which fundamental rights qualifying as liberty interests are made."

With all appropriate respect for the weight of tradition and history, is it unfair to consider here that prior to *Brown v. Board of Education* there was not "a single case old or new" that had done what *Brown* did, which was to discard *Plessy v. Ferguson's* "separate but equal" doctrine and racially integrate our schools?

§ 2.2   Equal Protection

Without pretending to be entirely accurate in this short space, the Equal Protection Clause of the Fourteenth Amendment (which simply states that "no state shall * * * deny to any person within its jurisdiction the equal protection of the laws") requires that legislation must operate equally upon all members of a group that is defined reasonably and in terms of a proper legislative purpose. The Clause thus does not forbid "unequal laws" and does not require every law to be equally applicable to all individuals. Of necessity, classification must be permitted; otherwise there could be no meaningful legislation. But a law does *not* provide equal protection if it applies only to part of a larger group that is similarly situated in relation to the purpose of the legislation. Such a law is "under-inclusive." If the criteria defining the covered group are such that individuals who are *not* similarly situated, are brought within this group, again tested in terms of the purpose of the legislation, the law fails the equal protection test because it is "over-inclusive." The inclusiveness test thus simply consists of a comparison of the group that is properly the object of the statutory concern with the group that is actually covered by the statute's reach. Both the over- and the under-inclusiveness of a group may be illustrated by *Skinner* which involved the statutory classification of habitual, hereditary criminals for purposes of sterilization. The classification was held under-inclusive in that it failed to include, along with habitual robbers, other offenders of "intrinsically the same quality," such as embezzlers. At the same time, the classification was over-inclusive because not all habitual robbers are hereditary criminals, quite aside from the question whether there is such a thing as hereditary criminality. A graphic example of a group once thought well-defined is furnished by *Plessy,* in which the plaintiff, a person of seven-eighths white descent, was told that he had no right to be treated as a white citizen if state law classified him as Black. The statute met the constitutional test because it applied to him just as it applied to other Blacks, and such an application was in direct furtherance of the purpose of the statute—racial segregation.

The Equal Protection Clause did not remain limited to this mechanical function, and the *Plessy* Court's deference to the statutory purpose has been overcome. Modern courts have realized that the purpose of the statute may itself be in violation of the Equal Protection Clause. Viewed in this light, it may be said that we ask not only whether the classification includes all who are situated similarly, but also whether the purpose of the grouping is proper. A statute which segregates Blacks passes the "inclusion" test if it applies equally to all Blacks, but fails the "purpose test," since there is no reason for classifying Blacks and Whites in separate groups, other than the improper reason of maintaining in an unequal position two groups that *for all rational purposes are situated similarly.* Likewise, since men and women are "situated similarly" for many (all?) rational purposes, it is not necessarily enough that legislation involving women applies equally to all women (§ 10.1). And to show that legislation discriminating against illegitimate children applies equally to all illegitimates, regardless of color, nationality or sex, does not prove the validity of such legislation (§ 11.8). The question thus becomes whether a superficially fully inclusive classification, such as race, sex or illegitimacy, actually is under- or over-inclusive when tested against *appropriate* statutory purposes, and the inquiry must determine whether the criterion in question may be used as the basis for a legislative classification. To do that, legislative purposes of individual laws must be clearly defined and rationally evaluated. Long ago, Justice Van Devanter stated the Supreme Court's traditional view concerning this process:

"The rules by which this contention must be tested, as is shown by repeated decisions of this court, are these: (1) The equal protection clause of the Fourteenth Amendment does not take from the State the power to classify in the adoption of police laws, but admits of the exercise of a wide scope of discretion in that regard, and avoids

what is done only when it is without any reasonable basis and therefore is purely arbitrary. (2) A
classification having some reasonable basis does
not offend against the clause merely because it is
not made with mathematical nicety or because in
practice it results in some inequality. (3) When
the classification in such a law is called in question, if any state of facts reasonably can be conceived that would sustain it, the existence of that
state of facts at the time the law was enacted
must be assumed. (4) One who assails the classification in such a law must carry the burden of
showing that it does not rest upon any reasonable
basis, but is essentially arbitrary" (*Lindsley*).

Justice Van Devanter expressed the Court's reluctance to interfere with state law where the Equal
Protection Clause is invoked to protect *economic*
interests. While this reluctance has been likened to
a presumption of constitutionality, this presumption has been said to be reversed where the "basic
civil rights of man" are at issue. When *fundamental rights* are involved, even a rational relationship
between the regulation and a permissible legislative
purpose may not suffice to uphold the regulation.
Instead, the regulation will stand only if it is "necessary to promote a *compelling* governmental interest" (*Shapiro*). In *Harper,* Justice Douglas said:

"In determining what lines are unconstitutionally
discriminatory, we have never been confined to
historic notions of equality, any more than we
have restricted due process to a fixed catalogue of
what was at a given time deemed to be the limits

of fundamental rights.   * * * Notions of what constitutes equal treatment for purposes of the Equal Protection Clause *do* change.   * * * We have long been mindful that where fundamental rights and liberties are asserted under the Equal Protection Clause, classifications which might invade or restrain them must be closely scrutinized and carefully confined.''

This "two-tiered" standard of constitutional inquiry was summarized in *Norton,* citing to *San Antonio*:

"The Supreme Court has emphasized two distinct standards for testing claims of denial of equal protection.   To determine which test applies, our initial inquiry is whether the statute '[1] operates to the disadvantage of some suspect class or impinges upon a fundamental right explicitly or implicitly protected by the Constitution, thereby requiring strict judicial scrutiny.   * * * If not, [2] the scheme must still be examined to determine whether it rationally furthers some legitimate, articulated state purpose and therefore does not constitute an invidious discrimination in violation of the Equal Protection Clause of the Fourteenth Amendment.'   There is little doubt that this once-settled differentiation is currently being critically reexamined * * * for symptoms of * * * giving way * * * 'to a more graduated sliding-scale test.' "

In the late 1970's, the Court's abandonment of the two-level standard of review became explicit. To illustrate, in connection with issues involving women's equality, the requirement of a "substantial relationship to an important governmental objective" became the coin of the realm (*cf. Craig*). But this did not herald the development of a "three-tiered" standard of review. The graphic metaphor of the "realm of less than strictest scrutiny" that nevertheless "is not a toothless one", was launched to govern illegitimacy cases (*Trimble*). Elsewhere, this was paraphrased as requiring "a close and substantial relationship to a permissible governmental interest" (Justice Marshall, dissenting in *Boles*). In short, the strictness of the scrutiny is directly related to the importance of interests at stake.

The Fourteenth Amendment says "no *State* shall * * * deny * * * ", and usually there is no difficulty in establishing "state action" as a source of the discrimination. Typically, the complaint goes against legislation or judicial or other official *state* action. With respect to *federal* legislation, another bridge must be crossed before the equal protection rationale may be applied because the Fifth Amendment does not express a requirement of equal protection. However, the judicial evidence is ample that, with respect to "Equal Protection," the Fifth Amendment is to federal legislation what the Fourteenth Amendment is to state action.

Two options arise when a discriminatory law is held to violate equal protection: The coverage of the law may be extended to the group discriminated against, or the advantageous treatment may be taken away from the favored group. The U.S.

Supreme Court explains: "We are left with the question whether the defect should be cured by extending the presumption of dependence to widowers or by eliminating it for widows. Because state legislation is at issue, and because a remedial outcome consonant with the state legislature's overall purpose is preferable, we believe that state judges are better positioned to choose an appropriate method of remedying the constitutional violation" (*Wengler*).

§ 2.3   Due Process

The line between Equal Protection and substantive Due Process analysis often seems blurred. We may take some comfort in the fact that U.S. Supreme Court justices sometimes have similar difficulty. One instructive illustration is Justice Marshall's majority opinion in *Zablocki*, when compared with Justice Stewart's concurrence in the same case. By contrast, the distinction between substantive and procedural Due Process typically is quite clear:

"The Due Process Clause of the Fifth Amendment provides that 'No person shall * * * be deprived of life, liberty, or property, without due process of law * * *!' This Court has held that the Due Process Clause protects individuals against two types of government action. So-called 'substantive due process' prevents the government from engaging in conduct that 'shocks the conscience,' or interferes with rights 'implicit in the concept of ordered liberty.' When government action depriving a person of life, liberty, or property survives substantive due process scrutiny, it must still be implemented in a fair manner. This requirement has traditionally been referred to as 'procedural' due process" (*Salerno*).

§ 2.4 The Privacy Doctrine

Equal protection and substantive due process were the main routes of constitutional attack on outdated family law. Another major infusion of constitutional doctrine into the family sphere began with *Griswold* in 1965. In that historic case, Justice Douglas invoked the "emanations" and "penumbras" of the 1st, 3rd, 4th, 5th, 9th, and 14th Amendments to construct a right of marital privacy to protect a married couple's right to use birth control advice and devices against a Connecticut statute which made the use of such devices a criminal offense. As lyrically expressed by Justice Dougles, the right recognized in *Griswold* seemed clearly based in the marital relationship: "We deal with a right of privacy older than the Bill of Rights— older than our political parties, older than our school system. Marriage is a coming together for better or for worse, hopefully enduring, and intimate to the degree of being sacred. It is an association that promotes a way of life, not causes; a harmony in living, not political faiths; a bilateral loyalty, not commercial or social projects. Yet it is an association for as noble a purpose as any involved in our prior decisions." While the Court had previously stressed the importance and constitutional dimensions of marriage and the family, it had not "discovered" so basic a right (*e.g., Maynard, Pierce, Meyer*).

In 1972, a Supreme Court case involving *unmarried* persons and their right of access to birth control, retreated from this family orientation: "It is true that in *Griswold* the right of privacy in question inhered in the marital relationship. Yet the marital couple is not an independent entity with a mind and heart of its own, but an association of two individuals each with a separate intellectual and emotional make-up. If the right of privacy means anything, it is the right of the individual, married or single, to be free from unwarranted governmental intrusion into matters so fundamentally affecting a person as the decision whether to bear or beget a child" (*Eisenstadt*). A Federal District Court has applied *Eisenstadt* to strike down a zoning ordinance that prohibited two unmarried persons from living together (*O'Grady, cf. French, Norman, Donahue*). Previously, the Supreme Court had upheld a zoning ordinance that forbade a "commune" from establishing itself in a residential area, but that ordinance did not preclude *two* unmarried persons from living together (*Boraas*).

Since then, the long chain of abortion cases (*Wade* to *Casey*) was decided. Numerous decisions have excluded husbands of pregnant wives and in most circumstances the parents of pregnant minors from the abortion decision (*e.g. Danforth, Belotti I and II, Matheson, Planned Parenthood of Rhode Island, Casey, Akron I and II, Hodgson*). Clearly,

the Court considers that it is dealing with the
woman's *individual* sexual privacy, rather than
with any right inherent in marriage or family association or parentage. Other cases that might (but
need not) be read as de-emphasizing the relevance
of marriage in constitutional terms are many of the
nearly three dozen illegitimacy cases that the U.S.
Supreme Court has decided since 1968 (§ 11.8),
even if the Court did proclaim in *Lehr* (and *Michael
H.* may be read to the same effect) that, "[t]he
institution of marriage has played a critical role
both in defining the legal entitlements of family
members and in developing the decentralized structure of our democratic society. In recognition of
that role, and as part of their general overarching
concern for serving the best interests of children,
state laws almost universally express an appropriate
preference for the formal family".

The issue of whether, *constitutionally,* there is a
distinction between married and unmarried individuals may also be pursued by asking whether law
criminalizing fornication and adultery remain constitutional. Before a more conservative U.S. Supreme Court upheld the constitutionality of criminalizing homosexual conduct in *Bowers* (§ 3.2), a
Federal District Court opined that a "statute criminalizing lewd and lascivious [heterosexual] cohabitation between persons *not* married to each other
cannot withstand constitutional scrutiny" (*Duling*).
At the state level, New Jersey's Supreme Court
struck down a criminal prosecution for fornication
on constitutional privacy grounds (*Saunders*).

Even adultery was suggested to be a private choice protected by the Constitution (Manderino, J., concurring in *Fadgen*) and, as a crime, prostitution seemed in jeopardy (*In re P., rev'd.* on appeal). The marital/nonmarital distinction has prevented prosecution of a married couple for sodomy or other consensual sexual activity carried on in the privacy of their home (*Cotner, cf. Bateman*), but the marital right to privacy is waived where a third party or a camera is present (*Lovisi*). On a more abstract level, the distinction in federal income tax treatment between married and unmarried taxpayers has been upheld. In the factual constellations of *Barter, Boyter*, and *Druker* this was to the *dis*advantage of *married* filers, but in *Jansen* it was to their advantage. Today, the conclusion may safely be reached that *Eisenstadt* will *not*—as was originally feared by some—go forth to destroy marriage as a legal status conferring special rights, privileges and responsibilities. This does not mean, of course, that other causes will not accomplish that, and perhaps quite soon.

§ 2.5 Variations on the Theme of Marriage

On the positive side, *Eisenstadt* should have been seen as an invitation to rethink our inherited and all too long unquestioned social goals and values in this sensitive area. Instead of questioning the continued validity of distinguishing between married and unmarried persons, the time has come to provide legal distinctions between different types of marriages that serve different purposes. Modern marriage has moved from the unitary concept that

it was even a generation ago when (most) people got
married, when children were considered a natural
corollary, indeed the purpose of marriage, when
there was almost no divorce, and when most women
had neither the opportunity nor the inclination to
work outside the home. Various ideas that would
create optional forms of marriage have been discussed for years. Proposals have ranged from trial
marriage which may be transformed into a full-
fledged marriage after the expiration of a certain
period of time or after the birth of a child, to a
three year renewable contract option that was the
subject of a proposal in the Maryland legislature.
Premarital contracts, defining the expectations and
respective rights and duties of specific spouses are
one route to the end of custom tailoring marriage
(Ch. 7). In a number of states cohabitation arrangements have serious financial consequences
and offer another alternative to the uniformity of
marriage (Ch. 6).

Legislation would be the better and more secure
route. In terms of formalities, ease of entry and
exit, as well as legal consequences during and after,
the following classifications should be differentiated: (1) Pre-child marriage in which young people
pursue their individual careers and set up housekeeping together which then may develop into, (2)
marriage with minor children in which one spouse
takes on primary responsibility for the raising of
the children, thereby sacrificing earnings and career
prospects, and the other is freed to build a career,
(3) post-child marriage where one partner has sacri-

ficed earnings and career to raise children and now has little property and faces limited employment prospects, (4) marriage without children, where both partners pursue their own careers, (5) marriage of elderly partners for financial convenience or social companionship, (6) "multiple" marriage (serial polygamy), of persons who have continuing legal, financial and social ties to prior partners and children.   Precisely what groupings are to be distinguished may not be as clear as the conclusion that the State cannot—reasonably or perhaps even constitutionally—justify dealing with these fundamentally different relationships as though they were one—the role-divided, procreative marriage of history.

This legislative task exceeds even the Supreme Court's legislative ambitions and, when pressed, the Court has favored interpreting the Constitution as concerned with *individual* rights.   We do not often see the Court balancing the social interest in the family against individual rights, nor even against that of other individuals intimately interested in the marriage relationship, such as the spouse or children (*cf. Danforth, Casey, Hodgson*), if they are not formally before the Court (*Yoder, Lassiter, Santosky*).   Interestingly, the Court did extend due process protection to the *extended* family—a grandmother and her grandchildren—in *Moore,* when it struck down a zoning regulation that limited occupancy of residences to immediate, nuclear families.

The diversity of (and confusion in) this new wealth of constitutional interpretation defies an attempt to define a consistent "constitutional family law." Three decades after *Griswold, Loving* and *Levy,* it remains too often unpredictable what constitutional constraints apply. Hair splitting examples are the many cases attempting to define permissible parental involvement with their minor child's abortion (*Danforth, Belotti I and II, Matheson, Akron II, Hodgson*), and the nearly three dozen cases sowing unnecessary confusion around the basically accepted proposition that illegitimate children may not be subject to discrimination (§ 11.8). The problem has been aggravated by the U.S. Supreme Court's changing personnel and resultant changes in policy. In the 1980's, several decisions and dissents seemed to signal a retreat from the "soaring" sixties and seventies (*e.g., Michael H., Bowers*). The premature disclosure of Justice Marshall's papers showed how close the right to abortion came to being severely restricted. Considerable credit for the confusing state of affairs remains due to the Court's fractious tendency to write overlong, multiple opinions rather than to compromise on one or at most two positions per case for the sake of the legal order. Dissents that point to a future in the tradition of Holmes' dissents should replace the many dissents that now fight rearguard actions.

§ 2.6 Legitimate State Interests in the Family

Sole reliance on individual rights threatens the social role of the family. In the absence of effective alternatives, the family must stand as more than the sum of its constituent parts. The conclusion that the Constitution does not affirmatively protect the family does not compel the conclusion that a state may not do so, or that the U.S. Constitution should not be interpreted to respect the state's legislated will if it has been expressed in reasonable legislation.

What is reasonable? Even in this sometimes more reckless than brave new world, important social functions are most effectively fulfilled by marriage and the family, consistently with modern pragmatism as well as our diverse culture, our political philosophy and universal human needs. There is ample room for argument about details, but the following social functions are obvious: Marriage and the family provide for (1) procreation in associationally stable and economically secure circumstances; (2) autonomous socialization of children in their early years, shared later by the schools and sometimes by day care; (3) rudimentary "social security," *i.e. mutual* (husband and wife, parents and children) economic insurance against economic adversity, relieving the taxpayers of potentially substantial economic responsibilities which they would have to assume in an environment in which man-woman pairings are impermanent, less partner-centered and more oriented toward "individual happiness"; (4) economic security and long run assurance that permit role division in terms of career and child raising without threat of ultimate destitution for the "at-home-partner" before or after the job is

done; (5) the "production" and raising of children
as guarantors of (a) the social security system, as
well as (b) the economic security of their own parents in old age, thus relieving society at large of
considerable risk; (6) provision of an efficient and
orderly setting for sexual activity, "efficient" in the
sense of regular availability without intensive ener-
gy and time consuming "wooing efforts," and "orderly" through permanent, publicized pairings, thus
signaling married persons to be at least presumptively unavailable and avoiding the disruptive potential of a permanent "open season"—disruptive
in terms of the other functions of marriage, as well
as the terms of efficient functioning at other levels
of economic and social activity; (7) "posthoney-
moon" companionship and mutual psychological
support in times of individual stress—which may
fulfill a more basic and quite different human need
than does the time and energy-consuming romantic
courtship likely to have to be maintained as the
essential glue of looser associations.

Today, marriage and the family are failing on
many of these "social assignments." One illustration is our liberal new divorce law produced by, as
well as producing, ever increasing social acceptance
of divorce. In rather a short time, society not only
has come to permit divorce, but divorce is seen as
the appropriate remedy when "the going gets
tough," when economic or other conditions of marriage turn "worse" instead of "better," or when a
new romantic attachment appears on the scene
that, not long ago, would have rated a short or even

a protracted affair, but not the basic shift in associ-
ational and economic loyalties and responsibilities
that is imposed by divorce. Other conditions also
have changed. Social welfare provisions and equal
job opportunities for women have reduced the importance of the "economic insurance" functions;
the cohabitation option raises doubt about the
whole idea of interpersonal associations with fixed
or any legal consequences—and so forth. Even
where the nuclear family still functions in terms of
its traditional role, it may be that it functions
inefficiently. There may be inefficiency in terms of
cost to its members (unhappy spouses, neurotic
children) as well as in the sense that the same
functions might be performed more efficiently and
effectively by other arrangements. The extreme
alternative, of course, involves communal child-
rearing at government expense, full equality and a
concomitant obligation in terms of economic self-
sufficiency for women, full social insurance for
health and adversity, including economic provision
for old age, plus psychiatric care to cope with loneli-
ness, although the latter may cost no more than
what is now expended on coping with togetherness.

Nearing the millennium (at least chronologically),
America does not seem ready for a broad, pragmatic
new view of marriage and the family. Less ready,
in any event, than it may have seemed in the
1960's, the 1970's and even the 1980's. Throughout the world, there is doubt about collectivism and
increased reaffirmation of individualism and indi-

vidual responsibilities. Looking forward, we must adapt the legal concept of marriage and family not only to the decline of the "welfare state," but also to the diversity of lifestyles that are lived and widely accepted. The traditional, unitary legal ramifications of marriage have not kept pace.

PART II

CREATION OF THE MARRIAGE RELATIONSHIP

CHAPTER 3
MARRIAGE REGULATION: SUBSTANTIVE REQUIREMENTS

§ 3.1 Introduction

With the injection of constitutional law into family law, traditional marriage regulation became subject to question. The states were forced to take a careful look at the rationality of their laws. Not all judges enjoyed the task, as expressed uniquely by Justice Henriod of Utah's Supreme Court in 1973:

"When and if the Supreme Court of the United States says the Fourteenth Amendment guarantees an unrestricted right for two persons of any character or status to marry, the 50 states to take it lying down simply because citizens or resident aliens or felons, or syphilitics, etc. profess to have unlimited civil rights, and that a felon has the same constitutional right to marry, and perhaps become a behind-bars father without any semblance of parental control, which also would deny

to the states a right to prevent a couple of homo-
sexuals, for example, from marrying, or condone
the switch of wives by swingers, this country then
will have switched to legalized indiscriminate sex
proclivities with a consequent rising incidence of
disease, poverty, and indolence, but worse, to
subject unwary citizens to the whim and caprice
of the federal establishment, not the states"
(*Goalen*).

Justice Henriod's outburst notwithstanding, the
U.S. Supreme Court has since held that prisoners
have a constitutional right to marry (*Turner*), a
prisoner has sued to allow him to provide sperm to
inseminate his wife artificially (N.Y. Times,
9/20/87), same-sex partners may become eligible to
marry in Hawaii (*Baehr*), and herpes and AIDS
have become epidemic.

The validity of State regulation of marriage depends on a balancing of interests. The individual's
interest in marrying the chosen partner is measured against possible State interests in regulation.
Spurred on by current social trends, reflected in
constitutional interpretation, the legislative and judicial balance has tipped in favor of "deregulation."
It also should be noted that due to the early preference of Church and State for marriage (even a
"bad" one) over illicit sexual activity and illegitimacy, traditional regulation of marriage was quite
lenient. As a practical matter, enforcement of marriage regulation has been so lax that it rarely has
stifled individual freedom of choice. Moreover, to
the extent a particular prohibition is not universal

throughout the United States, it often may be circumvented by a sojourn to a more hospitable jurisdiction (§ 5.6).

In evaluating this controversy, it is important to remember that most of our marriage regulation derives from a time in which unmarried cohabitation was illegal, and marriage was indissoluble by law or nearly so by social custom. Moreover, the procreation of children was an all but uncontrollable and almost universally desired incident and, indeed, the principal purpose of marriage. None of these conditions obtains today. This invites scrutiny of traditional regulation of marriage.

While *prohibitory* marriage regulation is dwindling, the states might do more to help the marrying public in the area of *advisory* regulation. Regrettably, education for marriage in school covers primarily physical aspects. Frightening aspects of "sex" are graphically taught in required AIDS curricula, even to grade school children. Condoms are widely distributed by schools. The equally important, although more complex and perhaps less "teachable" psychological, social, legal and financial dimensions of the sexual and marital relationship should receive more attention and could point toward greater marriage stability and enjoyment. Similar services for adults need attention and encouragement.

§ 3.2 Heterosexual Marriage

Publicity has gone to cases that have unsuccessfully challenged the most basic regulation of tradi-

tional marriage, requiring that marriage be between
members of opposite sexes. (Typically that requirement is not even expressed in the statutes, but
implied from the traditional and dictionary meaning
of "marriage"). Aside from seeking the social approval implicit in marriage, same-sex couples have
sought the right to file joint income tax returns, to
obtain marriage-related veteran's or social welfare
benefits and to adopt children, along with more
basic legal incidents of marriage, such as the right
to inherit and, yes, divorce. A nuance is added by
litigation involving "transsexuals" who have been
held unable to contract marriage before a sex
change operation was performed (*Anonymous*), but
whose marriage has been held valid if contracted
after the operation (*M. T.*). Same-sex couples have
so far failed to win their broad argument that the
"fundamental right to marry" expressed in *Zablocki* and *Loving* extends to the relationships they
contemplate (*e.g., Baker*). Nor may same-sex partners be divorced, based on a purported common law
marriage (*DeSanto*). In 1993, Hawaii's Supreme
Court asked a trial court to determine what, if any,
compelling state interests stand in the way of same-
sex marriage (*Baehr I, II*). In response, Hawaii's
legislators reaffirmed their original and continuing
intent to have the marriage laws apply only to
male-female couples and suggested that any change
must come from the legislature or a constitutional
convention. Nevertheless, the legislature set up a
commission to study whether and what legal recognition might be extended to same-sex partners.

More movement in the direction of recognizing same-sex unions in some legal respects is on the way, as increasing numbers of local governments and courts, corporate America, universities and even states recognize same-sex unions by providing specific legal benefits that resemble those provided for heterosexual unions (§ 6.3).

The fact is—the *law* is—that homosexual *conduct* remains a crime in many jurisdictions. In 1986 the U.S. Supreme Court affirmed a Georgia sodomy conviction involving consenting male adults (*Bowers*, § 2.1). At that time such statutes remained in effect in 24 states. Prior to *Bowers*, confusion in the lower state and federal courts as well as in state supreme courts had reigned regarding the constitutionality of criminalizing homosexual conduct. The uncertainty was the result of (1) the U.S. Supreme Court's affirmance of a Virginia sodomy conviction in 1976 (*Commonwealth*); (2) the denial in 1981 of review of a decision by New York's highest court that, relying on *Griswold*, *Eisenstadt*, *Wade* and *Stanley v. Georgia*, had held essentially the opposite of *Commonwealth*, *i.e.*, that the criminalization of consensual sodomy is indeed "violative of rights protected by the United States Constitution" (*Onofre*); (3) the refusal in 1984 to decide whether the right to privacy extends to homosexual solicitation (*Uplinger*—previously accepted for review and argued), and (4) affirmation in 1985 by an equally (4:4) divided Court of the right of public school teachers to advocate homosexuality (*National Gay Task Force*). Since *Bowers*, a number of states have reconsidered these issues reaching different results. In 1992, the Kentucky Supreme Court struck down the state's sodomy law (*Wasson*), D.C. repealed its sodomy statute, but the Texas Supreme Court let stand the state's prohibition of homosexual conduct in a civil case (*Morales*).

Where and as long as homosexual conduct remains criminal, recognition of same-sex marriage seems precluded in any event, but where (and when) it is *not* criminalized, it does not follow that same-sex marriage would or must be allowed. Even where a state had enacted an E.R.A., same-sex marriage was held not to be a necessary corollary (*Singer*).

The root of the difficulty may be that we adhere too tightly to an outdated definition of marriage. Originally, marriage in practically all cases was concerned with reproduction, and it legalized sexual activity that was otherwise punishable. The social purpose was to provide an orderly setting for child rearing and economic security to allow marital role division. Today, of course, a legal "license" is no longer needed for sexual activity. Fornication, adultery and even homosexuality statutes have given way or are not enforced, *Bowers* notwithstanding. Many modern marriages bypass both child rearing and role division. Thought processes triggered by cases such as *Baehr* perhaps should move us toward a more restrictive redefinition of "marriage," that makes special legal privileges and protections available only where it makes sense to give such an advantage, to parents, children, and arguably to career-forsaking, child-rearing, role-dividing spouses.

§ 3.3 Monogamous Marriage

The Mormons' claim that the First Amendment (freedom of religion) exempted their practice of polygamy from the bigamy law of the Territory of Utah provided an early preview of the current conflict between governmental interest in marriage regulation and the individual's constitutionally guaranteed rights. The U.S. Supreme Court held in 1878 that society's interest in regulating *action* superseded the Mormons' religious rights, leaving them with the consolation that they might believe in, but not practice polygamy (*Reynolds*). Although the Mormon Church banned polygamy in 1890, pockets of resistance remain in Utah, Arizona, Idaho, Nevada and Montana to this day. In 1983, Royston Potter (a policeman with two wives) initiated a renewed constitutional challenge to Utah's law, asserting polygamy is "necessary as far as theology goes" (N.Y. Times, 9/12/83). Potter was dismissed from his job, excommunicated by the Mormon Church, and the city attorney said "he's a felon." Bigamy charges, however, were not brought, and Utah's Deputy Attorney General said: "We've never asserted that polygamy is a demonstrable moral evil. Some of Utah's leading senior citizens are children of polygamists" (N.Y. Times, 4/29/84). His suit was dismissed by the federal district court and the Tenth Circuit Court of Appeals affirmed: "Monogamy is inextricably woven into the fabric of our society. It is the bedrock upon which our culture is built. In light of these fundamental values, the State is justified, by a compelling interest, in upholding and enforcing its ban on plural marriage to protect the monogamous marriage relationship" (*Potter*).

In 1991, the Utah Supreme Court ruled that polygamy, while still illegal, does not make a family ineligible for adoption (*Fischer*). And Elizabeth Joseph, a lawyer and one of nine wives of the mayor of Bigwater, Utah, opined: "I see it as the ideal way for a woman to have a career and children. In our family, the women can help each other care for the children. Women in monogamous relationships don't have that luxury. As I see it, if this life style didn't already exist, it would have to be invented to accommodate career women" (N.Y. Times, 4/9/91). On the other side of the equation, Elizabeth Taylor is said to have said: "Bigamy is having one husband too many. Monogamy is the same."

§ 3.4 Marriage Age

Age limitations on marriage originally were founded on the reasonable consideration that candidates for marriage should have reached puberty. Accordingly, the common law permitted males to marry at 14 and females at 12. While the ages were raised, differentiation on the basis of gender remained common until it was struck down under the Equal Protection Clause (*e.g., Phelps, Friedrich, cf. Stanton I, II*). State regulation continues to insist on setting a nearly absolute minimum age for marriage (the UMDA suggests 16) and a somewhat higher age (the UMDA suggests 18) below which marriage requires parental consent. Special circumstances, such as pregnancy, are allowed to undercut minimum age requirements in many states, upon petition to and approval by a court.

Today's substantially raised minimum age for marriage, well past the age of puberty, remains supportable by the need for contractual capacity. Moreover, marriage requires emotional maturity as well as the ability to be self-supporting. With the reduction of the age of majority to eighteen years, the requirement of parental consent is becoming less important, but was upheld against constitutional challenge on the basis of "New York's important interest in * * * preventing unstable marriage among those lacking capacity to act in their own best interest" (*Dinkins*). A parental consent requirement, however, is difficult to justify where it is not co-extensive with the parental obligation to render support and guidance. As a consequence of the reduction in the age of majority, that obligation now typically ends when the child reaches the age of 18.

§ 3.5 Incest and Affinity

An important prerequisite to marriage is that the intending spouses must not be closely related. Prohibitions on marriage within the immediate family (ascendants, descendants, siblings) are universal. Beyond that, the "incest prohibition" varies from state to state and may include a variety of relationships. Nearly all states forbid uncle-niece and aunt-nephew marriage, about one-half (but not UMDA § 207) forbid marriage of first cousins, and until recently a few states prohibited marriage of second cousins. Relationships of the half blood typically are considered the same as relationships of the full blood, and illegitimacy is irrelevant. In many states the civil marriage prohibition is co-extensive with relationships subject to criminal prosecution for incest, in others the civil prohibition extends further.

Various relationships created by a former marriage ("affinity") continue to be considered impediments to marriage in a small minority of jurisdictions. While there is a continuing decline in such prohibitions, a man may be forbidden to marry "the widow of his son" or the "daughter of his wife," and similar rules may or may not apply to corresponding relationships of women. Many states extend marriage prohibitions to step-relationships, and most cover adoptive relationships, with the prohibition continuing even though the relationship may have ended. The Colorado Supreme Court has allowed adoptive siblings to marry, holding the adoption impediment "illogical" (*Israel*). As the Colorado Court recognized in dictum, the prohibitions on marriage between persons related by a former marriage (affinity) seem at least equally vulnerable. Since some of these discriminate on the basis of sex—a man may be prohibited from marrying his son's former wife whereas a woman may not be prohibited from marrying her daughter's former husband—they should be void on that ground alone. A more direct case against such prohibitions can be made on the ground that there remains no "compelling state interest" that supports prohibition of marriage between former "in-laws".

Questions also arise with respect to at least some blood relationships. The very fact that about one-half of the states permit first cousin marriages may indicate that no *compelling* policy interest stands against such marriages even in the states that prohibit them. In any event, genetic considerations cut both ways. In the long run, prohibition of intermarriage does not solve the problem of recessive genes. The genetic argument favoring the incest prohibition involves little more than a shift of the "genetic load" onto future generations. (The success of modern agriculture, plant and animal, is based on incest). However, a convincing argument remains to uphold the incest prohibition within the immediate family: Family relationships must not be allowed to become a potential basis for sexual exploitation. There also is the historical fact that incest is an all but universal cultural taboo.

§ 3.6 Eugenics

Aside from the incest prohibitions, there has been no serious concern with genetic considerations in marriage regulation. Years ago, marriage prohibitions for epileptics were common, but when medical ability to control epilepsy progressed, all states repealed these provisions.

§ 3.7 Mental Condition

Parties to marriage must be of sound mind at the time of marriage. The primary or sole concern here is contractual capacity (§ 4.1) rather than ability to bear and raise children.

§ 3.8 Health

A test for venereal disease remains a widely enacted prerequisite for issuance of the marriage license. With the sudden advent of the AIDS epidemic, several states enacted AIDS testing laws, some for the purpose of *informing* the carrier and the proposed partner. Going further, Utah declared a marriage of "a person afflicted with [AIDS], syphilis or gonorrhea that [is or may become] communicable ... prohibited and void." On reconsideration, Illinois and Louisiana repealed their AIDS testing statutes, and Illinois threw out all other VD tests with it. Utah's Governor blocked enforcement of the law until the legislature would meet, and a federal court held Utah's statute unconstitutional in 1993 (*T.E.P.*). Several states also test for other conditions, such as tuberculosis, German measles, drug addiction or Rh compatibility.

§ 3.9 Waiting Period

Waiting periods between the issuance of a marriage license and solemnization are imposed by approximately three quarters of the states and range from 1 to 10 days, with three days commonly required. Given the obvious value of a waiting period in preventing at least some mistakes—if nothing else, marriages under the influence of drugs or alcohol or "on a dare"—and its minimal inconvenience, it is surprising that some 15 states do not impose a waiting period.

CHAPTER 4

MARRIAGE FORMALITIES AND INFORMAL (COMMON LAW) MARRIAGE

§ 4.1 Consent

Legally effective consent to marriage requires mental capacity to contract and actual intent to be married. By and large, principles of contract law dealing with capacity and validity of consent are applied in the marriage laws.

The question of capacity to contract (to be distinguished from eugenic considerations or ability to perform the contract) is the principal basis of statutory requirements forbidding the issuance of marriage licenses to persons who are "insane", "lunatics", "feeble minded", "imbeciles", "of unsound mind", "mentally incompetent", "idiots" or under the influence of liquor or drugs. (No statute seems to prohibit marriage between "fools".) Although the statutes commonly state a requirement of mental capacity, no effective mechanism is provided to ascertain the applicants' mental condition. Usually the matter lies in the hands of the persons (county clerks, etc.) authorized to issue marriage licenses, who typically are not qualified mental health professionals. A few statutes attempt to set a specific (but often questionable) standard of incapacity, such as previous confinement in a mental institution. Cases protesting the refusal of marriage licenses on grounds of mental incapacity are so rare that it is fair to conclude that licenses are very infrequently refused on this ground, or that, if refused, couples do not sue but travel to a more hospitable jurisdiction. In 1984, the Minnesota Supreme Court upheld the appointment of a conservator to give (or more likely deny) consent to the marriage of a mentally ill person (*Mikulanec*). The issue of mental capacity or condition typically is litigated not until there is an action to annul marriage (Ch. 21) or for divorce (§ 19.7).

In evaluating consent to marriage, courts generally limit themselves to inquiring whether, at the time of the marriage, the intending spouses were capable of understanding the nature of the act. If a marriage was entered into in jest or on a "dare" and, preferably, was not ratified by consummation, the weight of authority supports annulment. Only a few older cases inflicted continued marriage as a sort of punishment in such circumstances and when the traditional law of divorce was accessible only to a spouse complaining of marital fault, the parties were in difficult straits.

Consent procured by fraud invalidates the marriage, but typically only if the fraud goes to the essence of marriage. There is variation concerning what is considered to be of the "essence." For instance, false representations as to wealth usually are not considered to be essential, but a misrepre-

sentation concerning willingness to have children is
(§ 21.4). Similarly, consent procured under duress
(a shotgun, for instance) vitiates a marriage. On
what now is a historical note, a threat of criminal
prosecution for seduction, fornication or some such
outdated crime, was *not* deemed duress, and the
criminal law recognized subsequent marriage to the
victim of such crimes as a defense. There has
always been doubt whether marriage induced in
this manner is a socially desirable event, and changing social conditions—especially the demise of male
legal supremacy and the decline of the double standard that had extolled female "virtue"—have rendered the issue largely moot.

If the parties married with an ulterior motive, for
the purpose of legitimating a child or to secure an
immigration visa or to obtain an income tax advantage, the judicial response has varied. If the parties
sought to partake of an incident going to the essence of marriage (*e.g.,* legitimacy for a child), the
general rule is that their consent covers the full
relationship. They are validly married and, if they
wish to part legally, must do so by divorce. If the
parties only intended to secure a collateral advantage of marriage (*e.g.,* immigration status), annulment has been granted more readily (*Faustin*). Of
course, even if such a marriage were upheld against
challenge by a party, this would not necessarily
bind the immigration authorities. By 1986, U.S.
immigration authorities believed 30% of marriages
of U.S. citizen to aliens to be fraudulent, and the
immigration laws now define quite specifically what

sort of marriage will earn a visa (*Smith v. INS*). Even so, one private agency in New York arranged some 500 sham marriages that grossed $2.5 million (N.Y. Times, 7/22/94).

§ 4.2 Solemnization

Most states require compliance with specific formalities in order to effect a valid marriage, the modern objective being as much to impress the parties with the seriousness of their act as to provide witnesses and a permanent record for purposes of proof. At least the latter two purposes were served when a couple exchanged their wedding kiss in the heavens, after parachuting out of a plane, along with their wedding party (N.Y. Times, 6/18/84). To foretaste the upside as well as the downside of marriage, 46 couples exchanged vows during a roller coaster ride (Chicago Trib., 6/26/93).

Required formalities range from the issuance of a marriage license on the basis of an application which requests information related to marriage prohibitions (this being the control point where substantive marriage regulation is enforced), to details regarding the solemnization of marriage. The latter typically may be accomplished either by a civil or a religious authority, such as a judge, justice of the peace, other authorized public official or any "minister of the gospel" or, under UMDA § 206, "in accordance with any mode of solemnization recognized by any religious denomination, Indian Nation or Tribe, or Native Group". Marriage by proxy representing one party (in a few states even both parties) continues to be permitted in several states and is specifically recognized in UMDA § 206(b). Proxy marriage may be useful when a party is unavoidably unable to be present and there are good reasons to perform the ceremony at that time and place. The typical illustration is the pregnant bride whose prospective husband is a soldier overseas. More recent and more controversial examples involve inmates of penal institutions.

§ 4.3 Informal (Common Law) Marriage

Contrary to popular misconception, common law marriage does not necessarily involve prolonged cohabitation. Rather, in its historical form, common law marriage is as express a contract of marriage as is formal marriage, lacking *only* solemnization by an authorized official. All substantive marriage prohibitions apply. In the "pure" view, consummation of a common law marriage is not essential to its validity, the emphasis is on proof of the contract to marry in words of the "present tense". Words of contract in the "future tense", *i.e.*, an engagement, on the other hand, would produce a valid marriage only with consummation. No court now insists that common law marriage requires proof of the parties' express contract to live together as husband and wife in "words of the present tense." In 1907, the U.S. Supreme Court regretted that "no witness heard them say, in words, in the presence of each other, 'we have agreed to take each other as husband and wife, and live together as such'," but the Court inferred an actual contract from the parties' circumstances and allowed the marriage to stand (*Travers.*) In current usage in the upward of a dozen states that still allow common law marriage, the emphasis is on proof of the parties' cohabitation and their holding themselves out to the world as husband and wife. The resulting relationship is as fully a marriage as any other and must be distinguished from legal relationships that may arise from unmarried cohabitation in states that follow the *Marvin* case (Ch. 6). In 1987, Utah codified a modernized version of common law marriage: "(1) A marriage which is not solemnized * * * shall be legal and valid if a court or administrative order establishes that it arises out of a contract between two consenting parties who: (a) are capable of giving consent; (b) are legally capable of entering a solemnized marriage * * *; (c) have cohabited; (d) mutually assume marital rights, duties, and obligations; and (e) who hold themselves out as and have acquired a uniform and general reputation as husband and wife" (Utah C. A. tit. 30, § 1–4.5).

As long ago as 1753, England tired of the difficulties of proof and resulting confusion of status and inheritance rights created by these marriages and ceased to recognize them. Owing, perhaps, to the great distances confronted by our early settlers, a lack of accessible officials or clergymen and consequent difficulty in formalizing marriages, along with problems of proof resulting from poor recordkeeping, the institution of common law marriage continued to thrive in the United States. Arguments continue both ways: For instance, if a child's legitimacy or a survivor's right of inheritance from his or her *de facto* spouse of many years is involved, many policies coalesce toward giving legal approval to the facts of their life. In addition, modern lifestyles and increased awareness of cultural diversities have given renewed impetus to proponents of common law marriage. On the other hand, the abolitionist view is supported by the value of certainty and easy proof of relationships, even at the expense of occasional injustice. No general, "hard and fast" solution can reconcile these different policies, and the courts often have tailored their decisions to the facts and equities of the specific case before them.

Even those 35 or so states that themselves do not allow common law marriage generally recognize common law marriages validly entered into where legal (*cf.* § 5.6). In a few states, courts have extended this policy to more or less transient visits to common law marriage states by cohabitating parties who were not married where they came from. After such a visit, they were deemed married (*Renshaw*). It seems ironic that the number of common law marriage jurisdictions has been steadily shrinking, just when new lifestyles and "alternative forms of cohabitation" make this ancient institution of new interest and potential value.

CHAPTER 5

EFFECTS OF NON–COMPLI-ANCE WITH MARRIAGE REGULATION

§ 5.1 Void and Voidable Marriages Defined

The classification of invalid marriages into void or voidable marriages usually is (or at least should be) related to the intensity of the State's interest in the particular regulation that has been violated. For example, generally considered "void" is an attempted incestuous marriage, or one involving a party below the absolute minimum age of marriage, or one between persons one or both of whom have prior marriages subsisting (bigamy), or one between persons at least one of whom lacks the requisite mental capacity. On the other hand, less seriously defective marriages are usually classified as "voidable". These include an attempted marriage between partners above the minimum age who need, but lack, parental consent for marriage, or one entered into in violation of collateral or formal requirements, such as health checks. In addition, a host of impediments or defects that are of interest primarily to the other spouse (such as fraud) may make a marriage voidable.

To be distinguished further are situations best described as "nonmarriages". These may involve, for instance, a failure to comply with essential formal requirements, but even here some courts have been lenient. In Connecticut, a marriage may be upheld where either the license or the ceremony (though not both) are missing (*Carabetta*). In Missouri, by contrast, a marriage ceremony performed without a marriage license by a hospital chaplain the day before the groom died was held *not* to give his companion of twelve years the status of his widow (*Nelson*). Less, if any, hope is offered to an attempted common law marriage in a jurisdiction that does not recognize common law marriage (but *cf.* § 5.6) or, for the time being, an attempted marriage between partners of the same sex (§ 3.2). Neither gives rise even to the limited consequences that a "void" marriage may have (§ 5.3).

§ 5.2 Who May Attack?

If a "void" marriage is truly void, one would think that it may safely be ignored by all (§ 5.3). The situation is less clear with respect to "voidable" marriages. To illustrate, the trend seems to go against permitting parents to interfere with the marriage of an underage child who married without parental consent, the UMDA to the contrary notwithstanding. The role of the public, represented by the juvenile authorities or the state's attorney, would similarly be circumscribed in these cases. Whether potential heirs are permitted to attack the marriage of a decedent (so as to eliminate as a competitor the decedent's alleged spouse or a person claiming through that spouse) typically is decided on the basis of whether the challenged marriage was void or voidable. Challenge is permitted in the case of the former, but not in the latter.

In cases involving defects in the marriage that are of interest primarily to the spouses themselves, the spouse responsible for (or having) the defect usually is barred from raising the question, by something akin to the "clean hands" doctrine or estoppel. If the "offended" spouse has "ratified" the marriage, as by continuing the relationship with knowledge of the problem, he or she will be similarly barred.

§ 5.3 Legal Effects of Invalid Marriages

An attempted marriage that does not comply with substantive or formal state regulation may be void, voidable or—partially valid, *i.e.,* the purported marriage may have a limited effect in that the partners are deemed married for some legal purposes or in that certain incidents pertaining to marriage are conferred.

By definition, a void marriage is non-existent, has never existed and should require no formality to come to an end. Nevertheless, a declaratory judgment to the effect that a void marriage really is void may be useful, sometimes even necessary, to prevent unexpected claims, confusion, or the possibility of a prosecution for bigamy. A voidable marriage, on the other hand, is effective until it is formally voided, usually by means of a court order. Once a voidable marriage is voided, however, the effect usually is retroactive and, as in the case of a void marriage, the law deems that the marriage has never existed. This traditional theory is largely the product of contract doctrine.

Today it is generally recognized that certain facts, such as the birth of a child or merely passage of time, are realities that prevent restoration of the *status quo ante*. Traditional law held a child born in a void or in an annulled voidable marriage a "retroactive bastard". For some time, it had been generally recognized that the social harm from such a harsh result outweighs the social gain from strict insistence on the integrity of the marriage regulation process. (Today, of course, the legal equality of marital and non-marital children renders this issue largely moot § 11.8). Some states now validate some void marriages automatically, though not retroactively, when the impediment is removed. To illustrate, under UMDA § 207(b), the death of a prior, undivorced spouse validates a bigamous marriage to another partner. Similarly, an under-age marriage, void when contracted, may be validated by continued cohabitation after the proper age for marriage is reached.

Questions as to "partial validity" of an otherwise invalid marriage may arise in a variety of contexts. Various solutions have been offered. A few states have specific statutes allowing alimony and property rights to the "wife" of at least the voidable and sometimes the void marriage. The trend of modern statutes, spurred on by the UMDA, is to blur increasingly the line not only between void and voidable marriages but even between them and valid marriages in an attempt to equalize the consequences of termination of marital or near-marital relationships on whatever ground (§ 21.7, 8). In those states that recognize the *Marvin* doctrine as the ultimate safety net and give some legal rights to an unmarried cohabitant, certain (or, more accurately, uncertain) legal consequences may result simply from cohabitation, and "cohabitants" may of course include partners to an invalid marriage (Ch. 6).

§ 5.4　Common Law Presumptions Regarding Validity of Marriages

Even when there is no void or voidable marriage and even in jurisdictions where common law marriage is not recognized and quite aside from the *Marvin* doctrine, cohabitation of a man and a woman may produce certain incidents of marriage or the whole package. In certain factual situations, the common law *presumes* that a valid marriage exists, although a valid marriage has not been made out clearly. Proof that persons have cohabited as husband and wife raises a presumption of marriage, and the person attacking that presumption bears the burden of proof. Absence of a marriage record does not establish the non-existence of a marriage, and the presence of a marriage record raises a presumption that the marriage has continued. If two marriages are documented, courts will recognize the validity of the later marriage, by presuming that the earlier marriage was effectively dissolved.

In such cases, the defender of the first marriage must prove that his or her marriage was never and nowhere dissolved—at best a very tough assignment (Spearman).

Where applicable, the presumptions may operate to provide legal certainty of paternity (legitimacy) to a child whose status otherwise might be insecure, or to channel an inheritance or other benefit to a "widow" or "widower" who otherwise would go without. The matter goes deeper, however. Conflicting presumptions potentially apply in many situations, and the court must choose between them, technically on the basis of the better evidence. However, the presumptions sometimes seem to serve as a nearly discretionary device that allows the court to achieve the result it wishes, looking to the equities and social policies involved in the case (*Huff*).

§ 5.5 The Putative Spouse Doctrine

From the civil law of France and Spain, the "putative spouse doctrine" found its way into the laws of California, Louisiana and Texas. The UMDA has imported the doctrine into numerous common law states. Generally speaking, a "putative marriage" requires (1) a marriage ceremony in accordance with law and (2) belief, in good faith, in the validity of the marriage by one or both of the spouses. Since the UMDA does not expressly require a marriage ceremony as the basis of the belief, it seems at least possible that a mistaken belief held in good faith that common law marriage is recognized may create a "putative marriage" with consequent rights and obligations, in states that have abolished common law marriage. Illinois recognized that potential problem, and its statute specifies that a putative marriage can arise only if there was a marriage ceremony.

The rights of the putative spouse vary in the states that recognize the doctrine. Typically, the putative spouse will recover an equitable share of property that was accumulated while the relationship continued in good faith. Putative spouses also may share an inheritance and may be entitled to workmen's compensation, sue for wrongful death or be eligible for other benefits related to the partner. In short, for the duration of the relationship, there is a close approximation between the rights of the putative spouse and those of a legal spouse.

The putative spouse's protection extends only so long as the good faith lasts. Thus, the person who, in good faith, has married a bigamist, is protected only until he or she finds out the truth. No further rights accrue beyond that point, but rights accrued previously continue to be protected. Good faith is not determined solely from a subjective state of mind, but the court asks what a reasonable person would have concluded under similar circumstances.

The doctrine is intended to protect the rights of innocent parties. On the other hand, when the putative spouse successfully competes with the legal spouse, the doctrine interferes with the rights of perhaps an even "more innocent" party. This raises serious questions of policy, and the drafters of UMDA § 209 would have the court do the impossible: "If there is a legal spouse or other putative spouses, rights acquired by a putative spouse do not supersede the rights of the legal spouse or those acquired by other putative spouses, but the court shall apportion property, maintenance, and support rights among the claimants as appropriate in the circumstances and in the interests of justice." Arguably, the putative spouse doctrine thus condones a sort of economic polygamy.

§ 5.6 Conflicts of Laws

The law of conflicts of laws may help validate unions that otherwise would have no legal consequence. We can only touch on the complexities of this body of law. A first principle holds that the law of the place of celebration governs the validity of a marriage. This obviously is the only sensible solution with respect to domiciliaries of the place of celebration of the marriage, even if they later move. The situation becomes more interesting when non-domiciliaries, non-residents or mere transients are involved. Aside from (or along with) the interests of the parties, the conflict in such cases involves (1) the legitimate concerns of the parties' state of domicile, (2) the interest of the state where the marriage was performed in having other states respect its laws and (3) the interest of the state in which the litigation takes place. Still taking its cue from the policy in favor of upholding marriage, the general rule upholds a marriage valid at the time and place of celebration, unless an important policy requires non-recognition. Exceptions depend on how strongly the state asked to recognize an out-of-state marriage feels about the policies underlying its marriage restrictions (the existence or non-existence of criminal sanctions is a helpful but not conclusive test), as measured against the disarray caused by interfering with an existing relationship.

Opposite results may be reached on identical facts. To illustrate, recognition of a locally prohibited marriage between cousins that was contracted in a jurisdiction where cousin-marriage is permitted may depend on whether the question arises at a time when the forum's policy can still be effectuated. Thus, whereas a cousin-widow's claim for social benefits or an inheritance relating to her deceased cousin-husband may be granted, a declaratory judgment to the effect that the out-of-state marriage is valid may be denied to cousins who seek to "live" their marriage in the state.

If valid at the time and place where entered, common law marriages have equally been extended recognition. Depending on the court's perception of the equities, the benefit of this rule occasionally has been extended to transients from states not recognizing common law marriage who spent a short time, preferably more than a mere vacation, in a state recognizing common law marriage (*Renshaw, Laikola, Pecorino*).

A few states, however, have enacted the "Uniform Marriage Evasion Act" that specifically undercuts some of the conflicts rules just discussed. UMEA provides that "if any person residing and intending to continue to reside in this state and who is disabled or prohibited from contracting marriage under the laws of this state shall go into another state or country and there contract a marriage prohibited and declared void by the laws of this state, such marriage shall be null and void for all purposes in this state." Equally void is a marriage contracted by non-residents, though fully in compliance with the law of the place where contracted, if the home law of the non-residents would not permit their marriage. Intended to protect the integrity of the individual state's marriage regulation and its control over its citizens, the Act was doomed to create mischief when it did not achieve universal enactment. Facing this reality, the Act was officially "withdrawn" by the National Conference of Commissioners on Uniform State Laws, but this, of course, did not help in the few states that had enacted the law and did not repeal it.

CHAPTER 6

UNMARRIED COHABITATION

§ 6.1 "Alternative Lifestyles"

New attitudes toward marriage, family formation and sexual companionship emerged in the 1960's as a by-product of many other cultural changes. Women have achieved equality in the market place along with freedom from unwanted pregnancy, social disapproval of unmarried cohabitation has faded, and the legal and much of the social stigma of illegitimacy is gone. Many couples now believe that the commitments and burdens of marriage outweigh its advantages, and the number of cohabiting unmarried couples has increased from half a million in 1970 to 3.5 million in 1993, and 1.2 million such couples have children under 15 years (Bureau of the Census, CPT, P20–478 (1994)).

One very practical attraction of unmarried cohabitation is that potentially costly legal procedures are not needed to end the relationship, and the financial consequences of divorce are avoided. For the more sophisticated couple, unmarried cohabitation seems to afford an opportunity to define the terms of their relationship individually and precisely—an opportunity still restricted in marriage which may override contractual variation of essential rights

71

and duties deemed inherent in marriage. For tax-conscious co-earners, cohabitation can spell considerable savings over marriage (§ 28.8). For the feminist, cohabitation seems to promise freedom from millennia of gender-based oppression through traditional male dominance in marriage. For the unemancipated recipient of alimony or welfare benefits derived from a first marriage, remarriage may be costly if, as is likely, these benefits would be terminated by remarriage. For same-sex couples, unmarried cohabitation remains—for the time being—the only option. For unmarried fathers, however, cohabitation without marriage may lead to uncertain parental rights (§ 11.17).

§ 6.2 Leading Cases: *Marvin* and *Hewitt*

Even while extensive press coverage has conveyed the opposite impression, in most states the legality and enforceability of cohabitation arrangements remains very much in question. Not long ago, contracts involving money and sexual relations—if anyone was bold enough to sue—were struck down everywhere, without ado or sympathy. Today, the universal theory remains—even in avant-garde California which, in 1995, imposed a 3–year prison sentence on the "Hollywood Madam", Heidi Fleiss—that a contract providing for "meretricious sexual services" violates public policy and hence is void. Current social attitudes towards prostitution have hardened, due to a real, if unlikely, alliance of modern feminists and traditional moralists. Two cases illustrate the range of opinion:

Lee *Marvin,* while still married to Betty, had an affair with Michelle who became his companion for almost six years. When Lee stopped paying her one year and a half after he had "compelled plaintiff to leave his household", Michelle sued. The Supreme Court of California lip-served the traditional view: "The courts should enforce express contracts between nonmarital partners *except to the extent that the contract is explicitly founded on the consideration of meretricious sexual services.*" From there, the Court proceeded "on the principle that adults who voluntarily live together and engage in sexual relations are nonetheless as competent as any other persons to contract respecting their earnings and property rights." Indeed, absent an express contract, "the courts should inquire into the conduct of the parties to determine whether that conduct demonstrates an implied contract, agreement of partnership or joint venture, or some other tacit understanding between the parties. The courts may also employ the doctrine of *quantum meruit,* or equitable remedies such as constructive or resulting trusts, when warranted by the facts of the case" (*Marvin*).

The Illinois Supreme Court's decision in *Hewitt* is the antithesis of *Marvin.* A dentist had held out a woman as his wife for fifteen years. She had borne and raised their three children. When she sought a divorce, her dentist (whom she believed to be her husband) confronted her with the information that they had never been legally married. In fact, their cohabitation had started with her pregnancy, and no marriage ceremony had ever been performed. Apparently overwhelmed by the appellate court's full-scale embrace of the *Marvin* doctrine in favor of Ms. Hewitt (*Hewitt App.*), the Illinois Supreme Court held wisely that the situation was too complex for judicial resolution and should be left to the legislature. Unwisely and unnecessarily, the Court proceeded to conclude that Ms. Hewitt had no rights whatever (§ 6.6).

§ 6.3 Did the "Marvin Doctrine" Really Spread?

In most states the response to *Marvin* has been slow and hesitant, but generally negative. Since fornication or adultery remains a criminal offense in nearly one-half of the states—even if criminal enforcement ranges from exceptional to non-existent—the validity of cohabitation contracts or the enforceability of such arrangements should be fatally affected, at least in theory. Without much or any explanation, many courts have ignored this issue (*cf.* §§ 3.2, 9.9). Nationwide, decided cases fall into four major categories:

(1) Many courts forthrightly reject *Marvin* outright. Some refer to traditional policies against meretricious relationships or common law marriage or other (often similar or related) policies (*e.g. Hewitt*).

(2) Some courts waffle, giving lip service to *Marvin*, but hold cautiously that in *this particular case*, the contract was not proved, or not implicit, or the *Marvin* remedy not applicable (*e.g. Marvin II*).

(3) Much misunderstanding concerning the spread of *Marvin* was caused by many cases that *seem* to accept the doctrine by (*mis*)applying it to cases that do not involve facts that resemble *Marvin* at all closely:

(a) *Of course* there are judges who are pleased to grasp any legal justification for finding rights in relationships of very long standing, typically with children, or involving post-divorce relationships of partners previously married to each other, or involving premarital relationships of parties who have subsequently married. Invariably, these cases are of the type that would be upheld without argument and, more significantly, *without Marvin*, by the traditional common law marriage concept, a little loosely applied. Since common law marriage remains the law in only fourteen jurisdictions, courts in jurisdictions that have abandoned common law marriage are tempted to invoke *Marvin* instead. Many of these sympathetic cases involve claims by quasi-widows or quasi-widowers against the estates of *deceased* cohabitants, or for social security or other benefits relating to a *deceased* partner, and thus do not pose the different policy questions that arise when divorce-like settings are at issue.

(b) Numerous cases involving cohabitation invoke *Marvin,* but then limit themselves to disentangling commingled assets. In terms of validating the doctrine, these cases do not mean much either. After all, *someone* must "get the waterbed," as an exasperated judge in Minnesota put it. No matter what a state's attitude may be on the broader issues raised by *Marvin*, basic legal problems arising in such relationships must be identified and solved. These inescapable problems include legally binding identification of the paternity of the unmarried woman's children, the settlement of custodial rights, including rights of visitation, going specifically to the question of the father's position, parental support duties toward the children as well as to the ex-partners' property rights in relation to (joint?) acquisitions and gifts (express and implied) made during the period of cohabitation.

(c) A third main line of cases that invokes *Marvin* with approval (but even less relevance) involves situations in which there is a direct financial or business or special (such as nursing) service relationship between two parties, who also happen to have or have had a sexual relationship. While typically repeating—as indeed did *Marvin*—that meretricious relationships continue to be in violation of public policy, the courts have held—as of course they should—that a sexual relationship does not nullify the parties' otherwise valid business dealings. Recovery in these cases, however, typically is for the value of the *business* relationship and not for some undefined quasi-marital interest (*e.g.*, *Bass*).

(4) On careful analysis, surprisingly few cases apply the *Marvin* doctrine in its broad reach in circumstances that cannot be explained under the classifications suggested above. To illustrate, New Jersey's Supreme Court allowed an engaged woman standing to sue for her pain and suffering on the

occasion of her boyfriend's gruesome death in an accident she witnessed (*Dunphy*), and a few cases analogize from the state's marriage laws and impose a sort of community property (See *Michoff*, *Connell*, *Friedman*). California, of course, is bound to follow its own precedent. Even so, a California court *reversed* a lower court's award of $3,500 per month for four years to an actress who had agreed to serve as an executive's hostess, companion and confidante on the ground that the parties had *not* cohabitated, although or because they had had a sexual relationship. Actual domestic cohabitation was deemed an essential ingredient of *Marvin*-type claims inasmuch as otherwise "every dating relationship would have the potential for giving rise to such claims, a result no one favors" (*Bergen*).

Few other states are willing to derive property rights from the mere fact of cohabitation or promises relating thereto. To illustrate, New York held a man's promise of an apartment for his paramour in return for "love and affection" unenforceable because it implied adultery (*Rose*).

(5) Another line of cases goes to the applicability of civil rights statutes. In 1990 the Minnesota Supreme Court held that a landlord was not obligated to rent to an unmarried heterosexual couple. The majority wrote: "It is simply astonishing * * * that the argument is made that the legislature intended to protect fornication and promote a lifestyle which corrodes the institutions which have sustained our civilization, namely marriage and family life. * * * Before abandoning fundamental

values and institutions, we must pause and take stock of our present social order: millions of drug abusers; rampant child abuse; a rising underclass without marketable job skills, children roaming the streets; children with only one parent or no parent at all; and children growing up with no one to guide them in developing any set of values" (*French*). Similar decisions were reached in Wisconsin in 1993 (*Norman*) and in 1991 in California (*Donahue*).

Almost twenty years after its exploitation in the press and law journals had left a lasting imprint on popular misunderstanding, any broad interpretation of the *Marvin* doctrine (in the sense of "quasi-marital" rights arising from mere cohabitation) thus remains more the plaything of theorists than a tool of practice. Indeed, in the *Marvin* case itself, the trial court's final award of $104,000 to Michelle—rather unkindly termed "for rehabilitation"—was struck down on appeal as not in the purview of the vast array of potential remedies suggested by the California Supreme Court. Apparently tired of it all, the latter court acquiesced in the denial of any recovery whatsoever.

By contrast, professorial reaction to the *Marvin* doctrine has generally been favorable. Many commentators accept uncritically the California Supreme Court's self-perceived position that its holding adapts outdated law to current facts. As that Court put it, "the mores of the society have indeed changed so radically in regard to cohabitation that we cannot impose a standard based on alleged moral considerations that have apparently been so widely abandoned by so many." Acclaim *and* criticism both have emphasized the *Marvin's* perceived abandonment of traditional sexual mores. Amusingly, it has not been much noticed that acceptance of the *Marvin* doctrine would actually achieve quite the opposite: It would eliminate the option of cohabitation "without strings"—just when society seems ready to accept it. In a sense, *Marvin* would regress "free love" to a form of forced "mini-marriage" that is imposed upon the parties without their consent or, indeed, their knowledge. Pushing this point further, *Marvin* may be seen to resurrect something akin to the legal status of "concubinage" of medieval vintage and, with only a little more imagination, *Marvin* might be seen as remaking seduction into a compensable tort. Least pleasantly, *Marvin* has emerged as a legalized blackmail weapon for disappointed lovers, similar to, but potentially more troublesome than even the old-fashioned "heart balm" actions. To underscore this last point, numerous prominent figures (including Billie Jean King, Liberace and the Bloomingdale estate) have made expensive settlements—less perhaps because the paramour could not have been defeated in court, and more, probably, to avoid embarrassing publicity.

It *is* new and true that under *Marvin* same-sex couples may gain a measure of legal recognition for their relationships, having thus far failed in their quest for legal marriage. Illustrating the potential pitfalls even here, Martina Navratilova filed a malpractice suit against her attorney, blaming him for the support contract she signed with July Nelson, her lover, and claimed she had not understood the contract (Wash. Post 11/14/91). Here as well—or worse, for those who still desire to keep their sexual activities out of the public eye—a threat of suit under the *Marvin* doctrine provides staggering potential for blackmail. Nevertheless, the law of "contract cohabitation" is developing in connection with same-sex unions. As much as the right to marry, same-sex couples need a "right to divorce," in the sense of an orderly process to dissolve their relationship. Issues that have come to the fore include not only the "routine" cohabitation case, based on express or implied contract (*e.g.*, *Van Brunt*), but now range from intestate succession (no: *Petri*), to taking over the lover's apartment after the latter's death under New York's rent control laws (yes: *Braschi*), to the eligibility of a lesbian partner to act as legal guardian of her partner who suffered brain injury in an accident (yes: *Kowalski*), to a variety of child custody issues. In the latter arena, cases range from allowing the lesbian partner to adopt a child born to her lover (yes: *Evan*; no: *Angel M.*), to joint adoption of an unrelated child (*R.C.*, *Minor T*). After the termination of such relationships, some courts have denied, and others allowed, visitation rights to a lesbian domestic partner (*Kulla*, *Alison D.*, *Z.J.H.*). However, custodial rights to a Dalmatian puppy were denied to a lesbian ex-lover where her ex-companion was the owner of record of the dog as well as of the apartment. Rejecting also the ex-lover's claim for infliction of emotional harm, the court ordered her and her lawyer to pay $500 apiece to the dog's owner (*Malanga*).

§ 6.4   Problems With Proof

Acceptance of the *Marvin* doctrine poses many practical and policy problems. Since Lord Hard-wicke's Act of 1753, a chief purpose of requiring that marriages be solemnized publicly has been that this procedure provides the parties with a memora-ble event and the public with a permanent record. This makes it clear to all that a *legal* relationship with specific *legal* characteristics exists between two persons. Uncertainty of proof is the major argument that has defeated common law marriage in the majority of American states. Even so, the elements of common law marriage have long been fairly well defined (§ 4.3). By contrast, what inten-sity or frequency of cohabitation (with or without sexual relations?) is required to invoke *Marvin*? What may be expected of months or days or a long stretch of twice-weekly trysts? (*Cf. Bergen* § 6.3).

Moreover, the legal uncertainty regarding com-mon law marriage relates only to proof of the *exis-tence* of the relationship. Once found, the legal meaning of common law marriage is clear: It is the full equivalent of ceremonial marriage. By con-trast, the *Marvin* doctrine suggests enforcement of *whatever* relationship the parties may have chosen for themselves expressly, or tacitly, or by implied contract. This raises more delicate or, indeed, impenetrable issues of proof and may explain the seeming contradiction of the California and Illinois Supreme Courts, with the former noting specifically that *Marvin* does *not* resurrect long abolished common law marriage, and the latter noting emphatically that to decide the case in favor of Ms. Hewitt would indeed resurrect common law marriage. If we are *not* to generalize and are to respect the parties' individual relationships, how are we to approach proof of a "*tacit* understanding", in terms of implied contract?

Beyond contract, we must generalize of necessity. What is to be the reach of legal remedies *not* based on express or implied agreement between the parties, in terms of *quantum meruit* or equitable remedies? Will (or should) the parties be held to what a judge much later thinks they *should* have agreed? And would that not perforce be the equivalent of marriage—in many cases? In sum, to invite not only the very existence but even the legal meaning of the relationship to be established *ex post facto* is neither cost-effective, nor is it likely to be fair to the parties—or in any event to one of them.

The issue of proof is important because of the potential for fraud and imposition and the cost and inconvenience to the parties and to the judicial system. This objection to legalized cohabitation arrangements could be overcome by limiting allowable proof to writings, preferably formal documents, not the lurid love letters that figured so prominently in the widely publicized *Marvin* litigation. For good reason, most current statutes of frauds, as did the original in 1677, require a writing with respect to *marital* agreements, to produce certainty and to eliminate fraud and imposition. For the identical reasons, cohabitation contracts should be treated even more cautiously.

The very foundation of the *Marvin* doctrine, however, is that "agreements" may be inferred from facts or by law. Ironically, even without a *legal* writing requirement, the potential breadth of the *Marvin* rule thus imposes one *de facto*. Thinking cohabitants who really wish to have a relationship without legal consequences are well advised to have a written agreement that specifically so states. And if they wish to have a relationship with specific legal consequences short of (or other than) marriage, they had better define these consequences in writing and hope for the best. But what is best— should such contracts be binding?

§ 6.5 Problems of Policy

Solving the problem of proof does not solve basic policy problems. Even if there is perfect proof, a fundamental substantive question is whether the law should permit parties to enter into a contractual relationship resembling marriage, but providing different particulars. To rephrase the most important aspect of this issue more precisely: Should *unmarried* partners have greater freedom to arrange economic and other aspects of their relationship than most states now allow to *married* partners?

The short answer is that, to the extent the factual situations resemble each other, the same policies that (should) govern marital contracts should also apply to cohabitation contracts. One example makes this point: If the parties—married or unmarried—signed and sealed a comprehensive financial disclaimer twenty years ago, what court would or should enforce such an agreement after *children* and perhaps two decades of changed circumstances, when that old disclaimer now is oppressive, even if it seemed "reasonable" when it was made? (UPAA to the contrary notwithstanding, § 7.13). If, on the other hand, the cohabitation contract specifies anything significantly *more* or *less* or *other* than is "naturally implicit" in the kind of interpersonal relationship modern law understands modern marriage to be, we should be *very* careful indeed to consider literal enforcement—or we should reconsider the wisdom of our marriage laws.

A second, even broader policy issue that has largely escaped attention is that *Marvin* deals *solely* with the partner-to-partner relationship. To the extent it moves unmarried cohabitation to a level of recognition resembling that of marriage, it does so only between the parties. The next question should be what, if any, "public" legal consequences should attend unmarried cohabitation? For instance, should cohabiting partners be permitted to file joint income tax returns? Should they be *required* to file jointly if that would be to the advantage of the IRS? If unmarried cohabitants are allowed to waive mutual support liability, should the welfare authorities, *i.e.*, the taxpayer, be bound by such a contract and provide "welfare"—when even the UPAA would not permit one marriage partner to contract the other into welfare dependency (§ 7.13)? Should a dependency relationship based on unmarried cohabitation trigger welfare eligibility when the "provider" leaves? Should welfare and similar benefits be terminated when a *de facto* "provider" enters the picture? Should cohabitants have standing to sue for loss of consortium and wrongful death benefits? So far, these issues have not been approached thoughtfully or at all. Some courts have blindly extended the cohabitation relationship to include "third-party-effects", as when a California court approved the payment of death benefits to a gay lover who played the role of stay-at-home spouse.

The City of Berkeley was among the first to adopt a city ordinance assimilating marriage and cohabitation in terms of social and welfare benefits. Many cities, corporations, universities and even a few states have now followed suit, and "registration" of domestic partners of either sex has been permitted with varying legal benefits and ramifications. Notably, this move has extended exclusively to marriage-similar *benefits*. No legally enforceable burdens have been imposed, such as the marital partners' mutual support obligation that is enforced before the taxpayer will enter the picture.

Signaling perhaps a change of climate, in 1994, Governor Wilson vetoed California legislation that would have provided some incidents of marriage to unmarried couples, same-sex or heterosexual. He explained: "Government policy ought not to discount marriage by offering a substitute relationship that demands much less, and provides much less than is needed both by the children of such relationships, and ultimately much less than is needed by society" (N.Y. Times, 9/13/94). On the ground that state policy favors heterosexual marriage, a Minnesota court struck down Minneapolis' offer of health care benefits to the partners of gay employees (N.Y. Times, 2/3/95).

§ 6.6 Conclusion

The problems of proof and the problems of substance are indeed serious, but they must not lead toward a solution along the lines of *Hewitt*. To reach a result fairer to Ms. Hewitt, the Illinois Court did not *need Marvin*. The Court might have drawn on old-fashioned theories of estoppel (the dentist should not be heard to deny that he is married, but see *Watts*), or it could have played a little loosely with the fact that the parties' original cohabitation took place in Iowa which recognizes common law marriage (§ 4.3). Many of our courts have routinely (and sometimes not a little retrospectively) used the concept of common law marriage to do "the right thing" when they felt that strict adherence to legal norms would produce injustice. Indeed, as outlined above, most of the cases that seemingly accept the *Marvin* doctrine may be explained in just those terms.

The key to a sensible solution lies here: Where there has been a long-standing, marriage-like, role-divided, child-bearing and child-raising relationship between a man and a woman, a quasi-marital, legal relationship is properly thrust upon them, especially (but not only) in case of the death of one of them. In sum, nothing much short of the *Hewitt* facts should have spawned a doctrine protecting *"quantum-meruit-* cohabitation." The *Hewitt* situation merited protection (see especially *Watts*); the *Marvin* facts did not. Both leading cases were decided precisely wrong!

Postscript: Having carried his enthusiasm for "informality" too far, Marvin (really his name) Mitchelson, the attorney for Michelle Marvin and many other cohabitants, "the man who put the word 'palimony' into the legal lexicon, left a federal courtroom in handcuffs Tuesday after he was convicted of failing to report nearly $2 million in income. * * * Over the past 20 years, Mitchelson reported no taxable income, and has almost never paid taxes voluntarily, U.S. Attorney Terree Bowers said" (AP 2/10/93).

CHAPTER 7

VARIABILITY OF THE MARRIAGE CONTRACT

§ 7.1 Contract or Status?

Language in many cases might lead to the conclusion that marriage is a contract. More accurately, marriage is entered by means of a contract, but turns into a status. In 1888, the U.S. Supreme Court pointed out that "[o]ther contracts may be modified, restricted, or enlarged, or entirely released upon the consent of the parties. Not so with marriage. The relation once formed, the law steps in and holds the parties to various obligations and liabilities. It is an institution, in the maintenance of which in its purity the public is deeply interested, for it is the foundation of the family and of society, without which there would be neither civilization nor progress" (*Maynard*).

Spouses have argued that the dissolution of their marriage on newly enacted no-fault grounds constitutes an unconstitutional impairment of their contract rights or deprivation of property without due process. Arguing that "marriage is much more than a civil contract" a California court arrived at the curious conclusion that it merited less protection than a contract. Specifically, marriage was found not to involve contractual rights and obligations within the meaning of the Constitution, and was "deemed to incorporate and contemplate not only the existing law but the reserve power of the state to amend the law or enact additional laws for public good and in pursuance of public policy" (*Walton*). This expresses the prevailing rule.

Marriage may be compared with contracts of adhesion which subject the parties to extensive regulation, traditionally without adequate opportunity to vary terms, before or after entry. But even the most oppressive contract of adhesion spells out its significant terms, if only in fine print. Not so in marriage, where the idealistic promise "to love and to cherish, till death us do part" first translates into vast and often unexpectedly burdensome consequences and then is belied by our divorce statistics. In terms of nondisclosure of its legal effects, marriage may be the ultimate consumer fraud on unsuspecting innocents acting in an emotional fog.

In view of all this, it stands to reason that antenuptial contracts *should* be the norm, but they are not. Strong popular prejudice remains against such agreements, as expressed in a story reporting multibillionaire George Soros' second marriage:

> "[H]e is a singularly untrusting person, intent on not allowing others to take advantage of him. (Indeed, Soros is said to have presented his wife, Susan, with a prenuptial agreement. And, according to one longtime friend, the investment adviser Victor Niederhoffer, when, at Soros's

wedding, the minister recited the traditional vow for Soros to repeat— 'For better or worse, I do endow thee with all my worldly goods'—Soros turned to his personal attorney, William Zabel, and asked, wryly, whether he could state this without being bound, and, upon being told that he could, nonetheless muttered in Hungarian, 'Subject to any prior agreements with my heirs')'' (New Yorker, 1/23/95).

A fair, though fairly academic, question is *which* "contract of adhesion" the parties entered if they were married in a state other than the state where the litigation takes place. For instance, if a marriage is solemnized in a state with easy availability of divorce, does freedom of termination become part of the contract? If a marriage is contracted in a community property state, will community property be the economic basis of the parties' relationship even if they later move to a separate property state? Further undermining the notion that marriage is a contract, the courts have answered that the laws of the state of celebration merely create the status, whereas its incidents, including rights to support, property and grounds for divorce, are defined by the parties' domicile.

§ 7.2 Types of Marital Contracts

Entered by way of contract, once solemnized, marriage thus becomes a status with numerous wide-ranging personal and financial incidents prescribed by law. To what extent may the parties vary the conditions of their marriage by means of private agreement?

Distinguish between three major categories of marital contracts: (1) The antenuptial (or prenuptial or premarital) contract that is entered before marriage and looks forward to the conduct of the relationship or to its end through death or divorce; (2) a contract that is entered during marriage and that looks to the continuation of the marriage, sometimes as a "reconciliation agreement"; and (3) a contract that is made during marriage, but that anticipates separation and eventual divorce, *i.e.*, the "separation agreement" (Ch. 29). Different technicalities and policies apply to each of these categories.

§ 7.3 Antenuptial Contracts—Validity

While the advance of the Uniform Premarital Agreements Act is rapidly and radically changing the ground rules (§ 7.9), the continuing influence of the past cannot be ignored.

The typical antenuptial agreement sets forth special conditions relating to the contemplated marriage. These conditions seek to rule out, vary, or supplement legal consequences that would otherwise arise automatically. Since the relationship between the parties typically is not at "arm's length," great care must be taken in the negotiation and execution of such contracts. The courts carefully scrutinize the circumstances under which such contracts were procured. Provisions regarding the support or custody of children stand on still a different footing, as the court, as *parens patriae*, will not feel bound by anything it may view as adversely affecting the interest of a child (*cf.* § 15.3, § 29.8).

Traditionally, if the *wife* relinquished rights that otherwise would have resulted from marriage, she was jealously protected against overreaching. Courts spoke in terms of the *husband's* fiduciary duty. Some still do, and others have found a mutual duty. Husbands, by contrast, have not been protected nearly as well and often have been left to live with burdensome "deals". While this discrimination may be explainable in terms of a tradition of chivalry, it also may have made sense insofar as old-style, sex-role-divided marriage required that the law give the wife special protection and because men were generally more conversant with financial matters than women (*e.g., Sogg*). Today, equality of treatment is the goal in many courts.

If an antenuptial agreement is to stand up, the spouses either must make full and complete disclosure of their financial circumstances or must make such economic provision as a court, years later and with the benefit of hindsight, will consider "fair". "Fairness" in these cases often has depended on the "length of the chancellor's foot", *i.e.,* a judge will tend to play his or her own ideas. Contracts have been upheld if they fully met either requirement, but contracts meeting both requirements are more secure. In cases where a court feels that "unfair" provision was made, difficulties often surface with respect to *proof* of complete and full disclosure. It thus seems all but indispensable (and some statutes and many courts require this expressly) that each prospective spouse be represented by independent counsel to guard against an inference of over-reaching (*Hess*). "Duress" is often alleged in attacks on antenuptial agreements and has been found in any number of circumstances, such as the bride's pregnancy and the father's unwillingness to marry her unless she would sign an antenuptial agreement all but waiving alimony, child support and property rights (*Williams*).

Most antenuptial contracts do not raise serious problems with respect to the technical requirement of contract law that there be "consideration". The parties' mutual agreement to enter into marriage is sufficient. Even if the resulting marriage turns out to be invalid, some courts have found adequate consideration in the attempted marriage. Of course, in such circumstances an agreement may be unenforceable for other reasons or may simply have lost its relevance and applicability. The provisions of the English Statute of Frauds of 1677 that required antenuptial contracts to be in writing have been re-enacted widely. Even without statutory command, a writing is an essential precaution to protect against mistaken or fraudulent allegations regarding the existence or terms of an agreement. When, in a divorce proceeding, a husband raised the issue that the statute of limitations had run on his wife's attack on their antenuptial agreement, the court held that the statute was tolled during the marriage (*Lieberman*).

§ 7.4　Antenuptial Contracts—Subject Matter

If the antenuptial agreement meets these technical tests, the next question goes to subject matter. The most basic case involves the transfer of property to the prospective spouse in consideration of marriage. Such an agreement has long been held valid. Beyond that, courts have differed greatly in what else they have permitted antenuptial agreements to cover. The rules that have evolved turn principally on whether the agreement looks (1) to the death of a spouse in the ongoing marriage, or (2) to the termination of the marriage by divorce, or (3) to the regulation of the ongoing marriage relationship.

§ 7.5　Projected Event: Death

Antenuptial agreements relating to the distribution of property on death have long been upheld. Given independent counsel, full disclosure and/or fair provision, along with a writing satisfying the statute of frauds, each spouse may renounce or promise inheritance rights regarding the other.

§ 7.6　Projected Event: Divorce

Even today, agreements seeking to define the respective rights of the parties upon divorce may fail on grounds of the traditional public policy against "encouraging" divorce. While it should be recognized that it *restates* the law rather than looks forward, it is significant that the 1981 Restatement of Contracts (Second) § 190 still holds: "(1) A promise by a person contemplating marriage or by a married person, other than as part of an enforceable separation agreement, is unenforceable on grounds of public policy if it would change some essential incident of the marital relationship in a way detrimental to the public interest in the marriage relationship, * * * (2) A promise that tends unreasonably to encourage divorce or separation is unenforceable on grounds of public policy".

The traditional theory was that if any consequence of divorce were permitted to be defined in advance, the parties would be encouraged to seek divorce. The opposite argument seems equally plausible: If the parties only knew in advance the all too often ruinous financial consequences of divorce, fewer divorces might occur. The old rule remains true, however, when an agreement gives one party a "prize" for divorce. In *Noghrey*, the previously impecunious bride was promised a house plus half a million dollars in the event she decided to divorce. And, of course, she did—after seven months' of marriage. A more persuasive argument that has been used to impugn the validity of antenuptial agreements dealing with divorce is that the parties should not be allowed to *vary* the consequences of divorce, because these are imposed as a matter of public policy. Some sense remains in this. It also should be considered that in marriages of long duration the ultimate circumstances of divorce are usually so unforeseeable at the time of the antenuptial agreement as to render any agreement relating to it highly speculative at best.

Over the past several decades, a rapidly growing number of courts have upheld antenuptial agreements looking to divorce (*Marshall, Frey, Gross*), especially when high standards of fairness are met (*Osborne*) or when older parties and second marriages are involved (*Volid*), although others have clung to tradition (*Connolly*). Agreements relating to *property* settlements upon divorce have had a better chance of survival than agreements affecting *support* obligations, because the latter are deemed more of the essence of marriage and to involve public policy more directly. Where no reference was made to divorce, the Kentucky Supreme Court upheld *upon divorce,* a husband's antenuptial agreement to furnish his wife "a decent support during his natural life" (*Jackson*). Of course, with the considerable interrelationship of support and property arrangements on divorce (§ 28.2), it often is difficult to discern much practical difference between them. Some courts · enforce provisions in marriage contracts requiring the spouses to appear before a religious (rabbinical) divorce tribunal against challenges under the First Amendment (*Avitzur, Feuerman, Scholl*), or provisions to arbitrate upon divorce (*Kelm*).

Considerable care thus remains necessary (and is not necessarily sufficient) when drafting antenuptial agreements. Caution is indicated in the face of unpredictable outcomes here and now, and all the more where the attorney must project an outcome in a court sitting in the year 2020, when the decision-maker will have the benefit of 20/20 hindsight.

For the time being, even the very terminology may still make a difference: Some courts remain more likely to invalidate an agreement that expressly refers to divorce than one that does not, even if both accomplish substantially similar results. Of course, if the antenuptial agreement does not provide for the consequences of divorce or separation, the effect of divorce or separation on unexecuted aspects of the antenuptial agreement may become a problem. Once again, judicial answers vary with the court and the specific circumstances.

§ 7.7 Contracting for the Ongoing Marriage

Traditionally invalid were antenuptial agreements seeking to define or waive support obligations and other essential duties within marriage. Similarly, agreements relating to sexual practices, not to defend a fault divorce action, to raise a child in a particular religion or to send a child to a particular school have not been enforced, largely on the basis of the sound judicial policy against interference in the *ongoing* marriage (§ 8.1). Even though that policy no longer applies after divorce or separation, there may be technical questions regarding the survival of an antenuptial agreement past the divorce and, depending on the subject matter, there remain practical and policy questions whether such an agreement should or could be enforced by the judiciary.

In view of the new legal status of marital property and the frequently unpredictable, usually messy and nearly always (at least in the perception of one or the other spouse) unfair disposition of "marital" property that occurs upon divorce (Ch. 26), and in view of the unpredictable enforceability of some antenuptial agreements that seek to predict the consequences of divorce, it is surprising that antenuptial contracts regarding the property regime the spouses intend to follow in their marriage have found relatively little use in the practice of family law, at least in the common law states. By comparison, community property jurisdictions allow or encourage specific election by the spouses of a separate or community property regime (*cf. Stein–Sapir*). Traditional legal attitudes, of course, often have made a one-way street out of an antenuptial contract to follow a specific property regime: To the extent it improves property rights for the wife, it probably will be enforced. If on the other hand the agreement *limits* the wife's rights in a situation in which the court believes she should have more, the old argument against allowing antenuptial agreements to govern the consequences of divorce may resurface. Upon the *death* of one of the partners, on the other hand, the effect of such an agreement is more predictable: Ownership controls descent.

§ 7.8 Agreements During Marriage

If antenuptial contracts have travelled a rocky road, the fate of agreements concluded during marriage has been even more troubled. The first traditional hurdle is that all contracts need "consideration." When the parties are married, however, their mutual promises of marital support or housekeeping that almost inevitably supply consideration to antenuptial contracts are unavailable to serve as consideration because, upon marriage, these promises have turned into legal duties. A second hurdle is that a post-nuptial agreement may easily be subject to and struck down for undue influence or duress. A flagrant case is that of a husband who, after twenty years of marriage, presented his wife who was distressed over her father's recent death with a "deal" that would have given her only 7.5% of the parties' 40 million dollar assets, and in exchange for which he agreed not seek a divorce for two years. When the wife's first counsel advised her not to sign, her husband found her another lawyer who did (*Richardson*).

§ 7.9   Reconciliation Agreements

Where the spouses have had marital disagreements and their contract amounts to a "reconciliation", the courts have been disposed more favorably. Consideration has been found in the parties' agreement to continue or resume cohabitation or to abandon pending proceedings for divorce or legal separation. Moreover, the marital rift may reduce concern over the possibility of undue influence.

§ 7.10   Subject Matter

A further hurdle is the continuing unenforceability in some states of certain types of agreements between spouses during their marriage, *e.g.,* contracts for "services" or "labor". Most states today enforce agreements relating to a relationship be-

tween the spouses that is not inherently dependent
upon marriage, such as a business partnership between the spouses, or even an arrangement that
involves "extraordinary" personal services (§ 8.6).
Nevertheless, special technical problems cloud the
execution of such agreements. The very existence
of the marriage relationship implies a greater possibility of undue influence than might be present in a
premarital relationship. Finally, even if the agreement is validly executed and consideration is present, the courts' conception of permissible subject
matter has been at least as restrictive here as in the
case of antenuptial agreements. Again, agreements
that purport to affect details of the parties' marital
relationship, whether financial, sexual or social, are
likely not to be enforced.

§ 7.11 Separation Agreements

The type of contract most frequently executed
between spouses during marriage is the so-called
"separation agreement," attendant to imminent
separation or divorce. Although their usual purpose is to assure the consequences of divorce in
advance, the courts have long accepted these agreements, if executed with care (Ch. 29). If, on the
other hand, a "reconciliation agreement" is invoked
in a divorce, the Nebraska Supreme Court has held
that "to give binding effect to [a reconciliation]
agreement during a dissolution proceeding four
years later would operate to discourage reconciliation attempts. Agreements between husband and
wife concerning the disposition of their property,

not made in connection with the separation of the parties or the dissolution of their marriage, are not binding upon the courts during a later dissolution proceeding" (*Snyder*).

§ 7.12 Modern Legislation

Today it is accepted wisdom that the parties' wishes, expressed in an antenuptial agreements, should be respected—up to a point (*Marshall, Frey, Gross*). Given compliance with the requirement of full disclosure and/or fair provision and independent counsel, no rational reason continues to support the traditional, overly solicitous attitude to such contracts. Today's realities—at least in many cases— differ from the recent past when it was appropriate to bend over backwards to protect financially dependent wives from exploitation by unscrupulous husbands. Clear statutes are needed to provide certainty and predictability. The UMDA does not make specific provision for antenuptial agreements, although it allows them to be "considered" on divorce (§ 26.3). Until the Uniform Premarital Agreements Act (UPAA) became available in 1983, few states had passed legislation firmly establishing a reasonable, modern framework for the validity of antenuptial contracts.

§ 7.13 The Uniform Premarital Agreements Act

In 1983, the Commissioners on Uniform State Laws approved not just one, but two new model acts to govern antenuptial agreements. The Uniform

Premarital Agreements Act (UPAA) is directed specifically to this issue and covers all conceivable subjects. The Uniform Marital Property Act (UMPA) allows contractual variation, before or after marriage, from the essentially community property regime it imposes. Both acts allow modification of support obligations, except to the extent that welfare eligibility would result. Both Acts provide detailed guidelines to govern premarital agreements. By 1995, the UMPA had been adopted only in Wisconsin, whereas the UPAA had become law in 19 states. While UMPA may already be considered a failure in terms of wide-spread adoption, UPAA is likely to become prevailing law.

A crucial feature of *both* Acts is that an otherwise valid ante- or postnuptial agreement may be upset *only* if it was "unconscionable *when made* (UMPA § 10(f)(11)) or *when executed*" (UPAA § 6(a)(2)). Both acts require "fair and reasonable disclosure," *or* a voluntary and express written waiver of disclosure, or notice or adequate knowledge or reasonable opportunity for knowledge of the property or financial obligations of the other spouse. Neither Act specifically requires counsel, although agreements under both Acts would no doubt gain strength from the presence of counsel. Neither Act defines the term "unconscionable"; both leave that to the court to be decided "as a matter of law".

What law? Perhaps the ultimate issue here raised is whether "love" and sacrifice of advantage induced by "love" is unconscionable *per se,* or whether it is not the essence of at least some marriages? If the provisions of both Acts that mandate full enforcement of all agreements regarding property and support except to the extent that welfare eligibility would result, are not "unconscionable", what is? Quite aside from the complexity of determining welfare eligibility on a hypothetical basis, anyone familiar with the inadequacy of welfare provision must be concerned with the rigor of this limitation.

While it may be readily agreed that many or most of the old rules do not meet the needs of today, it is not nearly as clear what does, or that UPAA or UMPA do. While predictability is a virtue, it may be too facile to jump to the conclusion that *any* marital contract, not based on fraud or unconscionable imposition and between consenting adults, should be enforced. What starry-eyed eighteen-year-old can foresee what he or she might feel (or indeed be) twenty, thirty, or forty years later? Should *all* promises made "under the influence" of romantic intoxication be enforced decades later? In short, while a substantial tightening in the enforceability of premarital contracts is indicated to meet popular demand and a social need for custom-tailored marriages, there also is need for an explicit "retrospective" safety valve, preferably one more restrictive and specific than the one that was dropped out of the UPAA draft, as follows:

"If, after considering all relevant facts and circumstances, the court finds that enforcement of an antenuptial agreement * * * would be unconscionable under the *existing* facts and circumstances, the court may refuse to enforce the agreement, enforce the remainder of the agreement without the unconscionable provisions, or limit the application of the unconscionable provisions to avoid any unconscionable result." (Emphasis added).

Perhaps a court, called upon many years later to enforce an antenuptial agreement that *then* has unconscionable consequences, will "brutalize" the UPAA and hold that if the *current* circumstances had only been foreseen or foreseeable at the time the contract was made, the contracts would have been "unconscionable when made" and thus strike it down. Another escape might be to hold that the parties' conduct during the long-term marriage impliedly dissolved an antenuptial agreement that now has become unduly burdensome, but this contention may be difficult to maintain in the face of the writing requirement that applies to modifications in both statutes. Neither approach thus offers much promise. One "safety valve" that courts have often used in upsetting post-marital agreements—absence of consideration—is expressly ruled out by UPAA and UMPA, both of which expressly dispense with any consideration for antenuptial and, even more significantly, for postnuptial agreements.

Perhaps a careful retailoring for this unique context, of contract law dealing with "frustration" and "change in circumstances" may provide the needed remedy: A long-term marriage involves such vast changes in "circumstances" that "frustration" may not only describe the parties' attitude, but may also be present in an "equitable" sense, though perhaps not in the technical sense applied to commercial contracts. Notably, Illinois rephrased its version of the UPAA to the effect that if any contractual modification of spousal support "causes one party * * * undue hardship in light of circumstances not reasonably foreseeable at the time of the execution of the agreement, a court * * * may require the other party to provide support to the extent necessary to avoid such hardship" (750 ILCS 10/7(b)).

Agreements made *during* marriage, as well as the modification during marriage of antenuptial agreements, are governed by substantially similar rules under both Acts. They must be in writing, but no special consideration is given the parties' substantially changed circumstances. It is arguable that the term "unconscionable *when made*" should invite a stiffer test when applied to parties who are already married. Somewhat surprisingly, neither UPAA nor UMPA specifically address separation agreements which, of course, are the most common postnuptial contracts or are typical modifications of unexecuted portions of premarital contracts. Again, the proviso "unconscionable *when made*" may allow the court to take into account the rather different circumstances in which the parties find themselves when drafting a separation agreement, but a more detailed definition of *what* special considerations should apply at that point would have been useful.

Other unresolved issues arise under both Acts. Perhaps the most important of these is the interpretation of UPAA § 3(a)(8), which allows the parties to contract regarding—in addition to property, support, wills, life insurance, choice of law—"any other matter including their personal rights and obligations, not in violation of public policy or any statute imposing a criminal penalty." What is "public policy", and what criminal statutes regulating "personal rights" of marriage partners remain constitutional (*cf. Cotner*)? Indeed, the UPAA's listing of subjects for permissible contractual variation seems so complete that one may almost hypothesize that parties may contract *not* to be married in any legal sense that is not to their advantage. At the extreme, unless the nebulous reference to "public policy" comes into play, parties might contract to file joint income tax returns to obtain more advantageous rates, but negate by contract nearly all other legal consequences of their marriage. Lack of space forbids a more detailed critique, but the points already made demonstrate that in this area of reform, the Commissioners on Uniform State Laws did not fully succeed. Still, it is too early to conclude that *all* prenuptial agreements that meet the UPAA's terms will be henceforth and forever binding.

§ 7.14 Antenuptial Agreements and Third Parties

Antenuptial agreements are not limited to agreements between intending spouses. For instance, a member of either spouse's family may contract with the other spouse that certain payments will be made in the case of or after the marriage, or that the support of the spouse and offspring will be taken care of. Such agreements have generally been held enforceable. On the other hand, agreements with (or offers by) third parties in restraint of marriage or tending to induce divorce are deemed to go against public policy and are not enforced.

§ 7.15   Tax Consequences of Antenuptial Transfers

Transfers of property in connection with antenuptial agreements may have consequences under the income and gift tax laws. The Internal Revenue Service has taken the position that entry into marriage is *not* adequate consideration from the standpoint of the donor's gift tax liability, even if it *is* valid consideration to support the antenuptial agreement as an enforceable contract. At the same time, if it is not a "gift" for tax purposes (in which case the donor's basis is transferred), the transfer of appreciated or depreciated property may have income tax effects. Careful attention is needed to avoid unexpected and possibly unnecessary tax consequences of antenuptial arrangements. The move in the 1980's from limited exemptions to the elimination of gift tax consequences arising out of gifts between spouses has made it even more advisable that a gift be effective, under the gift tax laws, only after the parties are married.

§ 7.16 Conflicts

Marital agreements raise interesting problems in the conflict of laws. What law is to govern the validity of an antenuptial agreement entered into in State A which is sought to be enforced in State B in which the parties now are domiciled, if the parties were married in State A, B or C? Questions go to formalities as well as to the subject matter covered by the agreement. Answers depend on what policies the court believes to be applicable and what the court believes was the intention of the parties. Beyond geography, this area offers to "conflicts" a new dimension in time: An agreement doubtful or invalid where and *when* made may gain enforceability if sought to be enforced where and *when* such agreement is or *has become* valid. To understate the problem, results are not always predictable in advance. Some protection may be provided if the agreement expresses the parties' intent regarding applicable law. UPAA and UMPA expressly allow the parties to contract regarding "choice of law governing the construction of the agreement."

PART III

SPOUSAL RIGHTS AND OBLIGATIONS IN THE ONGOING MARRIAGE

CHAPTER 8
HUSBAND AND WIFE IN THE ONGOING MARRIAGE— SUPPORT AND PROPERTY

§ 8.1 Family Support

During marriage, *traditional* law required the husband to support his wife irrespective of the wife's own means, her own ability to support herself or even her own earnings which the Married Women's Property Acts (§ 8.6) gave to her, to do with as she pleased. The wife had no corresponding duty to support her husband; although many states imposed a conditional support duty on the wife if her husband was "in need." Today, either by express statute or by extrapolation from U.S. Supreme Court decisions requiring gender neutrality (*e.g., Orr*), an equal and mutual obligation of support applies. Support suits by husbands against wives remain rare, however, because the actuality of gender-based role division, still found in varying degrees in the majority of marriages, is that many a husband continues to perform as the principal "breadwinner".

The obligation of support owed to spouse or child is enforceable civilly as well as by means of criminal sanctions (§ 16.1, 28.2). Judicial definition of the support obligation goes to "necessaries," but different things are deemed "necessary" for rich and poor (§ 8.3). While the level at which the spouse is to be maintained during marriage should correspond to the couple's "station in life", successful litigation defining support obligations during marriage is rare. Few remedies apply during the continuance of marital cohabitation because the courts are thoroughly reluctant to interfere in ongoing marriages:

"The living standards of a family are a matter of concern to the household, and not for the courts to determine, even though [this] husband's attitude toward his wife, according to his wealth and circumstances, leaves little to be said in his behalf. As long as the home is maintained and the parties are living as husband and wife it may be said that the husband is legally supporting his wife and the purpose of the marriage relation is being carried out. Public policy requires such a holding" (*McGuire*).

It would indeed burden the courts past the breaking point if they were to try to settle family budget disputes which arise so frequently, nor would they be likely to succeed. Arguably, when a dispute over support becomes so serious that judicial enforcement is considered, the break-up of the marriage may not be far away, so that the complaining party may as well file for separation or divorce. Equally plausibly, however, *some* marriages might be saved if the law would not relegate the parties to divorce or separation proceedings, when all they wish to gain is some degree of financial certainty. Conciliation may help, but while the trend is growing, not enough courts have institutionalized the use of nonjudicial help (§ 22.6). To summarize, the law does *not* involve itself with support *enforcement* until the marriage is in trouble. For the *ongoing* marriage the law has set neither a conveniently usable standard nor is it providing means for assuring a fair allocation of the earning spouse's pay.

§ 8.2   Actual Agency

Within the *ongoing* marriage relationship, the spousal support obligation may be litigated indirectly. A merchant may sue for purchases made by the partner. Rules are borrowed from the law of agency: A spouse will of course be liable if the purchase in question was authorized *expressly*. Additionally, an ongoing marriage relationship *implies* a broad range of authority. The test is whether the merchant reasonably could have concluded that the spouse had adequate authority. To illustrate, in the absence of notice to the contrary, Mrs. Rich's charged fur coat would be a safe sale, even without her husband's specific approval. Generally, authority will be implied if one spouse, even without expressly making the other an agent, has simply let the other carry on and has raised no objections to past, similar purchases. This continues until potential creditors are notified of the end of the indulgence.

§ 8.3   Authority to Purchase Necessaries

In addition to *actual*— express or implied—agency, there remains the *wife's* traditional authority, *implied in law,* to purchase "necessaries." Under that rule, if a husband fails to fulfill his duty of support, his wife is authorized to proceed to purchase what necessaries she or their child needs, on the husband's credit and even against his express directions. "Necessaries" obviously include food, shelter and clothing, but they have, depending on the judge's own ideas and the parties' circumstances (and sometimes confusing "agency for necessaries" with "implied agency"), been held to include fur coats, gold watches, jewelry, or an expensive sofa (*Sharpe*). It is up to the merchant to show that the unauthorized purchases were in fact necessaries, and the merchant will not collect from the husband if he actually furnished appropriate necessaries to his wife and family.

It is noteworthy that even relatively recent cases still speak in gender-specific terms (*e.g., Sharpe* majority, *contra* dissent, and *cf. Stromstedt*). One may predict that the rule will either become gender-neutral by evolving to protect purchases by the *non-earning spouse* in *role-divided* marriages or disappear altogether because the increasing financial independence of marriage partners and the attendant obfuscation of role division may make it unworkable. Going all the way in 1983, the Virginia Supreme Court held:

"[T]he necessaries doctrine has its roots in * * * now outdated assumptions as to the proper role of males and females in our society. It therefore creates a gender-based classification not substantially related to serving important governmental interests and is unconstitutional. The hospital urges us to extend the doctrine so it applies to wives as well as husbands, rather than abolish it. Courts in other jurisdictions have adopted this view. However, this task, if advisable, is better left to the General Assembly" (*Schilling*).

§ 8.4 Medical Care

With the weakening of the marital support obligation (corroborated by the decline in awarding alimony after divorce), thought should be given to redefining the appropriate scope and outer limit of spousal support obligations. The parade example is medical care and, especially, nursing home care. Of course, medical care is a "necessary", but the marvelous capabilities of modern health care carry potentially ruinous cost. Should spouses continue to be fully obligated for each other in extreme cases? If so, will divorce become the only reasonable alternative for the sick and aged? For a moment in 1994, it seemed that universal health insurance would render the issue moot. That opportunity lost, we must face these questions. Some courts are loosening the support obligation in special cases. Where a couple had informally lived apart for four years before the husband incurred medical bills prior to his death, the court found it significant that the couple had not separated in order to allow the wife to avoid this liability, and despite recent precedent reaffirming the spousal duty to provide medical care (*Jersey Shore*), refused to hold her liable (*National Account Systems*). In 1993, the Indiana Supreme Court reviewed this trend and stuck by the traditional rule and held a wife liable for her husband's pre-death medical expenses even though she had filed for divorce (*Bartrom*).

With the "Spousal Impoverishment Act of 1989", Congress now requires the states to allow certain set-asides for the at-home spouse that vary from state to state, but still leave the at-home-spouse at the edge of poverty. Congress also has cracked down on so-called "Medicaid planning" that has middle class parents transfer assets to trusted children so as to qualify for Medicaid. Under 1993 legislation, gifts to family members may render the donor ineligible for Medicaid nursing care for as long as one month for each $3,000 transferred within the last 3 years. Moreover, certain "Medicaid Planning Trusts" may no longer stand up, and states must seek recovery from nursing home patients' estates, going particularly after a residence that was exempt during the at-home spouse's lifetime.

§ 8.5 Property Rights During Marriage— Common Law

Two centuries ago Blackstone declared that "the very being or legal existence of the woman is suspended during the marriage, or at least is incorporated and consolidated into that of the husband." More succinctly, husband and wife were one person and that person was the husband. All of the wife's real and personal property came under the husband's control upon marriage, although she received back her realty and personal belongings if her husband predeceased her. If she predeceased him, her estate went to her heirs, subject to her husband's right of curtesy which arose if a child was born of the marriage. This permitted the husband to retain possession of her lands for life. During the continuation of the marriage, the wife had no rights with regard to her husband's realty. If he predeceased her, she was entitled to dower which amounted to one third of all property which he had owned at any time during the marriage. She could also take under his will because a bequest would not take effect until his death had resurrected her legal existence. This is not the place to define the operation of the complex and outdated rules that governed marital property in the common law; suffice it to note that most of them favored the husband, grossly. The common law reality was tempered by trust devices that circumvented the more oppressive property rules and provided the wife a measure of financial independence and protection.

Further, by traditional "logic", a husband's contract with his wife was seen as a contract with himself. For the same reason, neither could sue the other. The wife could neither sue third parties nor be sued concerning injuries to her person or property, nor be sued by them for damage done. All this was the husband's right and responsibility. For good measure, Blackstone added that "the husband also (by the old law) might give his wife moderate correction. For, as he is to answer for her misbehavior, the law thought it reasonable to intrust him with this power of restraining her, by domestic chastisement, in the same moderation that a man is allowed to correct his servants or children." On balance, Blackstone solemnly concluded that "even the disabilities, which the wife lies under, are for the most part intended for her protection and benefit. So great a favorite is the female sex of the laws of England."

§ 8.6 Married Women's Property Acts

Blackstone's optimistic view was not shared widely for long. A movement to improve the rights of married women swept the United States in the last century, and "Married Women's Property Acts" were passed in most states. These acts ended the husband's takeover of the wife's assets upon marriage and, as they still stand today, permit the wife to own, convey and otherwise act with respect to her real and personal property. The acts also permit suits between the spouses when either has inappropriately obtained property of the other, and allow the married woman to sue and be sued without joining her husband. The husband is exempted from liability for his wife's torts, and neither is held liable for the non-marital debts of the other. The statutes disallowed a suit by either spouse against the other for a tort to the person committed during the marriage, but this "immunity" is disappearing fast (§§ 9.3, 25.6). The wife is given the power to contract and full rights to her own earnings, and contracts between husband and wife on matters of business are generally enforceable, especially when they work together in a *de facto* or *de jure* partnership. Contracts for *domestic* services, however, generally remain invalid, because such duties are deemed implicit in the marriage relationship, unless the services are quite out the ordinary, such as providing for a sick relative of the spouse, if the care provided goes well beyond what is normally understood to be domestic services. Even extraordinary nursing services provided to a spouse, however, are not generally compensable, the Virginia Supreme Court reaffirmed in 1994 in a divided opinion (*Dade, cf. Dept. of Human Resources*).

The "Married Women's Property Acts" were intended to improve the married woman's legal position. On their face, these acts approached equality, entitling husband and wife to their separate properties and to their own earnings. The detail that was overlooked was that when these laws were enacted and for a long time after, the typical married woman had no earnings. In consequence, so long as it remained the social norm that the husband was the

sole or principal earner, wives continued without or
with inferior marital property rights. Changed social conditions are belatedly putting meaning into
the separate property concept—one century later
and, ironically, at the very time when community or
marital property regimes govern marriage and,
more importantly, divorce in community and in
separate property states (Ch. 26).

§ 8.7 Joint Property and Presumptions of Ownership in Separate Property Jurisdictions

Though well-intentioned, the "Married Women's
Property Acts" failed to provide the non-earning
wife in the role-divided marriage any *property* interest in her husband's work product, as distinguished
from support rights. A non-earning wife could obtain marriage-related *property* only by *gift* from her
earning husband, in compliance with formal requirements attending gifts. If a homemaker had
saved money from her household allowance, she was
held *not* to own the savings, but to hold them for
her husband (*Hardy*). Even within this framework, however, the common law jurisdictions have
long recognized certain forms of community ownership by spouses. With regard to realty, a typical
method of taking title is by the *entireties,* a special
form of joint tenancy for husbands and wives.
Upon the death of either spouse, title to real or
personal property held jointly goes to the survivor
automatically.

Since legal title does not necessarily reflect actual (equitable) ownership, two presumptions were developed: If the husband had paid for the property but title was taken jointly, it was presumed that the husband intended to make a gift to his wife. The burden of disproving this presumption rested on the husband, and the courts applied strict standards (*Fraase, Ramsey*). If, on the other hand, the wife furnished the money for property taken in the husband's name, an opposite presumption of *advancement* arose, *i.e.,* that she did *not* intend a gift and, in the absence of clear evidence of a gift, a trust was imposed in favor of the wife. The obvious inequality expressed in these presumptions was held unconstitutional by the Pennsylvania Supreme Court under that State's Equal Rights Amendment (*Butler*). The question the court or, preferably, the legislator must decide is which of the two presumptions to extend equally to *both* parties, or whether the time has come to abandon both presumptions and deal with each case on its individual facts.

In separate property states, the traditional rules largely remain in effect *during* the marriage. Not much harm is done because property ownership in the *ongoing* marriage has no significant repercussions. The important question is what happens upon divorce. Recent far-reaching redefinition of the non-earning spouse's *property* rights upon divorce in most states ignores who owned the property during the marriage (§§ 26.3–7) and, in addition, an increasing number of states allow the concept of "dissipation of marital property" to be invoked.

Upon divorce, that concept may *retroactively* redefine the separate-but-marital property owner's rights in terms of dispositions he or she made during the marriage (§ 26.6).

§ 8.8 Property Rights During Marriage— Community Property

Long ago, civil law influence from France, Spain and Mexico brought community property to Arizona, California, Idaho, Louisiana, New Mexico, Nevada, Texas, Washington and Puerto Rico. Much more recently, the Uniform Marital Property Act brought community property to Wisconsin. In various ways, these ten jurisdictions give each spouse an immediate one-half interest in what is defined as community property. Community property generally is all property that is not statutorily defined as either spouse's separate property. Separate property generally is property each party brought into the marriage as well as property that came to either of them during the marriage by will, bequest or devise. From state to state there are a variety of differences in the definitions of community and separate property. To illustrate, earnings after the marriage on separate property are separate property in most states, but are community property in Texas and Louisiana. In characterizing property as separate or community, some states distinguish between income from and appreciation of separate property, while others do not.

Regarding *management* of community property during the ongoing marriage significant differences appear as well. Texas gives each spouse the sole management, control and disposition over his or her own earnings, the revenue from his or her separate property, recoveries for personal injuries and any revenue relating to community property that thus is under his or her control. Only such separate property as actually is combined with community property becomes subject to the joint management of both spouses, and that only if there is no agreement to the contrary. In short, during marriage the non-earning spouse's *de facto* situation regarding the other spouse's earnings does not differ materially from that in separate property states. In Arizona, on the other hand (and more in keeping with the theory of community property), "the spouses have equal management, control and disposition rights over their community property, and have equal power to bind the community." California provides a "business exception" to the equal management concept, whereby the spouse who operates a business has separate and sole management power, even though the business is community property. In *Kirchberg,* the U.S. Supreme Court invalidated Louisiana's community property statute that gave the husband, as the "head and master", the unilateral right to dispose of property jointly owned with his wife without spousal consent. That holding may affect the states' freedom to allocate community property management, certainly if management roles are assigned by reference to gender (which in the above examples they are not), but *possibly* even if it were shown that, in fact, husbands remain principal earners and thus manage the great bulk of community property (*cf. Kahn*).

Upon divorce or death, major differences appear between various community property systems. Even greater differences appear between community property regimes and the common law separate property systems, although recent reforms in the separate property states have reduced many distinctions—in the direction of community property concepts (§§ 26.3, 4).

§ 8.9 Survivor's Rights on Partner's Death

In separate property states, upon a spouse's death without a will, modern intestacy statutes typically give the surviving spouse all of the estate or one half, depending on whether the deceased spouse has left children or parents. The wife's former right of dower (which may have made sense when wealth was synonymous with real estate) has been supplanted by statutes permitting a disinherited spouse (formerly only the widow) to elect against the deceased spouse's will and receive a share of the estate, typically one third, regardless of the length of the marriage. However, protection of the widow(er)'s share against dissipation (by gifts or otherwise) during the marriage is scant. In 1978, the Illinois Supreme Court upheld *any* actual transfer without retention of an ownership interest, even if it is "for the precise purpose of defeating his spouse's marital property rights" (*Johnson*). An analogy has not generally been drawn to the concept of dissipation of "marital property" that is increasingly invoked on divorce (§ 26.6). By contrast, the Uniform Probate Code, adopted by 1994 in eight and in some portion or form in 40 states, has elaborate provisions defining an "augmented estate" which, among other things, disregards a variety of *inter vivos* property transfers for the purpose of computing the decedent's estate. By 1995, some five separate property states had adopted, and others were considering, important UPC revisions that put the elective share system on an accrual basis and that redefine the "augmented estate" to include the couple's combined assets. In that scheme, the elective share increases with each year of marriage until, after 15 years, the disinherited spouse may claim one half of the whole estate, whether separate or "marital" property.

As a practical matter, surveys indicate that disinheritance of a spouse occurs rarely and that, in contradiction to typical intestacy laws, most spouses actually wish their spouses to inherit the *entire* estate, regardless of the presence of children or parents. Spouses who write wills typically accomplish just that and leave it to the surviving spouse to provide for children.

In a community property state, the surviving spouse already owns one-half of the community property at the time of the death of the other spouse. Accordingly, only one-half of the marital property is at issue. No restrictions (such as the widowed spouse's indefeasible share provided in separate property states) govern the testamentary disposition of property owned by the decedent.

None are considered necessary, because the widow(er) is provided for by ownership of one-half of the community property.

§ 8.10 A Few Thoughts on the Relative Merits of Separate and Community Property

If the community property approach were to provide a distinct alternative to the historically dominant separate property system, each spouse would have to be given a one half (but not greater) interest in the other spouse's earnings during the ongoing marriage and in accumulated property upon termination of the marriage by death or divorce. A theoretically "pure" community property system would, in all respects, consider all property acquired by either spouse after marriage the property of both spouses, except gifts, inheritances and, *probably,* earnings and gains thereon. The "pure community" should feature joint powers of management, control and disposition. Upon the death of either party, only one-half of the community assets would be in the estate and subject to inheritance laws and taxation. For a variety of very practical reasons, however, no jurisdiction has adopted this "pure" approach.

The Problem with Joint Management: Joint decisions regarding the management of property imply a veto power in each party. If equal management or a system of joint management is seen as the logical community approach, the problem of management of business and investment property becomes crucial—as much to guard against spiteful interference as to guard against stubborn inexpertise of the non-active or non-earning partner. The obvious solution would be to exempt business and investment property from the operation of the joint management provisions, but what would remain? Not much more than household property. To assure certainty, it would then probably be practical not to exempt business property, but to rephrase the law in terms of joint or equal management of *household* property. If this view is sound, the Texas option of treating each spouse's community earnings as separate property so long as the marriage continues, emerges as the better idea. This goes far toward reducing what change the community property concept has to offer the separate property states.

Protection for the Disinherited Spouse: The obvious generalization is that community property regimes provide better protection for the disinherited spouse. Nevertheless, each case depends on its individual facts, and the result will vary also with the specifics of the community property system in question. For instance, if most of the deceased spouse's property has remained separate and there is little or no community property, the disinherited spouse will fare badly. In a separate property jurisdiction, on the other hand, she or he would take one third of *all* of the deceased spouse's property, however and whenever acquired. In separate property jurisdictions that have adopted the UPC's accrual share (§ 8.9), the outcome would somewhat more closely resemble the community property situation, although the UPC does include the decedent's non-marital property in computing the survivor's share. Conflict of laws problems may aggravate these difficulties (§ 8.12).

Divorce: Chapter 26 provides details, but this is the place to raise the much neglected issue of whether the ideal marital property regime should produce the same financial results on divorce from, as it does on the death of, the marital partner. A typical scenario is the case where, in a separate property jurisdiction, one spouse wishes to disinherit the other, thereby reducing the "disinherited" spouse's rights to one-third of whatever—even "marital"—property the owner or earner has not disposed of at the time of death. In the same jurisdiction, however, modern divorce law might entitle a spouse to one-half or even more of all marital property. The issue surfaces with particular poignancy when either party dies while a divorce is pending. Courts have held with considerable conviction that if the divorce was not final on the spouse's death, the survivor takes as the widow(er) (*Lawrence, Haviland*). But other decisions hold that the marital property distributable on divorce "vests" upon filing of the divorce (*cf. Jacobsen* where the husband had killed his wife before the divorce). For reasons with which some may and others may not agree, the drafters of the UPC "phased share" amendments deliberately chose *not* to equalize or closely approximate the divorce and death situations (Waggoner, 26 Real Property Probate & Trust J. 683 (1992)).

Tax Differences: Federal gift and estate tax issues were removed in the 1980's when an unlimited exemption became applicable between spouses. Under state laws, however, state gift and inheritance tax liabilities may continue. What is subject to tax may depend on ownership during the marriage and at the time of death which, as explained, may differ considerably depending on whether a separate or community property regime is involved.

With regard to the federal income tax, the community property systems *automatically* and all along provided the advantage of "income splitting". Since one half of the joint income belonged to each spouse, each spouse was taxed at the rates applicable to one half of the joint income. This resulted in ever more significant savings as the marginal tax rates increased. These savings did not go unnoticed in separate property states. In the 1940's, a number of legislatures responded by enacting some form of community property legislation so as to enable their citizens to enjoy the federal tax break. In some instances, the legislation was drafted haphazardly and produced considerable confusion concerning property rights. In one notable instance, the package was declared unconstitutional (*Willcox*). In 1948 and before matters had gone too far in too many states, Congress changed the law to allow "income splitting" to all married taxpayers, regardless of the property system applicable in their domicile. This resulted in repeal of community

property legislation in those states that had oppor-
tunistically adopted it. Remaining income tax differences between the property regimes chiefly ap-
peared in connection with the transfer of assets
between spouses and on divorce and revolved
around the characterization of property as separate
or community. In the 1980's, sensible tax reform
legislation essentially eliminated these differences
(§ 28.3).

§ 8.11 The Future of Community Property and The Uniform Marital Property Act?

The tide of reform proposals has moved many
separate property states toward community property concepts. The most far-reaching proposal is the
Uniform Marital Property Act (UMPA), approved
by the Commissioners on Uniform State Laws in
1983 and by the American Bar Association in 1984.
Wisconsin enacted it almost immediately upon its
promulgation, but soon amended it substantially.
The Act came under consideration in several states,
but had not been enacted anywhere else by 1995.
There is serious doubt whether community property
really does "speak to the realities and equities of
marriages in America in the Eighties." Does *typical* modern marriage still involve an "emotional and
perceived concept of 'ours' '", waiting to be "translated" "into a verified legal reality", as the UMPA's
drafters so romantically expound in the Act's Prefatory Note?

Community property may be an idea that came to us one hundred years too late, one that would have better fitted the times and circumstances when nearly all marriages involved a role-divided partnership that made the wife-mother financially dependent on the husband-breadwinner. Then the Married Women's Property Acts were enacted and their emphasis on separate property was somewhat of an empty gesture. Ironically, separate property may be more in tune with *current* marital lifestyles. Except to the extent that UMPA allows the parties to opt out by contract, that Act and community property do not speak intelligently to the "realities and equities" of the modern model of the two-career marriage with two separate bank accounts and sharing of expenses. Professor Glendon wondered long before UMPA was drafted:

> "There is still one small fact that gives rise to a nagging doubt about our reform efforts. This is that in West Germany and Sweden, home of systems like those we are trying to establish, discontent is being registered with the deferred community. In Sweden, law reforms are in progress which seem likely to result in the curtailment or abolition of the deferred community and its replacement with another system, more responsive to current needs and desires. What is this ultra modern system? Separation of assets. O tempora, o mores!"

The better questions today are not whether community property is better than separate property, but (1) whether the law should impose one specific marital property regime on all marriages and (2) if so, whether that regime should be imposed mandatorily or presumptively. In the real world, these questions lose some of their importance if, on *divorce,* the courts are not bound to follow the *marital* property regime (and by and large they are *not,* under traditional *and* reformed divorce law and even under UMPA which "takes the parties to the doors of the divorce court only"), and if the parties are allowed to "opt out" by reasonable antenuptial or postnuptial arrangements (and UPAA and UMPA allow just that).

Given this state of affairs, the question is reduced to whether the *presumptive* property regime applicable in the *ongoing* marriage, when parties have *not* exercised their "out-option", should be separate or community. The intelligent solution may be to impose neither property regime mandatorily *or* presumptively, certainly not on *all* marriages. Instead, marriage partners should opt into one regime or the other at the time of their marriage, with an appropriate mix of leeway and compulsion to adjust their choice during marriage and on divorce, if vital circumstances change during the marriage. A useful purpose might be served if the law would single out the role-divided child-bearing and child-rearing marriage as a special case, and mandate special protection of the "dependent" partner by limiting both partners' contractual freedom (*cf.* §§ 2.5, 6). In that case, however, a strict community property regime would not necessarily provide the best answer.

§ 8.12   Conflicts Problems

Many and varied conflicts of laws problems arise in relation to marital property. One illustration provides flavor: Consider the not too hypothetical case in which (1) the parties have lived long or all of their lives in a separate property jurisdiction, (2) the husband has been the sole earner (so that all "their" savings are his separate property), (3) they have retired in a community property state and (4) the husband has died with a will leaving nothing to his widow. In these circumstances, the disinherited widow might have no property rights at all upon her husband's death, as she has no legal interest in her husband's separate property and the community property states allow her no "forced share" that she might elect against her husband's will. Several community property states have dealt with this situation by enacting statutes that, for purposes of *inheritance,* consider property acquired elsewhere as though it had been acquired locally. Under such statutes, the disinherited widow in our hypothetical would receive one-half of her husband's property. Some such "quasi-community property" statutes cover only the treatment on divorce *or* death of property acquired in a common law state, but some deal with both death *and* divorce.

Conversely, if a couple had moved from a community property state to a separate property state, the disinherited widow would already own one-half of the community property upon her husband's death. Is she to be allowed to elect a further one-third in the husband's separate and his half of community property against his will? The Uniform Disposition of Community Property Rights At Death Act deals with several of these problems and, by 1995, had been enacted in fourteen states.

CHAPTER 9

HUSBAND AND WIFE IN THE ONGOING MARRIAGE— NAMES, TORTS AND CRIMES

§ 9.1 The Married Woman's Name

Tradition had the family and, more particularly, the wife, bear the husband's surname. An early breach in judicial reluctance to break with this patriarchal tradition was that, upon divorce and upon her request, the former wife normally would be allowed to retake her former name. More recently, many a prospective or continuing wife has mutinied against laws and practices which *seemed* to compel her to bear her husband's name during marriage. Actually, no *general* state statute has effected a change in a marrying woman's surname since Hawaii's statute was declared unconstitutional in 1975. The basic rule is that anyone may call himself or herself by any name—"Rose", for instance—so long as no fraud is intended and the name is not offensive.

The Supreme Court of Wisconsin has rejected any claim to common law status of the name-change tradition, saying that if a wife acquires her husband's name, it is as "the result of usage and her holding out to the world that the surname is the

same as the husband's" (*Kruzel*). Even if this
fascinating denouement is a correct interpretation
of existing, older law (and it may well be), it does
not wipe out numerous legal, quasi-legal and cus-
tomary instances in which even today many a wife
sees few convenient alternatives to using her husband's surname, whether the context be obtaining a
driver's license or credit. Hyphenated or dual sur-
names are on the increase, sometimes carried by
husband and wife, but typically only by the wife
(*e.g.*, Hillary Rodham Clinton). If there is a social
and commercial (credit) interest in identifying each
socio-legal family unit by a common appellation,
especially where there are children, the partners
should decide whether that name is the husband's,
the wife's or a hyphenated mixture. But custom
dies hard. As late as 1993, the Nevada Attorney
General had to order a local election clerk to register a married woman under her own name (Op. No.
93–12, 5/26/93), instead of her husband's, and a
federal district court judge told Ms. Wolvovitz, a 36
year old lawyer, that she must go by her husband's
name, Mrs. Lobel, in his courtroom. " 'Do what I
tell you or you're going to sleep in the county jail
tonight. * * * You can't tell me how to run my
courtroom.' * * * When her co-counsel * * * pro-
tested, Judge Teitelbaum found him in contempt
* * * for 'officious intermeddling' and gave him a
suspended sentence of 30 days in jail. * * * 'What
if I call you sweetie?' Judge Teitelbaum * * * said
when the trial resumed" (New York Times,
7/14/88). " 'I have always referred to married wom-
en by their married name,' said U.S. Senior District

Judge Hubert Teitelbaum, 73. 'This is the way my generation was taught to express respect to the institution of marriage and the family.' Teitelbaum went on to apologize to attorney Barbara Wolvovitz and * * * vacated [co-counsel's] sentence" (A.B.A.J., 9/1/88).

Rebelling against male surname supremacy, Ms. Cooperman sought to persuade a New York court to change her name to "Cooperperson". Judge Scileppi denied her request because he felt that to grant it "would demean the women's liberation movement and expose it to ridicule." He also was concerned that "those named Jackson would want to become 'Jackchild' and 'Manning' might have to be changed to 'Peopling'. The given name 'Carmen' would be converted to 'Carpersons' " (*Cooperman I*). He was overruled on appeal (*Cooperman II*). As far as is known, Ms. Cooperper*son* has not been back to have her name changed to "Cooperdaughter", after taking a closer look at what she had accomplished.

Challenges (*Schiffman, Jech*) also have arisen with regard to children to whom the common law gave their father's surname. In the case of a name change on divorce, the child's best interest controls (*Grimes*).

§ 9.2   Intra-family Tort Immunities

Taking into account the special nature of family relationships, the law of torts traditionally applied special immunities to disputes within the family. At the same time, tort law traditionally recognized certain causes of action uniquely based on family relationships (§§ 9.3, 4). Originally, the doctrine of "oneness" of husband and wife logically precluded any lawsuit between spouses since the husband would have to sue himself and any recovery would be both paid and received by him. Similarly, the husband was liable for his wife's torts to third parties. Since the Married Women's Property Acts were enacted, however, neither spouse has been liable for the other's torts, with few modern exceptions, such as the "family purpose doctrine" (§ 14.5).

The Married Women's Property Acts explicitly continued common law tort immunities between husband and wife, fully or in part. Tort suits between husband and wife (as well as between parent and child) were held to disturb family harmony, although there must always have been doubt whether, once litigation is considered, what harmony there was left to be disturbed. When many or most negligent torts today are covered by some form of liability insurance, the question became whether the mere circumstance that it was the spouse or parent who ran a car over the victim should prevent the victim from recovering damages from the tortfeasor's insurance company. Some courts held that the presence of insurance not only nullified the tired argument regarding family harmony but, indeed, that family harmony would be improved by obtaining cash to help with expenses relating to an accident. The presence of insurance also destroys the argument that tort liability would involve a meaningless shift of family finances from the left pocket into the right. Other courts, however, were persuaded that the very presence of insurance might lead to collusion and concluded that tort suits between closely related persons should not be allowed, to protect the insurance industry. Too few courts considered the sensible argument that insurance rates are based on potential liabilities under *existing* tort law, and that the presence of insurance should not serve as a bootstrap to find liability where none existed before. At the extreme end of the spectrum stood the Supreme Court of Oklahoma which decided in 1984 that tort liability applies *only* in the presence of insurance, thus putting the cart entirely before the horse (*Unah*). Whether tort law and liability insurance are sensible vehicles for the compensation of intra-family injuries is doubtful. In any event, insurance companies increasingly exclude intra-family tort liability, although some courts have held such exclusion clauses to violate public policy (*Jennings*). The spread of no-fault insurance and, eventually, universal health insurance will reduce the importance of this question.

The strong trend—in 1993 the Florida Supreme Court counted 32 states—is to eliminate the spousal tort immunity altogether. Notably, the Seventh Circuit Court of Appeals held that the immunity denies married persons equal protection (*Moran*). For a while, some legislatures and courts distinguished between intentional and negligent torts, but few still do so, and despite a tort suit's potentially contradictory relationship to *no-fault* divorce, divorces that settle the parties' property and support rights, are increasingly held *not* to supersede an ex-spouse's liability for a pre-divorce tort (*e.g., Goldman, Hakkila*).

§ 9.3 Rights of "Consortium"

Consortium actions have a complex history. The common law recognized the husband's right to his wife's "consortium", comprising services, company and the sexual relationship. Based on the doctrine of "oneness", the common law held that only the husband could sue for injuries relating to his wife. In addition to recovery for injury to the wife herself, the husband would be compensated for damage to his relational interest in his wife. When Married Women's Property Acts gave the wife her own suit for injuries to herself, they did not abate the husband's action for his loss of consortium. Today, loss of consortium actually has gained in importance as a factor in tort actions, because a majority of recent cases has concluded that the wife has an equivalent right to recover for loss of her husband's consortium (*Swartz*). Surprisingly few courts have gone the opposite and perhaps more sensible route, using the wife's right to equality as an opportunity to disallow recovery to the husband. To reduce the risk of double recovery, some states require that the spouse's consortium claim be joined with the primary victim's action.

§ 9.4 "Heart Balm" Actions

Derisively classified as "heart balm" actions, suits alleging "breach of promise to marry" (*i.e.,* of an engagement), "seduction", "alienation of affections" and "criminal conversation" may seem today archaic, but such suits are still brought where allowed. "Breach of promise" is not—as would seem logical—a contract action but is a tort. "Alienation of affections" involves turning the head of a married person, and "criminal conversation" designates rather more than talk, the term being a quaint euphemism for adultery. Each tort permits the "victim" to sue for damages and thus receive "balm" for his or her aching heart. The largely historical tort of "seduction" allowed the father of a "fallen" daughter the right to sue her paramour, rather remarkably on the theory of interference with the father's right to his daughter's domestic services. The consenting woman herself typically was not permitted to sue, although some states permitted her to do so, if the seduction was accomplished by fraud. More generally, seduction has figured as an important element in aggravation of damages in actions for breach of promise. In 1994, Georgia struck down its 1863 seduction statute in a suit filed by a parent against her child's 11th grade teacher, on the ground that only men could be held liable under the law (*Franklin*). Ironically, the thoroughly modern *Marvin* doctrine (§ 6.2) may in some circumstances be viewed as a newborn first cousin of the thoroughly outdated tort of seduction.

The traditional "heart balm" torts (and quite possibly the *Marvin* doctrine), hardly suit current social conditions, even if, in 1993, a Missouri appellate court upheld a $221,000 award to a cuckolded

husband against his wife's lover (*Miller*). Most
jurisdictions have abolished "heart balm" actions or
limited their operation (*Hoye, Neal, Russo*). A
Pennsylvania court found that the constitutional
right of privacy now prohibits such actions: "If the
plaintiff's wife has a constitutional right to secure
contraceptive devices, to undergo an abortion, to
undergo a hysterectomy * * * all without the consent of her spouse, it stands to reason that she
likewise has the right to engage in voluntary, natural sexual relations with a person of her choice"
(*Kyle, cf. Fadgen*). Taking a middle ground, the
Utah Supreme Court abolished criminal conversation, but left alienation of affections alive (*Norton*).
Stating that these actions have been "subject to
grave abuses and [have] been used as an instrument
of blackmail by unscrupulous persons for their unjust enrichment" and that "the award of monetary
damages in such actions is ineffective as a recom-
pense for genuine mental or emotional distress,"
Illinois has limited recovery of damages in these
actions to *actual* damages, prohibiting recovery of
"punitive, exemplary, vindictive or aggravated damages." The latter, of course, have provided the real
incentive for bringing these actions in the majority
of states that allow them. Even so, in 1994 a
federal court in Illinois awarded a jilted attorney
$118,000 in "actual" damages, including pain and
suffering, after an Oregon cattle rancher decided to
break off their six-week engagement because he
thought her to be suffering from "compulsive personality disorder" (*Wildey I*, reversed on the techni-

cality that she had failed to include the date of her engagement in her notice to sue, *Wildey II*).

Elsewhere disappointed lovers and imaginative lawyers have sought to resurrect dollar damages in such cases on grounds other than "heart balm." Recent cases include a divorce suit in which a husband, after a 13–year marriage, was awarded a $242,000 fraud verdict against his wife for inducing him to marry her by pretending to love him and telling him that she found him sexually attractive, whereas she really did not (reversed in 1994 as a "gussied up" breach of promise suit, *Askew*). In 1991, the Wisconsin Supreme Court held that a husband's suit against his wife's lover for the emotional distress he suffered when she gave birth to her lover's child was nothing else but an attempted revival of the tort of criminal conversation, the child being "no more than the natural and probable consequence" (*Koestler*). On similar facts, a claim for "intentional interference with contract"—where the aggravating twist was that the husband had inadvertently turned to the lover for marital counsel, and received "comforting advice"—failed to convince the Nebraska Supreme Court in 1993 (*Speer*). Similarly, a husband failed to recover in a 1993 medical malpractice action from a professional therapist who had had intercourse with his wife, on the ground that he was not the therapist's patient and that the therapist's conduct was not "directed at the plaintiff" (*Pust*). The Oregon Supreme Court dismissed a married couple's "clergy malpractice" suit against a minister and his church where the minister was "ministering" sexually to the wife (*Bladen*). Also in Oregon, a wife failed in all traditional causes of action when she sought to recover from her husband for his extramarital affair, but the Oregon Supreme Court recognized a potential battery action for her in that she had engaged in sexual relations with her husband without knowledge of the fact that he had been unfaithful (*Neal*).

Tort suits for infection with herpes and HIV have been more successful. These cases carry the "heart balm" tradition forward, even if the anatomical focus has shifted away from the heart (*Kathleen K.*). In Miami, $18,000,000 was awarded to the ex-husband of an exotic dancer who had infected him with AIDS. In Louisiana, an ex-wife was awarded $93,-676 for her husband's negligence in transmitting genital warts and herpes to her (*Meany*). And if the lover has no money, consider insurance: The Wisconsin Supreme Court upheld a lover's homeowners' insurance coverage for negligent transmission of herpes (*Loveridge*), and a Minneapolis woman obtained a $25,000 settlement for her herpes infection from her lover's homeowners' insurance company (N.Y. Times, 6/29/85, *contra* when the lover knew that his herpes sores were active, *Allstate, Milbank*). If, however, the jurisdiction criminalizes sexual intercourse between unmarried partners, tort damages for injury sustained while committing a crime are not allowed (*Zysk*).

In conclusion, it is worth noting that opposition to "heart balm" is not necessarily the most modern attitude: Professor Jane Larson proposes the following addition to the Restatement (Second) of Torts: "One who fraudulently makes a misrepresentation of fact, opinion, intention, or law, for the purpose of inducing another to consent to sexual relations in reliance upon it, is subject to liability to the other in deceit for serious physical, pecuniary, and emotional loss caused to the recipient by his or her justifiable reliance upon the misrepresentation" (93 Col. L. Rev. 374, 453 (1993)).

§ 9.5 The Husband's Consent to His Wife's Abortion?

In 1976, the U.S. Supreme Court answered in the negative the important question of whether state law might require the husband's consent to his wife's decision to have an abortion. The Court found:

"We are not unaware of the deep and proper concern and interest that a devoted and protective husband has in his wife's pregnancy and in the growth and development of the fetus she is carrying. Neither has this Court failed to appreciate the importance of the marital relationship in our society. [Citing *Griswold* and *Maynard*]. Moreover we recognize that the decision whether to undergo or to forego an abortion may have profound effects on the future of any marriage, effects that are both physical and mental, and possibly deleterious. Notwithstanding these factors, we cannot hold that the State has the constitutional authority to give the spouse unilaterally the ability to prohibit the wife from terminating her pregnancy, when the State itself lacks that right. [Citing *Eisenstadt*]'' (*Danforth*).

The next question was whether the State may require that the husband be *notified* if his wife wishes to have an abortion. In 1992, the U.S. Supreme Court provided another negative answer:

"The spousal notification requirement is thus likely to prevent a significant number of women from obtaining an abortion. It does not merely make abortions a little more difficult or expensive to obtain; for many women, it will impose a substantial obstacle. We must not blind ourselves to the fact that the significant number of women who fear for their safety and the safety of their children are likely to be deterred from procuring an abortion as surely as if the Commonwealth had outlawed abortion in all cases" (*Casey*).

The question remains whether notification *after* the abortion has taken place should be seen as an equally serious burden. Among husbands so predisposed, post-abortion notification may pose an even greater risk of violence. On the other hand, the wife's right to have the abortion should be balanced against the husband's procreative interest in knowing whether *this* wife is willing to bear his child or whether he should seek one more willing.

§ 9.6 Intra-family Crimes—Domestic Violence and Orders of Protection

Studies show a shockingly large incidence of domestic violence. Senator Biden's Senate Judiciary Committee was told:

"In 1991, at least 21,000 domestic crimes against women were reported to the police *every week*; almost one-fifth of all aggravated assaults (20 percent) reported to the policy are aggravated assaults in the home; these figures reveal a total of at least *1.1 million* assaults, aggravated assaults, murders, and rapes against women committed in the home and reported to the police in 1991; unreported crimes may be more than three times this total" (S. Prt. 102–118, Majority Staff Report, 102d Cong. 2d Sess. 1992).

In 1994 and 1995, the O.J. Simpson trial became the highest-rated and longest-running TV documentary, and it was all about domestic violence. An urgent new look is being taken at this dismal phenomenon and is bringing about a landmark change in legislative, police, prosecutorial and judicial attitudes. Many states have elevated spouse battering beyond assault by encoding it as a new felony and now require police officers to make immediate arrests. Many statutes are directed specifically at *wife* battering, but some have been extended to comprehend victimized husbands and unmarried cohabitants.

"Orders of protection" have become the most important tool to prevent and prosecute domestic violence. A detailed statute provides:

"(a) A person who is subjected to domestic violence may petition a superior court for injunctive relief restraining the infliction of further domestic violence against the petitioner by the respondent. (b) Upon receiving a petition * * *, the superior court shall schedule a hearing and shall provide at least 10 days notice to the respondent of the hearing and of the respondent's right to appear and to be heard either in person or by attorney. If, at the hearing, the superior court finds that the petitioner has been subjected to domestic violence by the respondent, the superior court may issue any order it determines to be necessary for the protection of the health, safety or welfare of the petitioner or of a minor child in the care of the petitioner. An order under this subsection may include provisions which (1) restrain the respondent from subjecting the petitioner to domestic violence; (2) direct the respondent to vacate the home of the petitioner; (3) restrain the respondent from communicating directly or indirectly with the petitioner; (4) direct the respondent to pay support for the petitioner or for a minor child in the care of the petitioner if there is an independent legal obligation of the respondent to support the petitioner or the child; (5) award temporary custody of a minor child to the petitioner; (6) direct the respondent to pay medical expenses incurred by the petitioner as a result of the domestic violence; (7) direct the respondent to engage in personal or family counseling; (8) restrain the respondent from entering

a propelled vehicle in the possession of or occupied by the petitioner. (c) An order issued under
this section remains in effect for a period of time
not to exceed 90 days. However, the petitioner
may petition the superior court for an extension
of a provision of the order * * *'' (Alaska Stat.
§ 25.35.010 (1983); *See Siggelkow*).

The police, prosecutorial and judicial handling of
intra-family disputes in criminal channels often differs from the handling of criminal offenses committed against strangers. Civil rights liability for inap-
propriate police conduct or ineffective police protection is another—though cautiously limited—legal
tool in the struggle against a sorry tradition of
inadequate police response to domestic violence.
To find liability, there must be a ''special relationship'' distinguishing the plaintiff from the ''general
public'' that imposes a duty to act on the police.
''The state's awareness of the victim's plight, by
itself, will not create a 'special relationship' ''
(*Thurman, Nearing, cf. Balistreri*).

A noteworthy complication raised by the U.S.
Supreme Court is that a criminal contempt conviction for violating a domestic protection order may
preclude, on grounds of double jeopardy, a subsequent prosecution for assault or another crime
based on the same facts (*Foster/Dixon*).

§ 9.7 Sex Crimes and Marriage—Rape

Until the 1970's, the rape of a wife by her husband typically was not prosecuted as such. If force
was used, a prosecution for assault and battery was

deemed appropriate. By contrast, even consensual marital sodomy was prosecuted as sodomy, although significant constitutional doubts regarding the criminality of such conduct (if consensual) arise from *Griswold* and the right of marital privacy (*Cotner*). In *Bowers*, involving gay sodomy, the U.S. Supreme Court expressly expressed "no opinion on the constitutionality of the Georgia statute as applied to other acts of sodomy."

In 1978, an Oregon case brought the subject of marital rape into popular focus. Inauspiciously, Mr. Rideout was acquitted of the rape charge brought by his wife (N.Y. Times, 12/28/78). Thus reassured of his innocence, the wife reconciled with Rideout and both rode off on a second honeymoon, although they divorced later (N.Y. Times, 3/10/79). Recently, marital rape prosecutions have been successful, either on the basis of newly enacted statutes, or an amendment removing a marital exception from the state's regular rape statute, or by simply asserting that the law of rape had never recognized an exception for a husband (*Smith, N.J.*). The New York Court of Appeals held the exception unconstitutional, finding "that there is no rational basis for distinguishing between marital rape and non-marital rape" (*Liberta*). By mid–1993, North Carolina was among the last states to repeal its rape exemption for husbands. Many problems, however, remain unresolved or are resolved differently in different states. To illustrate, Maryland's Attorney General ruled in 1994 that a rape prosecution against a husband cohabitating with and not separated from his spouse lies only if force is used. On a lighter note, a 1992 New York decision did *not* permit a Nigerian national to raise his polygamous Nigerian marriage to a 13 year old as a defense to a charge of statutory rape (*Ezeonu*).

In its 1980 Model Penal Code, the American Law Institute did *not* yet see fit to eliminate the marital rape exception, except where the parties are *judicially* separated. Indeed, the Code would extend the rape exemption to cohabitants "living as man and wife, regardless of the legal status of their relationship". The A.L.I.'s position continues to be worth a thought. While rape is a particularly grievous form of assault, it is punished so much more harshly than an ordinary assault *because of the invasion of sexual privacy*. As between marital partners, however, sexual privacy is not at issue in a comparable way—even if Sir Matthew Hale's 17th century pronouncement no longer has appeal: "But the husband cannot be guilty of a rape committed by himself upon his lawful wife, for by their mutual matrimonial consent and contract the wife hath given up herself in this kind unto her husband, which she cannot retract."

§ 9.8 Incest as a Sex Crime

Incest is punishable in varying degrees of severity. Traditionally, many states punished father-daughter incest more severely than mother-son incest. This "discrimination" has been upheld against constitutional challenge on the theory that the potential for duress and imposition is greater in the father-daughter case than in the mother-son situation and, moreover, that the daughter might become pregnant, thus potentially suffering more severe consequences than would a son. *Boyer* upheld a similar statute against Illinois' ERA, but the statute was amended soon after to eliminate the discrimination. Today, the issue of incest has gained high visibility in the form of alleged, perceived and actual sexual abuse of children, female and male, in the typical case by their fathers. Criminal charges of sexual abuse fly quickly in disputed custody cases (*e.g.*, Woody *Allen*), and the devastation wreaked on the victim (whether it be the child or, in the case of a false accusation, the father), has been termed the nuclear bomb of family law (§ 18.7).

§ 9.9 Sex Crimes—Fornication and Adultery

Traditionally, fornication and adultery were crimes. In about one half of the states this remains nominally so, even if many statutes hold criminal only "open and notorious" fornication or adultery and, as a practical matter, such statutes are rarely enforced. Subsequent marriage or even an offer of marriage has served as a defense to a prosecution for seduction and, to a limited degree, fornication and sometimes statutory rape, bastardy, or adultery. In today's environment, little can be said in favor of retaining fornication and adultery as "sex offenses". While serious questions have been raised regarding their constitutionality, the U.S.

Supreme Court has shied away from taking a clear position (§ 2.4).

§ 9.10 Testimonial Privilege

The law of evidence extends testimonial privileges to spouses which, originally, forbade one spouse to be heard in testimony for or against the other. Many exceptions have been carved into the old rule. For obvious reasons, a spouse may testify regarding injuries inflicted by the other on that spouse or a child. Other limitations on the privilege conform to its modern theoretical bases. These are the notions that one spouse's testimony against the other would produce family disharmony and, more importantly, that a spouse has a right to privacy regarding confidential, marital communications. The question of whether a spouse's voluntary testimony may be accepted, has sometimes been answered by deciding whose privilege it is, the defendant's or that of the potential witness (*Motes*). It should be noted that no such privilege applies in the parent-child relationship (*Three Juveniles*).

Divorce has often been held to destroy the privilege, even as to testimony concerning events that occurred during the marriage, on the theory that no family peace remains for protection. This seems wrong. If the basis of the privilege is the confidentiality of the marital relationship, *i.e.,* the right to privacy, divorce should *not* end the privilege any more than termination of the attorney-client relationship frees information communicated during its existence.

Current trends run toward restriction of the marital privilege or even outright abolition. While *Griswold* might have supported a broader view, the U.S. Supreme Court in *Trammel* restricted the privilege in the federal arena to *confidential* communications between spouses, following the examples of the Uniform Rules of Evidence (§ 23(2)) and the A.L.I.'s Model Code (§ 215). New Jersey, for example, has abolished the privilege even for confidential communications, but enough states recognize enough of the privilege to merit careful research under the facts of each case.

§ 9.11 The "Unwritten Law" and the "Battered Wife Syndrome"

Once upon a time, the so-called "unwritten law" was statutory in Texas, Utah and New Mexico. In Texas, the killing by the husband of the wife's paramour was designated "justifiable homicide", "provided the killing takes place before the parties have separated"—which called for very careful shooting (*Shaw*). In a few other states, similar notions were developed by court action. In the majority of jurisdictions, a spouse killing his or her spouse or paramour after discovering him or her in adultery is considered to have been sufficiently provoked to bring the killing into the category of "voluntary manslaughter", rather than murder. However, even where all elements of voluntary manslaughter are proved in such circumstances, many juries refuse to convict a cuckolded husband.

Of late, abused wives have turned the table and taken to killing their abusive husbands. In a modern twist of the "unwritten law", many juries and courts have excused the abused wives' behavior by taking a non-technical approach to "self-defense", especially by not insisting on immediacy, or by employing a subjective standard (how threatening did the situation look to *this* woman?), or a "reasonable woman" standard (how threatening would a reasonable woman perceive the situation to be?) (*Hodges*). Others have applied the defense of "temporary insanity". A history of prior abuse by the spouse may be a mitigating circumstance both in terms of offense charged and the sentence imposed. Where convictions are obtained, state governors may grant clemency. In response to clemency drives, 26 women were pardoned in Ohio and 8 in Maryland in late 1990 and early 1991 (N.Y. Times, 1/30/93). In an ominous nuance, an English court in 1984 allowed a wife to inherit from the husband she had killed, but in 1992 a U.S. federal court denied a wife who had killed her husband his pension plan's death and survivor benefit (*Newman*).

Courts now employ the "battered wife syndrome" to combat "general misconceptions about women". New Jersey's Chief Justice Wilentz believes that "the expert could clear up these myths, by explaining that one of the common characteristics of a battered wife is her inability to leave despite such constant beatings; her 'learned helplessness'; her lack of anywhere to go; her feeling that if she tried to leave, she would be subjected to even more merciless treatment; her belief in the omnipotence of her battering husband, and sometimes her hope that her husband will change his ways" (*Kelly*).

This new defense was not everywhere received favorably (*e.g., Norman*). While recognizing that the "battered wife syndrome" may have considerable validity as a diagnostic or therapeutic concept, it was found to be potentially prejudicial (*Thomas*). However, with opinions *upholding* the defense, a string of state supreme courts have provided considerable precedential support (*Hodges, Kelly, Norman, Allery*). Several states have passed statutes specifically permitting testimony regarding the effect of prior violence.

Just before O.J. Simpson's spouse abuse captured the nation's prurient attention, Lorena Bobbitt, the abused manicurist who cut off her sleeping husband's penis with a kitchen knife, had received substantial popular support and, of course, she was acquitted. The New York Times was moved to editorialize "A Million Mrs. Bobbitts" (1/28/94). Let's hope not—though at least one other woman was acquitted after castrating her husband with a pair of scissors (A.P. 3/19/94). The Bobbitt case moved the debate over domestic violence to a lower plateau. As the story unfolded, John Bobbitt's penis was found by the roadside just where Lorena said she had thrown it out of her car window. For better or for worse, it was surgically reattached (N.Y. Times 7/13/93). Making the best of his bad situation, John Bobbitt forgave his "estranged" wife (USA Today Int., 11/16/93) and, by 1994, had hired an entertainment lawyer who booked him on a world-wide media tour billed as "Love Hurts." In addition, he autographed steak knives in restaurants (N.Y. Times 3/11/94), and in August 1994, John asked the court to return to him the knife that had not only been used as evidence. The judge refused to let him have it, pending a determination of whether it was marital property (Newsday, 8/15/94). In a "good news" twist, he learned that he had fathered a son some ten months earlier, not with Lorena and just in the nick of time. The "bad news" was that he owed child support amounting to as much as 17% of his half-million dollar earnings (N.Y. Times 1/24/94; A.P. 4/22/94). Not to be outdone, Lorena had received three movie offers, and 105 separate news organizations had sought interviews with her (N.Y. Times 1/22/94).

CHAPTER 10

EQUALITY OF SPOUSES

§ 10.1 Equal Protection

No application of the Constitution to family law is as important to an understanding of the modern family as is its application to the question of equal rights for women. That subject, of course, is much broader than family law, but has had and will continue to have reverberations regarding family law. As do some of the other constitutional issues, this issue arises in many and varied factual contexts and, throughout this volume, is dealt with on a case by case basis. It should be noted here, however, that after a long string of decisions, including *Reed*, *Frontiero*, *Kahn*, *Taylor*, *Weinberger*, *Stanton*, *Ballard*, *Califano*, *Orr*, *Kirchberg*, and *Rostker*, the U.S. Supreme Court has failed to approach the gender cases from a principled perspective. The nub of the problem is that the constitutionality of certain benign classifications *favoring* women has been upheld, but it is difficult to predict what may be considered "benign" (*e.g.*, *Kahn*, *Rostker*), and what is not (*e.g.*, *International Union*), or even whether a specific instance of discrimination is against women or against men (*Wengler*).

Considering the dramatically changed composition of the U.S. Supreme Court since many of the

156

seminal cases were decided, we remain quite uncertain regarding the meaning of women's equality under the Equal Protection Clause and, particularly, its reach into family law. What *is* clear is that only a minority of the members of the Court ever have considered classification on the basis of sex "suspect" and would have subjected sex discrimination to the *strict* scrutiny that is applied to classifications on the basis of race, alienage and national origin. Instead, the Court has settled on an intermediate level of scrutiny in gender cases, requiring a *valid* gender-based classification to have a *substantial* relationship to an *important* governmental objective (*e.g., Craig*).

§ 10.2 The Equal Rights Amendment

The federal ERA proposed that "equality of rights under the law shall not be denied or abridged by the United States or by any State on account of sex". After a ten-year national battle, the (once extended) time for its ratification by the requisite number of states ran out in 1982. Similar proposals were reintroduced into Congress almost as soon as the original failed, but have not yet succeeded. Most probably, the ERA has only been postponed. It will not go away.

What is the difference between the ERA and the Supreme Court's equal protection analysis? The crucial question that has concerned academics, politicians, polemicists, feminists and male chauvinists was (and remains) whether the ERA would have required an absolute interpretation, so that *no* state

interest, however compelling, would have legitimated *any* classification by gender. The absolute language of the failed amendment seemed to leave no
room for anything but a very strict interpretation.
It was precisely the absoluteness demanded by
many proponents that mustered the substantial opposition that ultimately stalled the amendment on
the basis of perceived "horribles", such as "coed"
restrooms (long used in airplanes) or a combat role
for women in the armed forces (*cf. Rostker*, but now
available in most armed services, short of subma-
rines). In retrospect, it seems probable that the
ERA would have been ratified if its wording had
made it clear that a truly compelling and rational
state interest would continue to permit "common-
sense" classifications on the basis of gender. Since
most proponents of the ERA agreed that it would
have been necessary to apply rational interpretative
tools to prevent the utter nonsense that, in a few
instances, might have resulted from an absolutely
literal interpretation of the ERA, one may argue
that the ERA failed over a bogus issue. This is not
without irony because, if indeed it was the ERA's
absolute wording that brought about its defeat,
women now are left with the Supreme Court's
uncertain interpretation of the Equal Protection
Clause that has stopped short of treating gender as
a "suspect classification". Worse, it may be speculated that, during the ongoing political process of
ratification, the Supreme Court purposely refrained
from holding classifications by gender "suspect," so
as not to impose from the bench the equivalent of

an ERA. In 1973, Justice Powell intimated just that in (Frontiero).

§ 10.3 State ERA's

Numerous states have equal rights provisions in their own state constitutions. Interpretation varies from ignoring the state equality provision and relying instead on federal equal protection standards, to giving classifications by sex the "strict scrutiny" that would be applied under the federal equal protection clause, if sex had been held to be a "suspect classification".

§ 10.4 Sex–Specific Discrimination in Family Law

Specific instances of sex-related discrimination in family law are discussed within specific contexts. What follows is an incomplete sampling which suffers from the additional shortcoming that it does not fix a specific point in time. By now, most legislatures have changed the laws described below and many more such laws have been struck down by courts. Moreover, most of the cited instances already involve a substantial withdrawal from earlier common law positions which favored the husband more grossly (*cf.* § 8.5).

With that in mind, we might recall that lower minimum ages for marriage have traditionally been applied to women than to men, and that the same discrimination was carried over to the parental consent requirement. In 1973, a (female) New York judge still upheld and justified this discrimination because the male's legal duty to provide for his family requires longer training and preparation than the woman's marital role (*Friedrich,* reversed on appeal). Today, the U.S. Supreme Court's *Stanton* cases should be read as forbidding such discrimination.

Usually to the disadvantage of the female child, the support obligation owed boys and girls often differed, either by statute or by court decision. The *Stanton* cases remedied that specifically. Further, courts used to invoke tradition to hold that higher education is a "necessary" for a boy, but not for a girl (§§ 15.2, 15.5, *cf.* 15.7). The illegitimate child, finally, had limited or no rights vis-à-vis the father, but had long enjoyed full rights vis-à-vis the mother (§ 11.7). *Levy* and more than thirty other U.S. Supreme Court decisions have dealt with that (§ 11.8).

Once married, the man's support obligations both to his wife and to his child were greatly disproportionate to those that might be imposed on the wife (§§ 8.1, 15.1). *Orr,* imposing legal equality in matters of alimony, may be interpreted to mandate equality here as well, although as a *practical* matter, husbands who remain primary earners, remain primary obligors (§ 25.1). The husband's name once became the family name (§ 9.1), and he chose the family domicile. If his choice was at all reasonable, the wife would be required to follow him, lest *she* be guilty of desertion which might result in a divorce without economic support (*Smith,* PA). *Kirchberg* held that Louisiana law may not give the husband exclusive domain over community property and goes far to outlaw this type of discrimination. Under traditional tort law, the husband had consortium rights related to his wife, but not *vice-versa* (§ 9.3). All but universally today, equivalent rights are extended to the wife (*Swartz*) or denied to the husband. By contrast, in matters of child custody on divorce, the wife has long been greatly favored over the husband (if giving her the children is doing her a favor), and that attitude continues (§ 18.3).

§ 10.5   Inequality of the Spouses and "Family Facts"

However unpleasant, outmoded or unnecessary, whatever sex discrimination remains in family *law* is trivial in comparison with the inequality of spouses that results from family *facts,* from the traditional role division that places the husband into the money-earner role and the wife into the home where she acquires neither property nor marketable skills. Today and tomorrow, the considerable risk of divorce with inadequate economic provision may make traditional role division a quite unreasonable option. Much may be said in favor of easy divorce, but one argument *against* it is that, without divorce and under earlier forms of fault divorce, the role-divided marital relationship was more secure, at least in economic terms. In the past, when a woman married into role division, she did not take the all but unacceptable economic risk she would take today. If it is true that "women's liberation" and resulting "raised consciousness" have helped put some marriages over the brink, there is at least as much truth in the perception that the movement toward easy divorce has made women's economic emancipation a necessity based on self-preservation. And "family facts" *are* changing; most married women are gainfully employed, though often still only as the "secondary" earner (§ 1.1).

Concerning the—by now rare—argument that legal equality for women or, specifically, that an Equal Rights Amendment threatens the family as an institution, we may rest assured that while our current way of life poses many threats to the family as an institution, spousal equality is not one of them. Most men—some of whom seem tired of the burdens they have carried throughout history in payment for their privileges—today agree that family laws should be recast in gender-neutral terms, in terms of *spousal* rights and obligations, without tying specific rights and obligations to one sex or the other. Today and in the future, spouses should agree among themselves what internal role division, if any, they wish to maintain—by contract (Ch. 7) or by conduct. Certainly, there should be no question that the spouse opting for financial dependency in order to raise children should have correlative rights against the spouse opting for the "earner" role. This has nothing at all to do with (in)equality, except that it equalizes the spouses' positions, when their roles are different—à la "comparable worth", in a context in which that concept makes sense.

PART IV

CREATION OF THE PARENT AND CHILD RELATIONSHIP

CHAPTER 11
LEGITIMACY, ILLEGITIMACY, PATERNITY—AND THE UNMARRIED FATHER'S CUSTODIAL RIGHTS

§ 11.1 History

Blood ties are and always have been a principal determinant of personal relationships and resulting legal rights. Over the years, male dominance has assured that blood ties of *legal* importance, in terms of property and other civil rights, are traced to and through the father. As a refinement of the blood tie, the concept of legitimacy developed early. It distinguished the offspring of stable, permanent relationships (with certain paternity) from the product of casual, impermanent liaisons (with uncertain paternity). The former was allowed to trace his descent to his father and the latter was not. In past societies, in which the passing of property and

163

status from generation to generation of the same family was one of the prime functions of law, the illegitimate child was the loose thread in the social fabric.

Based on these considerations and on society's wish to assure that children would be born within institutional structures capable of raising them— *i.e.,* stable families—a preference for the child of legitimate birth emerged in early law. Later, the Christian Church reinforced these attitudes on a spiritual level. The Church insisted on monogamy, "sins of the flesh" were discouraged, and illegitimate (unlawful) children—bastards—came to be viewed as sin turned into flesh. Indeed, special discrimination was visited on the offspring of illegal marriages and legal distinctions were made between "adulterous," "bigamous," "incestuous," and simple bastards, to the disadvantage of the former. Some of that carried over into early American law and related primarily to the question of legitimation. An "adulterous," "bigamous" or "incestuous" bastard was more difficult to legitimate or, indeed, was incapable of being legitimated. In several Southern states, special discrimination against illegitimate issue of unions involving partners of different races continued well into this century.

Today, U.S. Supreme Court decisions and the Uniform Parentage Act have all but eliminated remaining vestiges of *legal* discrimination, even if social realities still lag behind. One of these is the fact that illegitimacy often is accompanied by poverty. Two married parents in a family setting are likely to provide a better economic climate for child-birth and child-rearing than an unmarried, all too often very young mother. 1993 statistics show that two-thirds of all children living with single mothers are "officially poor," compared with only 10% of children living with two parents. Worse, the rate of births for unwed women rose by 70% between 1983 and 1993. Still worse, the Center for Disease Control reported in 1994 that birth to teenage women increased 27% between 1986 and 1991, although there was a slight drop in 1992. Here is the major cause of the alarming increase in child poverty. It also seems plausible that much of the continuing economic disparity between our white, black and Hispanic populations is due to significant disparities in the numbers of nonmarital births. More than twice as many (57%) black as white (21%) children live with one parent who has never married, compared with 32% of "Hispanic" children (N.Y. Times, 7/20/94).

§ 11.2 Federal Legislation

A substantial boost in the fortunes of the non-marital child came as a result of Federal legislation concerning child support enforcement (§§ 16.2–4). As a condition to participation in the Federal program, the states are required to provide effective means for the establishment of paternity of non-marital children. In 1993 alone, this legislation was responsible for the ascertainment of more than one half million fathers of nonmarital children.

§ 11.3 The Definition of Legitimacy

Legitimacy is defined primarily by reference to the marital status of the child's parents, at the time of the child's birth. The parents' divorce or the husband's death prior to the birth of the child normally does not affect the legitimacy of the child, if the child is born within a reasonable period after the termination of the marriage, often set at ten months or 300 days. Legitimate status may sometimes be obtained without parental marriage. Whereas the common law denied legitimacy to the child of an invalid marriage, most states have agreed for some time that the child of almost any alliance that resembles a formal marriage is entitled to legitimate status. Covered may be children of parents whose marriage did not meet the test of legality by reason of their failure to comply with formal or substantive requirements, such as health checks, consent of a parent's parents, and similar details, or because of legal disabilities of a parent such as a continuing prior marriage (bigamy), consanguinity (incest), nonage, idiocy or insanity, and the like. A large area of potential illegitimacy was thus eliminated.

Only the legitimate child was a full-fledged member of the family of both parents, with rights and reciprocal duties of support, a reciprocal inheritance relationship with both parents and members of their families, entitled to the father's name, and in the custody of both parents.

§ 11.4   Presumption of Legitimacy

The law presumes that a child born to a married woman was fathered by her husband. The purpose of this presumption is to stabilize family relationships. To the extent that an attack on legitimate status is made difficult or prevented, a socially based, legal family relationship that transcends biology may be created (*cf.* Justice Scalia in *Michael H.*). Even so, the definition of legitimacy is only secondarily involved with social relationships and its primary focus is on biological ties.

§ 11.5   Rebutting the Presumption of Legitimacy

Disproof of the presumption that a child born to a married woman was fathered by her husband long was made difficult or impossible. English law once required proof that marital intercourse during the critical period was absolutely impossible, as by the absence of the husband "beyond the four seas," which, according to Coke, meant outside of the jurisdiction of England. Later, other proof of impossibility or high improbability of marital intercourse was admitted. For instance, it might be shown that the husband had been imprisoned at the time of conception or was impotent. In American jurisdictions the requisite improbability now is shown if husband and wife were separated at the probable time of the child's conception under circumstances making it improbable that they had intercourse. However, if a challenge to the presumption of legitimacy is not timely, the husband may be held to be estopped (*Watts*).

When there was marital cohabitation at the time of the child's probable conception, only the advent of blood typing evidence made it possible to rebut the presumption of legitimacy. If the husband really is *not* the father, such evidence will all but conclusively show his nonpaternity in the vast majority of cases (§ 11.15).

Older law also imposed restrictions on the *means* by which the impossibility or improbability of intercourse may be proved. Under "Lord Mansfield's Rule", the spouses were not permitted to testify so as to impeach the legitimacy of a child born after their marriage and that included testimony as to non-access. "Lord Mansfield's Rule" has been abolished by statute or case in most jurisdictions because—in the words of a Pennsylvania judge— there is "no justification or morality in a rule which tends to absolve the rightful father of his duty of support, while imposing such an obligation upon an innocent husband merely because of his marital relationship" (*Savruk*).

The Uniform Parentage Act maintains the traditional restriction on the unmarried man's right to prove his paternity of a child born to a married woman. Impetus to opening up the question of the legitimacy of children born in wedlock came from U.S. Supreme Court cases providing broad substantive rights to the illegitimate child vis-à-vis its natural father (§ 11.8). The Colorado Supreme Court allowed an "outsider" a constitutional right to attack the legitimacy (and assert his own paternity) of a child born to a married mother in an ongoing family setting (*R. McG.*). Other state courts ruled to the contrary. (*e.g.*, A v. X, Y, and Z). The U.S. Supreme Court finally took on the issue squarely in *Michael H.* At the *husband's* insistence—a plurality of the Court *upheld* the presumption of legitimacy in a married setting. The Court thus continued to recognize the State's interest in protecting the integrity of the family unit against an unmarried father's attempt to assert his biological paternity.

§ 11.6 Illegitimacy

The definition of legitimate status automatically provides the definition of illegitimacy. A child who is not legitimate is illegitimate. Traditionally, such a child had a far more tenuous, if any, legal link with its father than that possessed by a legitimate child. Today, constitutional interpretation provides all but complete legal equality to the nonmarital (illegitimate) child (§ 11.8). As a practical matter, the traditional definition of legitimacy now serves primarily to distinguish cases in which paternity is established "automatically" from cases in which special procedures must be used to ascertain paternity.

§ 11.7 Traditional Legal Discrimination

In Blackstone's words, at common law "[t]he incapacity of a bastard consists principally in this, that he cannot be heir to any one, neither can he have heirs, but of his own body; for, being *nullius filius,* he is therefore of kin to nobody, and has no ancestor from whom any inheritable blood can be derived." Accordingly, in the eyes of the early common law, the nonmarital child had no parent at all, neither father *nor mother.* Long ago, most aspects of the mother and child relationship were equalized by law, but most states continued to discriminate heavily in the substantive relationship between father and nonmarital child.

§ 11.8 U.S. Supreme Court Intervention

Since 1968, the U.S. Supreme Court has decided more than thirty cases involving illegitimacy on the basis of the Equal Protection or Due Process Clauses of the Federal Constitution (*e.g. Levy, Glona, Labine, Weber, Gomez, Cahill, Jimenez, Mathews, Trimble, Fiallo, Lalli, Boles, Stanley, Quilloin, Caban, Lehr, Parham, Mills, Pickett, Clark, Rivera, Reed, Michael H.*). Together, these cases and uncounted state court decisions that followed in their wake establish the principle that the nonmarital child is entitled to all but complete legal equality with the legitimate child in practically all substantive areas of the law. Innumerable state statutes discriminating against nonmarital children have been declared unconstitutional, and the Uniform Parentage Act and similar statutes have implemented the Court's mandate. In return—and to the dismay of some—the unmarried father has gained custodial rights (§§ 11.17, 12.6).

§ 11.9 Establishing Paternity

To have meaning, legal rights must be enforceable. In the context of illegitimacy, enforceability implies first and foremost that someone be identified against whom the right can be asserted. While the mother and child relationship typically is established by the fact of birth (*mater semper certa est,* but see § 13.3), proof of nonmarital paternity is not so simple. Judicial means of ascertaining paternity have long been available in nearly all states. From its inception, the "bastardy" or "paternity" action was designed to help the welfare authorities on whom would fall the burden of supporting the child if the father could not be held responsible. The action was of limited scope and its history was in the criminal law. To illustrate, in a prosecution for the crime of bastardy or fornication, the father's support obligation was imposed only incidentally, as a condition to probationary suspension of the criminal penalty.

Today, the paternity action is a civil proceeding. The U.S. Supreme Court has held that proof of paternity need measure no higher than a "preponderance of the evidence" (*Rivera*), and safeguards applicable in the criminal process do not protect the alleged father. Still, a number of states try to have the best (and sometimes get the worst) of the civil and criminal law. New York requires that proof of paternity, in what otherwise is a civil proceeding, be "clear and convincing" whatever this may mean in practical application. The U.S. Supreme Court failed to comment on the constitutionality of this increased burden of proof when it had an opportunity (*Lalli*) and, of course, *Rivera* merely held that a state is not constitutionally required to demand such increased proof. Most states allow the alleged father a jury trial on the issue of paternity, and many state constitutions guarantee it (*B.J.Y.*). In some states, specific statutes authorize the declaration of family relationships, and elsewhere, a declaratory action may be allowed under a general statute authorizing declaratory judgments.

The judgment in a paternity suit normally includes an order against the father for the support of the child. Periodic support payments are the rule, in accordance with federally mandated state child support guidelines (§§ 15.3, 16.2–4). In addition to the child's support, the cost of the mother's confinement and other expenses incurred by her in connection with her pregnancy usually are allowed, as are the expenses of prosecuting the paternity action.

§ 11.10   The Uniform Parentage Act

The Uniform Parentage Act was promulgated by the National Conference of Commissioners on Uniform State Laws in 1973 and approved by the American Bar Association in 1974. Its guiding principle is full equality for all children in their legal relationship with both parents, whatever their parents' marital status. The Act emphasizes that the right in question is the right of the child, whereas traditional paternity acts had viewed the action to be the mother's. By 1995, UPA had been adopted in nineteen states and adapted in many more.   The Act abandons the concept of legitimacy. All children are equal in terms of their relationship with both parents, married or unmarried.   Marriage between the parents retains meaning as the most important indication of paternity, but has no further significance in this context.   An elaborate network of presumptions identifies circumstances in which it is more likely than not that a particular man is the child's father.   These presumptions cover (1) the basic situation in which the parents are married; (2) the case in which the man and the child's mother have attempted to marry prior to the child's birth but the marriage is void or voidable; (3) the case where the man and the child's mother have married or attempted to marry after the child's birth and the father has given some additional indication of recognizing the child; (4) the case where the man receives the child into his home and openly holds it out as his own; and (5) the case where the man acknowledges his paternity of the child in a formal writing without objection from the mother.   In all situations in which paternity is desired to be judicially established or disputed, specifically defined (interested) parties (in some circumstances limited to the mother, her husband and the child) may bring a formal action to ascertain or disaffirm paternity or to confirm one of the formal presumptions.   Efficient informal, administrative procedures are provided to reduce, where possible, the unpleasantness, cost and time that was involved in the traditional paternity case.

§ 11.11 Defenses

The traditional "defense" to a paternity charge was an allegation that the mother had had sexual relations at the critical time with a man other than the putative father. It was the all but universal rule that the mother's allegation of paternity could be discredited by corroborated testimony showing (or the mother's admission concerning) such sexual relations. In the light of advances in blood typing tests, evidence of this sort is much less potent today and, indeed, may backfire under the Uniform Parentage Act. That Act allows evidence regarding another man's sexual relationship with the mother only if blood tests do not exclude the other man and, if jurisdiction can be obtained, he is made a party to the litigation with a view to establishing *his* paternity. Some fathers have sought to escape responsibility by pleading "involuntary causation." Such arguments have been rejected in cases where the mother-to-be had deliberately misrepresented that she was using contraception (*Pamela P.*), or that she was infertile (*Linda D.*), or, indeed, where a sixteen-year-old baby-sitter had (statutorily) raped a twelve-year-old boy (*Hermesmann*).

§ 11.12 Statutes of Limitation

Short statutes of limitation had long restricted the right to bring a paternity action to one or a few more years after the child's birth. The Uniform Parentage Act—in analogy to the tolling of other statutes of limitations during minority—provides for a period of three years after the child reaches majority, although an earlier action is strongly encouraged. Since 1982, the U.S. Supreme Court has struck down periods of one year (*Mills*), two years (*Pickett*), and six years (*Paulussen, Clark*). These cases removed most lingering doubt as to the invalidity of *any* periods of limitation that would cut short a *minor* child's rights. The issue now is moot because federal child support legislation (§ 16.2) in 1984 required the states to "permit the establishment of the paternity of any child at any time prior to such child's eighteenth birthday."

§ 11.13 Settlements and *Res Judicata*

In the past, the paternity obligation could be the subject of a binding contractual settlement between mother and father. Most statutes required that such settlements and compromises be approved officially, either by a court or by the state's attorney, or they prescribed minimum, usually inadequate, terms for a settlement. The traditional view followed logically from statutes that allowed only the mother to bring the paternity action, in her own right and not as guardian of the child. Although the requirement of official approval, where applicable, was intended to compensate for this shortcoming, it has not been an effective safeguard of the child's best interest—nor of the taxpayer's. Responding to relevant U.S. Supreme Court decisions, state courts have upset traditional law that would hold the child to such a settlement (*Gerhardt, Cox*), even while, as the child's natural guardian, the mother continues to have broad powers regarding her child's welfare. Taking the idea one step further, a successful attack on an earlier paternity action in which a man was found not to be the father has come from a child who was not represented in the earlier action (*M.C.*).

A settlement of sorts occurs when the mother and putative father marry, if their marriage extinguishes the paternity claim. Since the parents' marriage is not necessarily tied in with legitimation of the child—an express acknowledgment of paternity being required in many states—the child may be the loser. In some states, an infant whose parents were married after its birth may obtain a declaratory judgment establishing its legitimacy and changing its name to that of the parents.

§ 11.14 Acknowledgment

States give the unmarried father the opportunity to accept responsibility for his nonmarital child by voluntary acknowledgment, typically only if the mother consents, or by bringing a suit to establish his paternity. The Uniform Parentage Act requires a *married* mother's husband's consent to such an acknowledgment.

§ 11.15 Blood Tests

Paternity actions are tied to the use of modern blood typing techniques. Initially the courts were slow to adapt their decision-making processes to this newly available technology. Today, blood tests have lifted the paternity action from an emotion-charged, perjury-ridden affair to the level of scientific fact finding. Procedures provided in the Uniform Parentage Act facilitate the use of such evidence. In 1976, a joint committee of the A.M.A. and A.B.A. developed authoritative guidelines to lead physicians, lawyers and judges through this complex and, if inexpertly handled, dangerous area. Reliance on these guidelines extends from trial courts to the U.S. Supreme Court (*Mills, Pickett, Little*). State courts have held that blood tests may be compelled (*Meacham*). In *Little*, the U.S. Supreme Court held that to deny free blood tests to an indigent paternity defendant was to deny him due process. *Little* may have had a lot to do with Congress' 1988 assumption of ninety percent of "laboratory costs incurred in determining paternity." More recently, and well before *O.J. Simpson* made "DNA" a household word, DNA testing has been employed in paternity cases. Illustrating the potency and longevity of DNA evidence, a North Carolina court ordered the exhumation of an alleged father's corpse for DNA testing (*Batcheldor*). In other paternity cases involving a deceased alleged father, DNA testing was extended to his living relatives (*Sandler, M.A.*).

Quality control of laboratories is another issue. Under federal auspices, the American Association of Blood Banks developed comprehensive "Standards for Parentage Testing Laboratories" (*Kofford*). The AABB also operates an accreditation program for laboratories. Similar controls have been put in place for DNA testing, spurred on by the growing use of DNA evidence in paternity cases.

§ 11.16 Calculating the "Probability of Paternity"

Many laboratories or experts calculate, and most courts accept in evidence, statements of the "mathematical probability" of a specific man's paternity. A note of caution is in order. The cumulative probability of excluding a non-father should not be—but often is—confused with a percentage statements of a non-excluded man's "probability of paternity." The former simply measures the exclusion power (based on a general population) of the tests that have been used in a given case. The latter is a complex statistical calculation based on a comparison of the child's, the mother's and the accused man's genetic markers. The former yields some, but quite uncertain, "evidence" regarding paternity to the effect that if tests were run that would exclude, say, 95% of the general population, and this man is not excluded and has been sexually linked with the mother, then it seems quite probable that he is the father. The latter, however, purports to present a precisely calculated statistical probability of paternity. Alas, experts are not of one mind on the proper method of calculating this probability. No lawyer or judge should deal with statistical evidence of paternity without being thoroughly acquainted with the literature (*e.g.*, 253 JAMA 3298), and the confusion in decided cases (*e.g.*, *Flieger*). At least at first glance, statements of probability ranging up to more that 9 billion to 1, as were solemnly discussed in the O.J. Simpson case, tend to boggle the mind and therefore may be less than useful. The statistically impaired layman may wonder whether, since creation or throughout evolution, there *ever* have been that many people, and even statisticians may question the adequacy of population samples and the appropriateness of methods (see AABB, Inclusion Probabilities in Paternity Testing (1983)).

§ 11.17 The Unmarried Father's Custodial Interest

With fewer preconceptions regarding male and female role division and an increased incidence of cohabiting, unmarried parents having children, along with significantly increased financial responsibility, many unmarried fathers show interest in their children's custody or visitation. Some seek a voice in adoption, or even a veto. The question is what substantive rights should accrue to the father from a determination of paternity? At issue are (1) the father's power to veto the child's adoption arranged for by the mother, (2) the father's opportunity to obtain custody of or visitation with the child (a) if the mother is seeking to release the child for adoption or (b) in competition with the mother, and (3) the definition of the circumstances under which the father might prevail in the cases listed under (1) and (2) above (*cf.* § 12.6).

In the constitutional quest for rationally based actual differences between married and unmarried fathers, the logical starting point is the definition of the *married* father's rights vis-à-vis his child. Given the closer factual situation, the legal rights held

by a *widowed*, *divorced* or *separated* father are to be
defined. "Subtractions" from these rights should
then be made in the case of the unmarried father
only to the extent lesser rights can rationally be
justified by objective differences arising from existing or previous marital status. This may be sound
analysis, but the U.S. Supreme Court has defined
the unmarried father's rights in terms of his *actual
relationship* with the child (*Stanley*). In the married father's case, by contrast, his actual relationship with the child may only affect the outcome of a
custody battle, not his right to wage one. Further,
the Supreme Court has said that the "mere existence of a biological link does not merit equivalent
constitutional protection" (*Lehr*), and this also is at
odds with the legal position of a married father in
otherwise the same factual circumstances—the married father's biological link is protected even if he
has never seen his child. Of course, the father's
marriage to the mother may be compared with the
Lehr test of "coming forward" (explained below).

Before the U.S. Supreme Court got involved, the
nonmarital child's custody, including any decision
on adoption, had in most states been wholly under
the mother's control. Only a few states heard the
unwed father on the question of adoption when he
had acknowledged the child in some way, when he
had adequately contributed to the support of the
child, or when paternity had been established by a
court. By now, the U.S. Supreme Court has had a
significant effect on adoptions of children born out
of wedlock even while some uncertainty remains

concerning the precise meaning of Equal Protection as well as substantive *and* procedural Due Process in this context.

Since 1972, the U.S. Supreme Court has rendered a variety of decisions dealing with the unmarried father's rights concerning his child, including custody, visitation and consent to adoption. In *Stanley,* a father who had long lived with the mother and his nonmarital children in a *de facto* family unit was held constitutionally entitled to notice and to a hearing in proceedings involving the custody of his children. In *Rothstein,* the Court remanded a case involving an unmarried father challenging a *completed* adoption, for decision in the light of *Stanley* but "with due consideration for the completion of the adoption proceedings and the fact that the child has apparently been living with the adoptive family for the intervening period of time". In *Vanderlaan,* the Court remanded to an Illinois court a case involving a father's claim to visitation rights concerning his nonmarital children. One problem that has stayed with us is the proper interpretation of Footnote 9 in *Stanley*:

> "We note in passing that the incremental cost of offering unwed fathers an opportunity for individualized hearings on fitness appears to be minimal. If unwed fathers, in the main, do not care about the disposition of their children, they will not appear to demand hearings. If they do care, under the scheme here held invalid, Illinois would admittedly at some later time have to afford them a properly focused hearing in a custody or adop-

tion proceeding. Extending opportunity for hearing to unwed fathers who desire and claim competence to care for their children creates no constitutional or procedural obstacle to foreclosing those unwed fathers who are not so inclined. The Illinois law governing procedure in juvenile cases provides for personal service, notice by certified mail or for notice by publication when personal or certified mail service cannot be had or when notice is directed to unknown respondents under the style of 'all whom it may concern.' Unwed fathers who do not promptly respond cannot complain if their children are declared wards of the State. Those who do respond retain the burden of proving their fatherhood."

This footnote became more important than the Court might have thought. In the ensuing scramble to reduce its impact on adoptions, numerous legislatures were stampeded into passing sometimes hasty legislation. A number of states require the unmarried father who wants to protect his parental interest to file, *prior* to the child's birth, what might be called a "notice of fornication" whenever he suspects that a sexual partner may be pregnant by him. In a more cautious response to *Stanley*, the 1973 Uniform Parentage Act proposed a procedure by which the rights of the *uninterested* unmarried father may be terminated with reasonable efficiency. Delay and interference with the adoption process are kept to the minimum consistent with a reasonable interpretation of *Stanley*, as follows: When a mother seeks to surrender her child for adoption, the court must try to ascertain the identity of the father (*See CAM*). Speedy termination of his potential rights may be had if he shows no interest in the child or if a *reasonable* effort would provide no clue to his identity. Publication is resorted to only when *and where* (*CAM*) it is likely to lead to identification. In the typical cases, the great majority of children can thus be freed for adoption very quickly. On the other hand, if the natural father or a man representing himself as the natural father claims custodial rights, the court has authority to determine custodial rights. When the man alleging himself to be the father is clearly unfit, the court would terminate his potential parental rights without troubling to decide whether he is the father of the child. The grounds generally defining parental "unfitness" control (§ 17.4), and "demonstrated disinterest" within a reasonable time of knowledge of birth constitutes "abandonment". If, on the other hand, the man alleging himself to be the father and claiming custody is *prima facie* a fit parent, the Parentage Act allows him an action to ascertain his paternity and assert whatever substantive rights he may have.

Numerous states require a *published* notice of the birth of the nonmarital child, addressed "to unknown father" or "to whom it may concern", before an adoption may proceed (*See CAM*). Some clarification came in 1978. The U.S. Supreme Court denied an unmarried father a "veto power" over the adoption of his nonmarital child, when for eleven years he had had, but had not availed himself of, the opportunity under Georgia law to legitimate the child, had supported the child only irregularly and had never lived with the child in a *de facto* family setting (*Quilloin*). In *Caban,* decided in 1979, the unmarried father had lived with the mother and two children for five years, had contributed to the children's support and had seen them frequently after he and the mother separated. Emphasizing the father's *de facto* relationship with his children, the U.S. Supreme Court allowed him to block the adoption of his children by the mother's new husband. In a crucial case decided in 1983, an unmarried father had not supported and rarely seen his two-year old child, but sought to have the child's adoption by the mother's husband invalidated on the ground that his right to due process was violated when he was not given advance notice of the adoption proceeding nor an opportunity to be heard (*Lehr*). The Court found the distinction between *Caban* and *Stanley* on one side, and this case and *Quilloin* on the other "both clear and significant":

"When an unwed father demonstrates a full commitment to the responsibilities of parenthood by 'com[ing] forward to participate in the rearing of his child,' *Caban*, his interest in personal contact with his child acquires substantial protection under the due process clause. At that point it may be said that he 'act[s] as a father toward his children.' But the mere existence of a biological link does not merit equivalent constitutional protection. * * * The significance of the biological connection is that it offers the natural father an opportunity that no other male possesses to develop a relationship with his offspring. If he grasps that opportunity and accepts some measure of responsibility for the child's future, he may enjoy the blessings of the parent-child relationship and make uniquely valuable contributions to the child's development" (*Lehr*).

In *Michael H.,* an unmarried father had briefly enjoyed "the blessings of the parent-child relationship" while he cohabited with the *married* mother. But when he sought custodial rights to his daughter, the mother's husband objected, and Justice Scalia was not amused. He upheld the traditional presumption of legitimacy (§ 11.4). The Supreme Court's warring factions battled over the relative weight in constitutional adjudication of historical analysis and recent precedents that have given new meaning to "Due Process." That did little to clarify what position the *un*married father now occupies in the more typical case where the mother is *un*married. If anything, *Michael H.* muddied further the none-too-clear waters of *Lehr, Caban, Quilloin,* and *Stanley* (*See C.A.S.* for an attempt at clarification.).

It *is* clear, however, that the unwed father has very real rights regarding his child in the increasing number of cases involving cohabitation without marriage, and that he enjoys "substantial protection under the due process clause". *Lehr* had not conclusively answered the question that is most important to the effective functioning of the adoption process: What are the *interested* and *responsi-*

ble, though unmarried father's rights *immediately* after the child's birth to an unmarried mother, before he has had a chance to "grasp" the opportunity to "accept some measure of responsibility for the child's future"? If he does not know of the birth of the child, how is he to grasp his opportunity? If, by placing the child for adoption, the mother denies him any opportunity to "accept some measure of responsibility for the child," should he not be heard at all? In *Caban*, the Court had emphasized that "because the question is not before us, we express no view whether [the difficulties of locating and identifying unwed fathers at birth] would justify a statute addressed particularly to newborn adoptions, setting forth more stringent requirements concerning the acknowledgment of paternity or a stricter definition of abandonment."

Under the Parentage Act, the California Supreme Court has held that "[i]f an unwed father promptly comes forward and demonstrates a full commitment to his parental responsibilities—emotional, financial, and otherwise—his federal constitutional right to due process prohibits the termination of his parental relationship absent a showing of his unfitness as a parent. Absent such a showing, the child's well-being is presumptively best served by continuation of the father's parental relationship. Similarly, when the father has come forward to grasp his parental responsibilities, his parental rights are entitled to equal protection as those of the mother" (*Kelsey S.*).

Two cases in which the mother deliberately frustrated the father's interest in coming forward have attracted national publicity: "Baby Jessica" and "Baby Richard". In both cases, the unmarried mother had surrendered her child for adoption without informing the father. Baby Jessica's mother had lied about the father's identity, and Baby Richard's father had been told that Richard had died after birth. In each case, the father asserted his paternal rights as soon as he found out the truth. In both cases, the mother subsequently married the father. There was a significant difference between the two cases: Jessica's adoption had been denied by the trial court. While the intending adopters appealed, they held Jessica in Michigan for some two years, in defiance of the Iowa court's contempt ruling. Ultimately, the Iowa Supreme Court ordered Jessica given to her father (*B.G.C.*) and the Michigan courts refused to intercede (*Clausen*). In Richard's case, the trial court had ordered the adoption despite the mother's refusal to name the father, and the adopters retained custody of Richard for more than 3 years. In 1994, the Illinois Supreme Court voided the adoption (*Kirchner I*).

In both cases, the press and public were captivated by the notion that adoption by nice, apparently stable, middle-class couples would be in the "best interests" of the two children. The outpouring of journalistic concern all but totally disregarded fundamental legal issues of parental rights and the role of Due Process in creating and terminating family relationships. The regrettable fact is that adoption by nice and well-off people may well be in the "best interest" of many children born to married or unmarried parents in unstable or less than affluent circumstances. That view of the child's "best interest," however, does not accord with our culture's long-standing respect for the primacy of natural parents. Our law presumes conclusively that it is best for a child to maintain the *legal* parent-child relationship with its natural parent, *unless that parent is unfit or has surrendered parental rights.* The "child's best interest test" that governs *custody* disputes between the two natural parents (or even between a parent and a biological or legal "stranger") must not be carelessly transferred to cases where *termination* of parental rights is at issue. In 1995, the Delaware Supreme Court explained this difference in *Reed* where the child had been with would-be adoptive parents for eight years:

"Acceptance of a best interest of the child standard as the exclusive basis for termination of parental rights, however, would be at clear variance with a succession of decisions of this Court which, implicitly at least, permit consideration of the best interest element only after there has been [proof of an enumerated statutory ground and a determination that severing the parental tie would be in the best interest of the child]. Apart from the break with precedent, moreover, acceptance of a best interest of the child as the exclusive or dominant ground for termination of parental rights raises a serious due process and equal protection concern. It is now firmly established that the parental rights of biological parents, including unwed fathers, may not be abrogated through State action without a full opportunity to be heard on the question of parental fitness. * * * [W]here, as here, a parent has sought to assert and maintain a parental relationship over an extended period of time, adherence to established statutory standards for determining unfitness is a sine qua non in any effort to extinguish parental rights."

The legal issue in both Jessica's and Richard's cases (as well as in *Reed* quoted above) was whether the father's justifiable ignorance of his child's birth was a circumstance that should weigh in his favor when measured against the U.S. Supreme Court's (*Lehr*) standard of giving him at least a chance to "grasp" "the opportunity to develop a relationship with his offspring". Neither Baby Jessica's nor Baby Richard's father had had any such chance. This contrasted with the "borderline" case of *Robert O.*, where the father's ignorance of the birth of the child and his consequent delay in asserting his rights was due to his failure to keep in touch with the mother during her pregnancy. New York's highest court had no sympathy with that father and upheld the adoption even though the mother had never been asked by the court about paternity, and she had filed a (in the Court's view technically accurate) statement that no one else was entitled to notice or required to consent to the adoption under New York law. It should be noted that in *Lehr*, the majority and the dissenters dif-

fered not so much on the law as in their interpretation of the facts of the case, *i.e.*, whether father
Lehr actually had had an appropriate opportunity
to assert his due process right to an "opportunity to
be heard 'at a meaningful time and in a meaningful
manner'" regarding his daughter, coincidentally
also named Jessica.

In both cases, the state supreme courts appropriately, if belatedly, gave the fathers their opportunity to be heard. To be heard, however, does not
necessarily mean to be given one's way. Both cases
involved mothers who had voluntarily surrendered
their children and who had deceived the court (Jessica) or the father (Richard). Once the fathers
came forward, it did not follow at all that the
mothers' rights had to be reinstated. And without
such reinstatement, the fathers' claims might well
have been adjudged against them. Both cases involved extended periods during which the child had
lived with the intending adopters. In Richard's
case, the adoption had been ordered at the trial
level and more than three years of seemingly lawful,
if disputed, custody by the would-be adopters had
intervened. Jessica's case was burdened further by
the complex issue of what weight should be given
the would-be adopters' less than lawful custody.

Surprisingly, neither the Iowa nor the Illinois
Supreme Court referred to the U.S. Supreme
Court's 1972 remand to the Wisconsin courts of the
Rothstein case—involving quite similar facts—with
the important admonition to give "due consider-
ation [to] the completion of the adoption proceed-

ings and the fact that the child has apparently lived with the adoptive family for the intervening period of time". Nor did the U.S. Supreme Court see fit to elaborate on *Rothstein* in Jessica's or Richard's cases. With Justices Blackmun and O'Connor dissenting, the Court refused to grant a stay in Jessica's case. Justice Stevens followed Iowa Justice Larson's advice that "as tempting as it is to resolve this highly emotional issue with one's heart, we do not have the unbridled discretion of a Solomon. Ours is a system of law * * * ". Justice Stevens coolly and correctly added that "neither Iowa law, Michigan law, nor federal law authorizes unrelated persons to retain custody of a child whose natural parents have not been found to be unfit simply because they may better able to provide for her future and education" (*DeBoer*). The U.S. Supreme Court refused to grant a stay in Richard's case, with Justices O'Connor and Breyer dissenting (*O'Connell*). This time, Justice Stevens said that he had no authority to consider "the regrettable facts that an Illinois court entered an erroneous adoption decree in 1992 and that the delay in correcting the error has had such unfortunate effects on innocent parties". Dismissing "child's best interest" legislation enacted after the Baby Richard debacle was under way, the Illinois Supreme Court finally ruled in 1995 that the father was entitled to immediate custody of Baby Richard:

"The Does' final argument is that Richard has a liberty interest in the familial relationship he has developed with them. However, they fail to address the liberty interest he may have in being with his natural father. Attempts to assert such a right on behalf of children who have become psychologically attached to a non-parent have not met with success, see *Clausen*. We likewise hold that no such liberty interest exists as to Richard's psychological attachment to the Does" (*Kirchner II*).

The most important issue in these difficult and potentially tragic cases is *speed*. If a procedure were in place to decide such disputes quickly and finally, the Baby Jessica and Baby Richard cases would not have become problems. Another attempt to interest the U.S. Supreme Court in Baby Richard was filed in April, 1995 (and rejected in June), father Kirchner obtained custody of Richard in May while enduring the jeers of some 200 neighbors of the would-have-been adopters who had thoughtfully been alerted to the event by their attorney (A.P. 5/1/95). It is difficult to see how Justice Heiple of the Illinois Supreme Court will not have the last word on the basic principle governing not only these cases but also statutes that would hold otherwise:

"If * * * the best interests of the child is to be the determining factor in child custody cases, persons seeking babies to adopt might profitably frequent grocery stores and snatch babies from carts when the parent is looking the other way. Then, if custody proceedings can be delayed long enough, they can assert that they have a nicer home, a superior education, a better job or whatever, and that the best interests of the child are with the baby snatchers. Children of parents living in public housing or other conditions deemed less than affluent and children with single parents might be considered particularly fair game. The law, thankfully, is otherwise. * * * We must remember that the purpose of an adoption is to provide a home for a child, not a child for a home" (*Kirchner, I*).

Many observers worry that adoptions are made insecure by the decisions in Jessica's and Richard's cases. The better argument goes to the contrary: Adoptions will be much *more* secure if these cases finally persuade over-eager adoption lawyers and courts to follow proper procedures to ascertain the identity of and, where appropriate, deal with (*i.e.,* terminate or recognize) the unmarried father's potential rights.

The Uniform Law Commissioners' Putative and Unknown Fathers Act of 1988 and their 1994 Adoption Act provide guideposts that clarify the unmarried and unknown father's rights. Neither Act had been enacted anywhere by 1995. If and where enacted, these Acts will help avoid disputes—as would compliance with the 1973 Parentage Act's paternal notice provisions after which both newer acts are patterned and which they would update. UPUFA § 3 provides:

"If, at any time in the proceeding, it appears to the court that an unknown father may not have been given notice, the court shall determine whether he can be identified. The determination must be based on evidence that includes inquiry

of appropriate persons in an effort to identify him
for the purpose of providing notice. The inquiry
must include: (1) whether the mother was married at the probable time of conception of the
child or at a later time; (2) whether the mother
was cohabitating with a man at the probably time
of conception of the child; (3) whether the mother has received support payments or promises of
support, other than from a governmental agency,
with respect to the child or because of her pregnancy; (4) whether the mother has named any
man as the biological father in connection with
applying for or receiving public assistance; and
(5) whether any man has formally or informally
acknowledged or claimed paternity of the child in
a jurisdiction in which the mother resided at the
time of or since conception of the child or in
which the child has resided or resides at the time
of the inquiry."

§ 11.18 The Unmarried Father's Right to Visitation

With respect to the unmarried father's right of
visitation, statutory direction remains scant, although the Uniform Parentage Act specifically provides for visitation. Some courts all along would
have granted visitation in appropriate circumstances. After *Stanley* and the *Vanderlaan* remand,
many courts and legislatures have gone this route
(*White*). In any event, a court that would not even
hear the unwed father regarding visitation, if he is
a fit person and is supporting the child, would make
a mistake.

CHAPTER 12

ADOPTION

§ 12.1 Social Functions

Not long ago, the adopting couple's interest in "normalizing" a childless marriage was emphasized. Today, adoption is seen primarily as an institution that helps place the child into an improved environment. The Uniform Law Commissioners' 1994 Uniform Adoption Act "is premised on a belief that adoption offers significant legal, economic, social and psychological benefits not only for children who might otherwise be homeless, but also for parents who are unable to care for their children, childless adults who want children to nurture and support, and state governments ultimately responsible for the well-being of minor children" (*Prefatory Note*).

An increasing number of states permit adoptions to be subsidized, and adoption thereby has matured as a social tool to improve the lot of "hard-to-place" children, often handicapped or with "special needs". The subsidy encourages adoption by suitable parents who could not otherwise afford to adopt, or would not otherwise adopt a child involving extraordinary expense. Subsidized adoption thus helps children whose sole alternative may be long-term institutionalization or foster care without permanence—both more expensive and less satisfactory in terms of the welfare of the child. Federal involvement has been of recent origin, but noticeable, extending from the drafting of a "Model Act for the Adoption of Children With Special Needs" to the "Adoption Assistance and Child Welfare Act of 1980" and amendments, and the "Antifraudulent Adoption Practices Act" proposed in 1984. When formulating their Adoption Act, the Uniform Law Commissioners recognized this trend by expressing "reluctance to impose substantial fiscal or administrative burdens on the states through laws that may more appropriately be addressed by Congress" (Prefatory Note). In April, 1994, the ABA's Adoption Committee reported that two dozen pieces of adoption-related federal legislation were pending.

§ 12.2 Adoption Agencies

In contrast to the State's relaxed and permissive approach to natural parenthood—where only a violation of the minimal standards of neglect and dependency laws gives rise to official concern (Ch. 17)—adoptive placement has been taken very seriously. Adoptions lie largely in the hands of specialized state and private agencies. A number of states have outlawed private placements with non-relatives, and other states require an investigation by a social work agency to be conducted in cases of private adoptions involving unrelated (or even related) persons, or require notification of child welfare agencies. Demands are made concerning the personal and financial qualifications of adoptive parents that many natural parents could not meet. Criminal prosecution may lie if compensation in cash (or a car, *Douglas*) is provided in connection with an adoptive placement. Typical exemptions include medical expenses, legal fees, or appropriate charges of the adoption agency.

The shortage of "desirable"—as defined by intending adopters—babies and pervasive agency control of the supply, raise the question whether would-be adoptive parents have "standing" vis-à-vis an agency. The 1994 Uniform Adoption Act would allow judicial review of an evaluation that a person is "not suited to be an adoptive parent."

Numerous cases emphasize that prospective adoptive parents have no legal right to challenge an agency's refusal to consider them. A few cases have allowed a potential adoptive parent to challenge an agency's blanket policies, such as the requirement that the applicant be of any or of a particular religious faith. Such holdings, of course, merely enter the applicants into the pool of available adoptive parents for further consideration and probably have little bearing on whether they will ultimately be selected to receive a child. "Standing" (in terms of the right to sue) has been recognized more readily if foster parents had received a child for temporary care, even if a contract with the agency expressly negated any "rights" to the child. In 1977, the U.S. Supreme Court issued a thoughtful opinion exploring in some depth the complex relationship between foster parents, child, and child welfare agency, but did not definitely resolve the foster parents' "claim to a constitutionally protected liberty interest", because New York provided adequate procedures "to protect whatever liberty interest [the foster parents] may have" (*Smith v. OFFER*).

§ 12.3 Who May Adopt Whom?

Statutes typically provide that any person, or any proper person, or any adult person may petition for adoption. Adoption by a single person generally is permitted, but a married person must normally adopt jointly with the spouse. As a practical matter, an adoption by a couple is preferred, simply by reason of the likelihood that a couple will provide a more "normal" family environment than could be provided by a single adopter.

All states allow the adoption of minors and a substantial number of states also allow the adoption of adults. In some of the latter, adult adoption is viewed as a separate category and a variety of additional conditions may be imposed, ranging from a prohibition on adopting a spouse (in an attempt to qualify her as a "child" for purposes of a trust or an inheritance), to specified age differences between adopter and adoptee (to maintain a family-like generational age difference), or keeping a married father of two from adopting his girlfriend by whom he had a child (*Jones*), or a professor from adopting his cousin so as to gain free tuition (*M.*), or a gay male from adopting his lover (*Robert Paul*). Recently, efforts by one partner in a same-sex relationship to adopt the other's *child* have sometimes been successful (*B.L.V.B., Tammy; contra Bruce M.*).

§ 12.4 Religion as a Factor

The issue of religion has arisen in numerous ways and has caused significant difficulty. Many statutes still prefer that the child be placed with a person of the same religion, often with the caveat "when practicable". Agency practices involving religious discrimination have been challenged. In 1972, a state agency's refusal to allow adoption solely on the ground that the intending adopters did not have any religious affiliation was upheld against challenge on the basis of the First and Fourteenth Amendments. The U.S. Supreme Court dismissed the appeal for "want of a substantial federal question", although Justice Douglas would have heard the case (*Dickens*).

The factor of religion enters at four levels: (1) The natural parent may have stipulated that the child be placed with adoptive parents of a particular religious persuasion or may have implied the same by surrendering the child to a placement agency affiliated with a particular religion; (2) the child may have reached an age at which a change in religion might jeopardize its psychological welfare; (3) some rite may have been performed upon the child which committed the child to a particular religion; or (4) in determining the intending adopters' "moral fitness" or suitability as adoptive parents, the agency or the court may wish to weigh their religion as a relevant circumstance.

Looking at these factors pragmatically, the natural parent's expressed choice should be considered primarily because *not* to consider it might discourage some parents from giving up a child, even if adoption would be in the child's best interest. Where the child's own and conscious religious affiliation is in question and the child's psychological well-being may be affected adversely by placement into a home with a different religion, religion also is a significant and legitimate factor. The performance of baptism or an equivalent rite on a baby unable to understand, however, would seem to involve an interest that is substantially less serious (if entitled to *legal* recognition at all). Finally, the practice of using "religion" as a gauge for the "moral fitness" of prospective adopters is most problematical. The presence or absence of any or a particular religion certainly cannot be the sole determinative factor in judging the "fitness" of adoptive parents, and courts have so held. But may the fact that the prospective adopters are or are not religious *never* be considered along with other evidence of their character? A concurring judge felt strongly that, as a matter of constitutional law, there is no difference between the obviously unconstitutional practice of allowing the applicant's religion to play the decisive role and letting religion enter as a factor—to be "the destruction of a man's good character or merely a blot upon it" (*Adoption of "E"*). Abstractly, this view makes more sense than when it is applied to real people. The same judge asked the all-important question: "If the belief may be considered as the majority say it may, then how much may be charged against an applicant who is a Jehovah's Witness and therefore opposed to blood transfusions, or a Christian Scientist, who, as I understand his faith, would turn to medical aid only as a last resort?" With that, he overstated his case. While thoughtful courts have allowed the placement of children with adherents of religions following unconventional views concerning medical therapy, on condition that conventional medical treatment would be available to the child, there is legitimate concern with such placements. It also should be noted that there are cases in which particularly zealous adherence to an unusual religion or cult may be evidence less of a good than of a bad environment in terms of the child's best interest.

§ 12.5   Race as a Factor

As in custody disputes among natural parents (§ 18.4), race has figured in adoption. When put in absolute terms, such as formerly employed in several Southern states which prohibited adoptions between persons of different races, the answer is that such discrimination is absolutely impermissible. However, when put in terms of the child's best interest and the question is what effect might this particular interracial situation have on the development and welfare of this particular child, consideration of race as one factor in the whole picture has been viewed as permissible (*Compos, Drummond*). What effect the U.S. Supreme Court's decision in *Palmore* ultimately will have on adoption is still unclear.   Of course, obvious differences between adoption by strangers and post-divorce custody call for cautious interpretation of the Supreme Court's mandate in this context.

Today's racial attitudes have swung to the opposite extreme.   The National Association of Black Social Workers has labelled interracial adoptions "racial and cultural genocide."   Efforts by agencies to block interracial adoptions stand on dubious legal ground, but have met with practical success (*Mansour*, *cf.* Minnesota's 1993 Racial Heritage Preservation Act).   In 1994 Congress enacted the "Multiethnic Placement Act" (42 USC § 5115a) that prohibits any agency receiving federal assistance from discriminating "in making a placement decision, solely on the basis of the race, color, or national origin of the adoptive or foster parent, or the child," though the agency "may consider the cultural, ethnic, or racial background of the child and the capacity of the prospective foster or adoptive parents to meet the needs of a child of this background as one of a number of factors used to determine the best interests of a child".

Remarkably, Congress was very much concerned with race and ethnicity when it enacted the 1978 Indian Child Welfare Act that made the adoption of Native American ("Indian") children by non-Indians all but impossible (*Indian Tribe*, *S.E.G.*).   Even more remarkably, the U.S. Supreme Court upheld this law and endorsed these practices in *Holyfield*, without discussing Due Process or Equal Protection considerations that one might think would arise when "Indian" children must be dealt with on a wholly different level than children of other races— although all are U.S. citizens. Most remarkably, the *Holyfield* opinion was authored by the otherwise child-friendly and liberal Justice Brennan, with Justices Stevens, Rehnquist and Kennedy dissenting. In short, *Holyfield* effectively denies "Indian", and even only half-Indian, children equal access to and treatment in American courts. There is a legal explanation though no satisfactory justification why "Indian" children do not merit protection under our Bill of Rights. (See Nowak & Rotunda, Constitutional Law 132–36 (4th ed.1991)).

§ 12.6　Consent to Adoption

Given the law's strong protection of relationships by blood, parental consent to adoption is essential. Both parents must consent to the adoption of their child, unless parental rights already have been terminated judicially or are terminated in the adoption proceeding because a parent has reached a level of unfitness that is sufficiently serious to terminate parental rights (§ 17.4). The unmarried father has posed a special case, in terms of ascertaining his identity, his right to notice and his substantive right to custody or visitation (§ 11.17). Grandparents have recently been held entitled to notice of and to intervene in an adoption proceeding involving their grandchild (*Brown*).

To cope with the social reality of increased incidence of divorce and remarriage as well as to facilitate the integration of the child of a former marriage into the custodial parent's new marriage, some courts and statutes now seem to permit adoption by a stepparent against the non-custodial parent's will more readily than in the case of a "normal" termination of parental rights. Given a stepparent ready to adopt, the non-custodial father's failure to contribute substantially to the support of a child for a given period and in accordance with ability may suffice for termination (*Jackson*). "Abandonment" by a non-custodial divorced parent may be found more readily than, for instance, when a mother's rights to a child in *foster care* are in question. In the latter situation even a periodic postcard or its equivalent has often been held to document her intent *not* to abandon the child. The *withdrawn* Revised Uniform Adoption Act contained the radical and probably unconstitutional proposal to permit adoption without the consent "of a parent not having custody of a minor [who withholds his consent] unreasonably * * * contrary to the best interest of the minor." This idea—very probably in violation of the noncustodial parent's Due Process rights (§ 11.17)—was not resurrected in the 1994 Uniform Adoption Act.

§ 12.7 Other Consents

A great majority of states set specific age limits other than the age of majority at which a child must consent to its own adoption (from 10 to 14 years). If the child is placed through an agency, the agency's consent is required and may be dispensed with only if the agency withholds consent unreasonably. If the child is in the custody of a guardian, the latter needs to consent.

§ 12.8 Form, Timing and Revocability of Consent

Consents are required to be in writing and may be required to be acknowledged or notarized. To hinder or prevent marketing of babies "endorsed to bearer," many states require the consent to identify the intending adopter, except when the consent is given to an authorized adoption agency. In only a few states, consent may be given prior to the child's birth and such a consent remains revocable until a period after the child's birth. In most states, valid consent may be given only after the birth, with some states requiring expiration of a specific period of time, such as 72 hours.

Provisions that regulate the time and form of consent so closely intend to balance mature consideration on the part of the consenting parent with the equally important interest of finality. Similar considerations apply to the revocability of consent. Most states provide that consent is irrevocable— barring, of course, fraud, undue influence or duress. While that sums up the better view, some states allow, with court approval, a consent to adoption to be revoked for a broad variety of reasons.

§ 12.9 Legal Effects of Adoption

In the eyes of the law, adoption increasingly duplicates the natural parent and child relationship. In most states, the legal assimilation of the adopted child into the adopter's family is complete in all respects. This means, in turn, that all legal ties between the child and its biological parents and family are cut. The legal integration of the adopted child into the adoptive family includes change of the child's name to that of the adopting parents and extends to the issuance of a new birth certificate that does not indicate the adoptive origin of the child, though date and place are usually kept unchanged.

Until recently, a few states imposed a subsidiary support obligation on natural parents in case their adopted child should ever fall on hard times. In a number of states the adopted child still retains inheritance rights in respect of its natural family, although it is also entitled to inheritance rights within the adoptive family. Conversely, although inheritance from the adopted child usually remains within the adoptive family, in some states property that came to the child from its natural family may pass back to the natural family. As a practical matter, of course, a continuing inheritance relationship between the adopted child and its natural parents means little, since the still prevailing (though currently eroding) practice of anonymous adoptions typically prevents the adopted child or its natural parents from knowing when or whether an inheritance is due. A few states limit the adopted child's intestate succession rights to the adoptive parent and do not extend them to the parent's relatives, and inheritance by will or benefits under trusts may be limited to natural children by judicial interpretation of words such as "child" or "descendant" (*Nunally*). Recently, some states have extended rights of visitation to biological grandparents even after their grandchild has been adopted by the new spouse of a former son or daughter-in-law (*C.G.F.,* § 18.17).

§ 12.10 Revocation of Adoption

If revocation of adoption is permitted, all other provisions of law defining the adopted child's relationship with its adoptive parents must be read with that in mind. A few states provide specifically for the revocation or annulment of an adoption order. In these states, grounds for revocation may include the fact that the child is feebleminded, epileptic, insane or has developed venereal disease as a result of conditions existing at the time of the adoption that then were unknown to the adoptive parents. The effect of revocation is to restore the child to its original biological family or to a responsible social agency. Of late, several states have allowed distraught adoptive parents to bring tort actions against agencies, when an agency had deliberately or negligently misrepresented the health of the child or failed to make relevant disclosures (*M.H., Burr*).

§ 12.11 Equitable Adoption

The concept of "equitable adoption" recognizes an inheritance relationship between a child and an "adoptive" parent, if nonrecognition would work an obvious hardship. Equitable adoption provides a remedy where a legal adoption did not take place, but where the would-be parents at one point contracted for legal adoption or at least gave the impression that they would legally adopt the child, and the child has occupied the position of an adoptive child *de facto* (*e.g., Singer*). A number of states favor adoption by estoppel, a number of courts have spoken out against it (the difficulty of knowing where to draw the line is great), and other states have not ruled on the issue. For purposes of imposing a support obligation on a divorcing husband, a sort of adoption by estoppel has been applied where the husband did not object to (or went along with) his wife's procurement of an infant for adoption (*Wener*).

§ 12.12 Anonymity of Adoption?

In recent years, many adoptees have challenged the laws under which most states maintain adoption records in complete confidentiality. Access typically is possible only by court order and for good cause—which does not include the adopted person's "search for identity". Strong opposition to "open adoption" focuses on the privacy interest of the natural mother who gave up her child for adoption perhaps two decades ago, the fear of adoptive parents that their relationship to the child they raised would be jeopardized, and concern that the mere availability of the information would entice adoptive children to become (potentially morbidly) interested in their (often not so happy) backgrounds. Attempts to have adoption records opened on the basis of constitutional challenge generally have failed (*e.g., Roger B.*). Recent legislative efforts, however, were partially successful in more than a dozen states, in addition to a few states that have long had open records. The modern compromise is exemplified by "registry" laws, under which the opportunity to register is offered to adult adopted persons and natural parents who are interested in meeting. If both come forward, they are matched. After a protracted battle between the "open adoption" and the "anonymous adoption" forces, the Uniform Adoption Act would maintain anonymous adoption and recommends release only of *non*-identifying, typically genetic, information. It also provides a matching registry that is to be available to adopted children over 18 years of age and their former parents, along with the quaint proviso that after 99 years, all files will be unsealed. Good-bye kid, see you in 2095!

§ 12.13 International Adoption

The shortage of "adoptable" babies in developed countries, the unfortunate circumstances in which some children and parents in developing countries find themselves, along with greatly increased international mobility, have given rise to the new phenomenon of intercountry (international) adoptions.

In 1992, approximately 6,500 children were adopted into the United States from abroad.

Actual, rumored and feared abuses of the adoption process for unsavory purposes have ranged from not-at-all improbable allegations of child prostitution (fear of AIDS is increasing the demand for younger prostitutes, N.Y. Times, 2/19/92), to the cold-war-era, Soviet-planted lie that the U.S. uses the international adoptions process to provide a cheap supply of organs to be "harvested" for transplants. More amusing is the rumor—still widely believed in some Latin American countries—that children are adopted to serve as unpaid household help. What is true is that the payment of compensation in connection with international adoption, both to intermediaries—sometimes lawyers—or to parents remains a problem. Indeed, there have been reports of the theft and abduction of babies for international sale.

In this volatile context, the Hague Conference on Private International Law developed a new Convention to regulate and secure international adoptions. Completed in 1993 and going into effect in 1995, the Convention stresses the value of providing a permanent family and home for a child for whom no suitable alternative can be found in its country of origin. The Convention governs all intercountry adoptions of children by adults "habitually resident" in a signatory country. All such adoptions must comply with the Convention's procedural and substantive rules. Compensation in connection with adoption is prohibited, although certain legitimate fees and expenses may be paid. Private (independent) adoptions are permitted, but intermediaries and intending adopters are regulated by the Convention. "Central Authorities", to be established in each signatory country, will supervise all intercountry adoptions. Once the appropriate authorities certify an adoption to be in compliance with the Convention, the adoption must be recognized in all signatory countries. Some 70 nations negotiated this treaty and in early 1994, the United States became the tenth country to sign. By June 1995 twenty-two countries had signed, and the five countries had ratified it so that the Convention entered into force on May 1, 1995. At that time, it was not yet clear when the treaty would be ratified by the U.S. Senate.

CHAPTER 13

ARTIFICIAL INSEMINATION, *IN VITRO* FERTILIZATION, EMBRYO TRANSFERS AND SURROGATE MOTHERHOOD

§ 13.1 New Children, New Issues

Legal relationships created by the modern techniques of artificial insemination, *in vitro* fertilization (IVF), and embryo transplants stand somewhere in between legitimate, illegitimate, and adoptive relationships. Combined with these techniques, the spreading practice of "surrogate" motherhood, typically by artificial insemination but possible also by *in vitro* fertilization and embryo transplant, introduces further complications. Estimates of the incidence of children born in consequence of artificial insemination run to 20,000 children per year. Poor reporting makes it impossible to estimate the true figures. The number of children born as a result of the more recent techniques, worldwide, is believed to range only in the low thousands, even while more than 1,000 IVF clinics offer the technique. In 1992, the success rate for births after *in vitro* fertilization stood near 17%. Some health insurance plans cover the procedure.

The morality of applying these new techniques is under ardent debate. In terms of family *law* and in terms of the interests of the children thus brought into being, however, the morality of what led to "creation" is not relevant. Enough children are "artificially" conceived to take this matter out of the genre of science fiction and philosophical speculation. Real answers are needed here and now. The important question goes to the child's status, which here is meant to encompass both the child's rights against, and the claims on the child by, the various actors in the typical scenario. These include: (1) the married mother's husband when the mother conceived the child by artificial insemination with semen donated by a third party; (2) the woman ("surrogate" mother) who carried the child to term and gave birth to it where the pregnancy resulted either from (a) her artificial insemination with the "order-placing" father's semen or (b) the transplantation of a fertilized ovum (embryo) stemming from another woman such as the wife of the couple "placing the order"; (3) the donor of the semen; and (4) the donor of the ovum or embryo.

§ 13.2   Artificial Insemination

In the situation—now widely accepted—where a married woman, with her husband's consent, has conceived a child by artificial insemination from a donor other than her husband, early cases branded the child a bastard and the mother an adulteress. Today, the judicial and legislative consensus holds that the resulting child is the husband's legitimate child. In many such cases, of course, the presumption of legitimacy that applies to children born in wedlock (§§ 11.4, 5) gives the child legitimate status vis-à-vis the mother's husband. Alternatively, old-fashioned estoppel (*Anonymous*) or the quickly fading "Lord Mansfield's Rule" (a married mother may not impugn the legitimacy of her child, § 11.5) has produced the same result.

Where there is statutory treatment of the question, it generally has followed that suggested by the Uniform Parentage Act. The Act provides that a child born to a married woman, as a consequence of artificial insemination from a donor other than her husband, is legally the husband's child, if the insemination was performed by a licensed physician with the written consent of husband and wife. The sperm donor is specifically dealt out of the picture and "treated in law as if he were not the natural father". Similar provisions are now contained in the laws of a majority of the states. Where a statute does not provide otherwise, liability of the sperm donor for support of the child, or even full legal responsibility as a parent, remains at least a technical possibility.

Inadequate regulation has led to many problems. There is the case of a Virginia physician who was criminally convicted for using his own sperm in as many as 75 successful inseminations (N.Y. Times, 9/8/93)—while his professional liability policy covered him (*St. Paul Fire*). More importantly, many states still do not require testing of "donated" sperm for the HIV (AIDS) virus, even while the

Center for Disease Control recommends that sperm donors be tested at the time of donation, their sperm be frozen for six months, and the donor be retested before his sperm is used.

§ 13.3 *In Vitro* Fertilization and Ovum Transplant

In vitro fertilization has become an accepted treatment for infertility. Various factual scenarios result in the implantation of a fertilized embryo into the "carrier" or "birth mother:" (1) The wife's own ovum may be fertilized with her husband's sperm *in vitro*, to overcome her inability to conceive naturally; (2) A donated ovum may be fertilized *in vitro* with the husband's sperm; (3) A prospective ovum donor may be artificially inseminated with the husband's sperm, and the fertilized embryo removed for transplantation; (4) A fertilized embryo may be used that is a biological stranger to both husband and wife.

§ 13.4 Surrogate Motherhood

Adoptable children deemed "desirable" by intending adopters are scarce. It is therefore not surprising that "surrogate" motherhood by way of artificial insemination has gained sudden prominence. Despite considerable controversy, "surrogacy" involves nothing particularly new—*artificial* insemination with the husband's sperm has simply cleaned it up a bit. The Old Testament tells of Hagar who helped "alleviate" Abraham's wife's (Sarah's) infertility, though even then not without considerable unpleasantness (Genesis Ch. 17). Confusion proliferated when Jacob got involved with Rachel's maid Bilhah and Leah's maid Zilpah, *et cetera* (Genesis Ch. 30).

The most significant cases have been concerned with the establishment of a legal family relationship between the child carried by and born to a "surrogate" mother and the "purchasing" couple, along with the termination of the legal relationship between the child and the "surrogate" mother and her husband. Michigan's Supreme Court allowed a married sperm donor to use the paternity act to establish his paternity with a view of bringing the child into his home. He had paid the "surrogate" mother $10,000 plus expenses (*Syrkowski*). In the District of Columbia, the Superior Court referred to the adoption laws to investigate the suitability of the "purchasers," and suggested that the paternity of the purchasing husband be verified by blood tests (*In re R.K.S.*). In a thoughtful opinion, the court considered many serious legal issues in a context involving a commercial agency, a $25,000 "surrogate" mother contract, and artificial insemination of the "surrogate" with the husband's sperm. A Kentucky circuit court denied the surrogate mother and her husband the opportunity to come into court under the law relating to the termination of parental rights and thereby to transfer legal custody to the "purchasing" biological father (*Baby Girl*). Later, however, the Kentucky Supreme Court held that the statute prohibiting the sale of children for adoption does not apply to "surrogate" parenting

(*Surrogate Parenting*). All four cases struggled with laws quite unsuited to the purpose to which they were sought to be put. They are striking examples of the need for thoughtful legislation.

Good reasons favoring prohibition of commercial surrogate motherhood range from the aesthetic to the moral, ethical and religious—and include the practical. On balance, commercial surrogacy surely raises more intractable dilemmas than its supposed benefits would justify. In the cases just discussed, all went well. In a variety of publicized surrogacy arrangements, however, the transaction did not go smoothly. In one celebrated early case, the "purchasers" (on the live Phil Donahue TV show), refused delivery of a "defective" child. The surrogate mother turned out to be in breach of the surrogacy contract because the child had not even been fathered by the "purchaser" (*See Stiver*). In California, Lucy Thrane decided to keep her and James Noyes' child in violation of her contract with Noyes and his wife. The contract covered her medical expenses, but provided no fee. The case was settled by entering Noyes' name on the child's birth certificate as the father, but he was not allowed visitation (N.Y. Times, 4/18/81, 6/6/81; 7 Fam. L. Rptr. (BNA) 2351 (1981)). In 1990, in an emotion-laden interracial scenario, a ("black") *true* surrogate carrier sued for custody of the child she had borne for a couple whose own ("white") sperm and ("oriental") egg had been employed. By 1993, California's Supreme Court held that the child's "natural mother" was not the carrier, but the provider of the ovum (*John-son*).

In 1990, a Tennessee appellate court awarded a divorcing couple joint custody of their fertilized and frozen-stored eggs (*Davis I*). Ignoring the husband's complaint that he did not want to procreate, nor be held to a child support obligation, the trial court had awarded the "embryos" to the wife. In 1992, Tennessee's Supreme Court held:

"[D]isputes involving the disposition of pre-embryos produced by in vitro fertilization should be resolved, first, by looking to the preferences of the progenitors. If their wishes cannot be ascertained, or if there is dispute, then their prior agreement concerning disposition should be carried out. It no prior agreement exists, then the relative interests of the parties in using or not using the pre-embryos must be weighed. Ordinarily, the party wishing to avoid procreation should prevail, assuming that the other party has a reasonable possibility of achieving parenthood by means other than use of the pre-embryos in question. If no other reasonable alternatives exist, then the argument in favor of using the pre-embryos to achieve pregnancy should be considered. However, if the party seeking control of the pre-embryos intends merely to donate them to another couple, the objecting party obviously has the greater interest and should prevail. But the rule does not contemplate the creation of an automatic veto. * * * This ruling means that the Knoxville Fertility Clinic is free to follow its normal procedure in dealing with unused pre-embryos, as long as that procedure is not in conflict with this opinion" (*Davis II*).

After its ruling, the Court discovered that the clinic's "normal procedure in dealing with unused pre-embryos" was indeed "in conflict with this opinion," specifically that the clinic's procedure was to "donate" unwanted pre-embryos to other childless couples. Since that was precisely one of the possible outcomes that the potential father had sought to avert and that the Court had precluded, the parties were ordered to return to court and agree either on donating the pre-embryos to approved research, or discarding the pre-embryos (*Davis III*).

In California, a lawyer committed suicide and left 15 vials of his frozen sperm to his girlfriend—a bequest his children of a prior marriage contested unsuccessfully, California's Court of Appeal holding that the sperm was property and thus properly in probate, and that posthumous artificial insemination of the unmarried girlfriend would not violate public policy (*Hecht*). In December 1992, a grandmother gave birth to her own grandchild: "The Wesolowskis considered advertising for a surrogate, but Dr. Cooper said they were more likely to attract kooks. * * * 'What about your mom?' * * * The Wesolowskis named the boy Matthew—meaning the gift of God" (N.Y. Times, 2/16/93). Yet another twist was featured by Phil Donahue: The ovum of Jim Mack's sister-in-law had been fertilized *in vitro* by Jim's sperm and implanted in Jim's sister, making for a potential "three-mother" jackpot for the baby boy who was born in 1993, in Illinois. Jim and his wife expected to legalize their relationship to the child by adoption and said: "The Lord plays practical jokes. Just when you think you know your limitations, he'll surprise you" (C.U. News–Gazette, 3/17/93).

In 1987 *Baby M* became the most publicized conflict spawned by the commercialization of reproduction. A sperm-donor father sued to force the surrogate (but natural) mother, who had been hired for $10,000 to carry his child, to turn over the child as agreed in their contract. High drama included the surrogate mother's flight to Florida, threats of suicide and harm to the child, seizure of Baby M by police, and criminal charges against the surrogate mother. A New Jersey judge held "that the surrogate parenting agreement is a valid and enforceable contract pursuant to the Laws of New Jersey. The rights of the parties to contract are constitutionally protected under the 14th Amendment of the United States Constitution." Further, the court found "by clear and convincing evidence, indeed by a measure of evidence reaching beyond reasonable doubt that Melissa's best interest will be served by being placed in her father's sole custody" (*Baby M. I*). The judge also terminated the surrogate mother's parental rights, so that the father's wife would be able to adopt the child. Next, book and movie rights were in dispute, an appeal was taken to the New Jersey Supreme Court, and limited interim visitation rights were restored to the surrogate mother. The mother's legal fees, without the appeal, were reported at $250,000—the equivalent of 25 surrogate pregnancies at market price. Ultimately, a series of appeals gave unsupervised, uninterrupted, liberal visitation to the mother. The court also enjoined the parties from publicly discussing their relationship with the child, or selling "movie rights" without prior approval of the court (N.Y. Times, 3/26/87). The Court concluded:

"Legislative consideration of surrogacy may also provide the opportunity to begin to focus on the overall implications of the new reproductive biotechnology—*in vitro* fertilization, preservation of sperm and eggs, embryo implantation and the like. The problem is how to enjoy the benefits of the technology—especially for infertile couples— while minimizing the risk of abuse. The problem can be addressed only when society decides what its values and objectives are in this troubling, yet promising, area" (*Baby M. II*).

§ 13.5 Surrogacy Legislation

For a while, commercial surrogacy was practiced openly in many states. Advertisements were carried by respectable publications. Women willing to carry a child for others were paid handsomely, although—given not only their relative efforts, but also the fact that the surrogate mother would be "occupied" with just one child for more than nine months—the middle persons profited most, such as Michigan attorney Noel Keane who netted $184,000 from his practice in 1983 (Am. Lawyer, 6/1984).

While *Baby M* and *Davis* spotlighted the void in our laws, widely divergent legislation was proposed in several states to deal with surrogacy. In 1992, Governor Wilson vetoed a California bill that would have regulated surrogacy and "found" surrogacy contracts not violative of public policy. Michigan now bans surrogate motherhood for pay and renders such contracts unenforceable (*Doe v. Attorney General*). By now a significant number of states have enacted a variety of laws banning surrogacy contracts or providing for their unenforceability, several states have expressly or implicitly recognized surrogacy by regulating some legal consequences, and various proposals have been considered, but so far rejected, by Congress.

In 1988, the Uniform Laws Commissioners offered their "Status of Children of Assisted Conception Act", to cover the whole field. The Act—at least as an alternative—would regulate surrogate motherhood and, as regulated, allow it. By 1995, however, only North Dakota and Virginia had enacted it.

Even if they are unenforceable, it is likely that surrogacy arrangements will continue to be entered into. The need, as perceived by infertile would-be parents, is just too great. In the absence of specific legislation, the parties to such arrangements will be subject to the controls of the adoption laws. Actually, those controls are reasonably adequate to deal with most cases, especially when they include a prohibition—as many do—against giving consent to the adoption of a child prior to its birth, and—as most do—prohibit paying compensation to mother or middleman (lawyer, physician, etc.), and—as all do—allow the court to make an appropriate investigation of the prospective adopters' home. If the purchaser-husband's own sperm was used to inseminate the surrogate mother, he may be able to establish himself as the legal father by operation of the paternity laws. Of course, paternity does not equal custody (§ 11.17).

*

PART V

THE PARENT AND CHILD RELATIONSHIP

CHAPTER 14
PARENTAL AUTHORITY AND CUSTODIAL OBLIGATIONS

§ 14.1 Introduction

Historically, parental or more accurately, paternal, power over offspring until the age of majority (now typically eighteen years), was all but unlimited and unchecked. As in other areas of family law in which the United States Constitution has played a role, no specific constitutional provision applies to define the parent's legal right to his or her child, nor the child's own rights that may limit the parent's. Over and over, however, our courts have emphasized the existence and constitutional dimensions of parental rights and, more recently, the child's. Recent U.S. Supreme Court cases deal with the rights of unmarried fathers (*Stanley*, *Quilloin*, *Caban*, *Lehr*, *Michael H*), race and custody (*Palmore*), termination of parental rights (*Lassiter*, *Santosky*), commitment for mental treatment (*Par-*

ham) and the minor's right to birth control and abortion (*Danforth*, *Bellotti I*, *II*, *Matheson*, *Akron II*, *Hodgson*, *Casey*).

In our culture, rights of family privacy and freedom from governmental intrusion rank among the highest values. We remember with horror how Fascist and Communist regimes set young children against parents. We view with unease the increasing transfer to the State of the ideological, moral, cultural and intellectual education of the young, as practiced in many modern societies. On the other hand, we have become aware that the socio-cultural background of a child's family environment may irrevocably stamp the child for life, for better or for worse. We debate which is the greater value, full equality of opportunity (which can be realized only if "bad" *and* "good" parental influence is minimized), or freedom from interference with family autonomy in child rearing practices. How can we properly balance these values?

The law has approached the subject gingerly. Legislation concerning compulsory school attendance, child abuse and neglect and dependency sets minimal standards. Often the laws speak uncertainly and some harbor conflict with specific constitutional guarantees, such as the right of freedom to religion. Traditionally, the parent was king. Of late, however, courts and legislatures have defined many specific instances in which the child is treated as an independent entity, especially in relation to outsiders, such as potential employers, juvenile and school authorities, and even parents, particularly in situations involving birth control and abortion. Dissenting in *Yoder,* Justice Douglas said: "Recent cases * * * have clearly held that the children themselves have constitutionally protectible interests. These children are 'persons' within the meaning of the Bill of Rights. We have so held over and over again."

§ 14.2 Parental Authority

In the first instance, parents are entitled to the custody of their children. They are free to make all decisions relating to the welfare of their child as they see fit, short of violating limited protective laws (Ch. 17). Modern statutes and courts have abandoned the father's traditional primary role and now give equal "powers, rights and duties" to both parents. In the case of divorce or separation, *all* rights of decision and control over the child go to the parent awarded custody, except when joint custody is awarded (§ 18.14). In the case of the death of one parent, custody "devolves" on the other. In the case of death of the second parent, the second parent may all but "will" the child to a person of his or her choosing, by appointing that person "testamentary guardian." Such appointment is subject to judicial confirmation, but usually not much investigation. In the absence of a parent or (testamentary) guardian, or in the case of the legally established inadequacy of a parent or, in some jurisdictions "whenever necessary or convenient," or at the request of a minor above the age of 14, the court will appoint a guardian of the person and of the estate of the child. As may be appropriate, different persons may serve as guardian of the child's person and as guardian of the child's estate.

§ 14.3　Emancipation

Through certain acts and activities on his or her part and on the part of the parents, a child may be emancipated earlier than at the statutory age and thus "escape" parental custody. There are no set procedures by which emancipation may be accomplished. Generally, enlistment in the armed forces, marriage or becoming self-supporting will effect emancipation. Typically, the inquiry is *ex post facto,* and if the minor is in fact independent of the parents, emancipation probably has occurred. As in other areas where courts have broad discretion, judges have tended to evaluate the circumstances of individual cases with a desired result in mind, except in the clearest of circumstances—and sometimes even then.

One important meaning of emancipation is that it ends the parental obligation of support. Children institutionalized "for their own good" usually remain chargeable to the parents, but the State typically cannot obtain reimbursement from parents for the cost of keeping children held for delinquency, or for public assistance payments made to children after they have left the family home (*Parker*). In one case, a drug-using daughter had borne the illegitimate child of a convicted criminal, consequently was unemployed, had rejected an offer that she return to the family home with her child and instead had chosen to live separately with the help of public assistance. The Court refused to require the father to reimburse the social services department for support given the twenty-year-old daughter, finding it "incomprehensible that a parent should be required to contribute toward the support of a child where the child commits acts in total derogation of the relationship of parent and child" (*St. Lawrence County Department of Social Service*). Similarly, a minor mother's eligibility to receive AFDC benefits in her own right was upheld against the welfare department's claim that minor mothers are the responsibility of their parents (*Devino*). Welfare reform proposals targeted in 1995 at "teen-mothers" may reverse these trends.

Another important meaning of "emancipation" relates to the effect of commercial dealings of persons who, but for emancipation, would have been minors. Once a nearly absolute defense, modern law (sometimes resorting to subterfuges drawn from the law of torts, such as misrepresentation, or from quasi-contracts or "unjust enrichment") has significantly restricted the effect of minority as a legal defense to contractual obligations to third parties. Different rules govern a child's or juvenile's tort and criminal liability, and "emancipation" has not played a significant role. Finally, the all but universal move to an age of majority of eighteen years has robbed emancipation of much importance, since the most serious questions concerning emancipation involved precisely the age-spread from eighteen to twenty-one years.

§ 14.4 Parent and Child Tort Immunity

Although the (all too real) fiction of legal identity that governed the husband and wife relationship (§ 8.5) never applied to the relationship between parent and child, the situation was similar. Supposedly to preserve "family harmony", the law disallowed tort suits between parents and children. Again, more than thirty jurisdictions have abrogated the immunity in varying degrees, as in automobile negligence (*Dellapenta*), or a father's sexual abuse (*Henderson*). The immunity typically has survived where an alleged negligent act involves an exercise of parental authority over the child, especially with respect to the provision of food, clothing, housing, medical services and other care, or when an intentional act involves the *appropriate* exercise of parental discipline.

§ 14.5 Parental Liability for Torts of Children

At common law, parents were not responsible for torts their children committed against third parties. When they had neglected their duty of supervision, parents could be held liable for their *own* negligence. This largely remains true today, although many statutes now hold parents vicariously liable for torts committed by their children, for a limited amount. Another exception to parental immunity from liability for their child's torts is the "family purpose doctrine" that has allowed third parties to recover from parents when they were injured by children driving the family car.

§ 14.6 Recovery for Wrongful Death

The dependent child is entitled to recover for the wrongful death of its parent. In the case of the death of a minor child, however, the courts have had difficulty allowing the parents recovery, because traditional tort law was concerned with the measurement of *money* damages. The argument against a monetary recovery in a situation devoid of monetary harm should not be rejected out of hand, considering the overburdened insurance system and the many monetary claims that go unfilled. Modern courts and legislatures, however, have been swayed by the emotional appeal of these cases, and parents now generally may recover for the loss of "society and companionship" of a child or for their mental pain and suffering upon the loss. The further question of whether the parent may recover for loss of enjoyment of a child in case of injury to the child (such as blindness, the *child's* own right to recover not being in question) has been answered affirmatively in some states, and in the negative in others (*Shockley*).

§ 14.7 "Wrongful Life"?

In 1963, a nonmarital child sued its father for having caused it to be born into the damaging status of illegitimacy. An Illinois Appellate Court flirted with the novel claim, found that there was indeed a "tort", but held that any remedy should come from the legislature. The court playfully speculated that to allow recovery in this instance might spark suits for being born into a destitute family (of course with scant chance of collecting a judgment), or being born "of a certain color" and thus be subject to discrimination, or being born with a hereditary disease (*Zepeda*).

The "wrongful life" cases began to get serious when parents sued physicians for malpractice resulting in the birth of *healthy* children. (There is of course no question that negligence resulting in the birth of a defective child is actionable.) Cases have involved faulty sterilization, failure to diagnose a pregnancy or, in the case of a pharmacist, dispensing the wrong "pills". In the majority of states, the courts refuse to entertain such suits, partly on grounds of public policy and partly on the theory that the benefit of having and keeping the child outweighs any damage (*Coleman, Turpin*). Other courts have allowed recovery, some holding that the probable enjoyment the child will bring must be offset against the cost of having and raising the child. The Michigan Supreme Court set this trend with a lengthy opinion rejecting the defendant's claim that the mother should have mitigated her damages by having an abortion or by giving up her child for adoption (*Troppi*). Compensation for the cost of pregnancy and the pain and suffering of pregnancy and childbirth has been upheld more readily (*O'Toole*).

§ 14.8 "Heart Balm" for Children

While "heart balm actions" brought by spouses are now disfavored (§ 9.4), and the traditional common law knew no such remedy for children (*Zarrel-*

la), a few children have been allowed to recover where a lover has alienated a parent's affections (*Wrangham*). Most courts, however, continue to reject such claims.

§ 14.9 Compulsory Schooling and Parental Control

Since the last century, laws compelling school attendance have been common. Today, many states require school attendance between the ages of 7 and 16, unless high school is completed earlier. The U.S. Supreme Court has been concerned with constitutional limitations on the State's power to compel school attendance. In 1925 the Court held that a state may not require attendance at *public* schools, but that equivalent private schooling is a satisfactory alternative (*Pierce*). In 1972, the Court decided that the sanctions of Wisconsin's compulsory school attendance law may not be applied to Amish parents whose children have completed the eighth grade. Various interests were asserted, especially the parent's constitutionally guaranteed freedom of religion, and were evaluated and balanced against each other. Unfortunately, the interest most directly involved, that of the child, was held *not* to be before the Court (*Yoder*). What *is* the State's interest in compulsory education? In the first instance, the State acts in the best interest of the child in requiring that it attain a reasonable level of educational achievement. This makes it all the more regrettable that *Yoder* excluded the child from consideration. As Justice Douglas put it in his partial dissent:

"While the parents, absent dissent, normally speak for the entire family, the education of the child is a matter on which the child will often have decided views. He may want to be a pianist or an astronaut or an ocean geographer. To do so he will have to break from the Amish tradition. * * * If he is harnessed to the Amish way of life by those in authority over him and if his education is truncated, his entire life may be stunted and deformed."

Secondarily, society as a whole has a legitimate interest in an informed citizenry, in terms of the exercise of the vote as well as in terms of economic self-sufficiency. In *Yoder,* Justice Burger insisted that the Amish are a "highly successful social unit" and that "it cannot be over-emphasized that we are not dealing with a way of life and mode of education by a group claiming to have recently discovered some 'progressive' or more enlightened process for rearing children for modern life."

Somewhere below the threshold of *Yoder* lurks the question of parental control over what and how their child is taught in school. This issue relates to the U.S. Supreme Court's long-standing willingness to allow a child to attend a private sectarian school (*Pierce*), to learn a foreign language (*Meyer*), as well as to the cases that forbade prayer or even a bit of silence (with the stated option of silent prayer) in school (*Engel, Wallace*). Related cases include the

use of school premises for voluntary prayer groups
(*Bender*). Courts have given parents the right to
withdraw their child from sex education classes
(*e.g., Medeiros*), and a New York appellate court
held the give-away of condoms in a school unconstitutional. The program was viewed as the provision
of health services without parental consent, rather
than education (*Alfonso*). To comply, New York
developed a parental "opt-out" program. Students
derided the idea: "Students are going to keep on
having sex unless parents chain them to the radia-
tor" (N.Y. Times, 1/11/94). Actually, a desperate
parent had previously tried out just that idea, but
faced child abuse charges even though the child had
unlimited access to "VCR, T.V., music, and a
fridge." ("Teen-ager discovered chained to an iron
pipe * * * to protect her from drugs; * * * She
liked the fast life * * * her mother was afraid she'd
get raped" (N.Y. Times, 9/19/91, 9/20/91)).

Some schoolbooks mirror the parents' ideas on
curriculum content, others do not. In 1992, New
York City schools Chancellor Fernandez suspended
a community school board for objecting to a mandated first grade "rainbow curriculum" that included stories such as "Heather Has Two Mommies,"
"Daddy's Roommate" and "Gloria Goes To Gay
Pride" (N.Y. Times, 10/3/92, 12/3/92, 12/12/92).
The controversy led to the chancellor's dismissal
(N.Y. Times, 2/11/93). At the other extreme, the
dispute on evolution vs. creationism—of "Scopes
Monkey Trial" fame, and thought buried with *Ep-
person*—resurfaced when the U.S. Supreme Court,

in 1987, invalidated a Louisiana law that barred the teaching of evolution unless taught alongside creationism (*Edwards*). In 1995, the governor of New Hampshire commented: "There are worse things taught in our schools" (N.Y. Times, 2/13/95). An explosive issue remains whether the parents' interest (right?) in sending their child to a neighborhood school outweighs the social interest in integration when it is effectuated through busing. So far, the Supreme Court's answer has been that it does not (*Swann*, *Milliken*).

The question of the minor student's rights in school, especially his or her position and that of the parents (which may be in conflict) vis-à-vis the school authorities has been the subject of much interest and innumerable state court cases. Reaching the U.S. Supreme Court were cases protecting the minor's freedom of political expression (*Tinker*), the use of lewd and offensive language (*Bethel*) and censorship of a high school newspaper (*Hazelwood*). New hearing requirements govern suspensions (*Goss*). Students were allowed to bring tort damage suits against school officials for being summarily expelled for "spiking" punch at a school picnic (*Wood, cf. Piphus*). Teachers are allowed to spank school children even over their parents' objection, if certain safeguards are followed (*Baker, Ingraham*). Intriguing, though not entirely consistent with the U.S. Supreme Court's cautious view on spanking, is the practice of teachers bearing firearms in school. So, of course, do students—a nationwide Harris survey in 1993 indicated that 9%

of 6th–12th grade had themselves shot at someone, 11% had been shot at, 40% knew someone who had been shot, and 15% had carried a gun within 15 days of the survey (N.Y. Times, 7/20/93). While some viewed the survey as "alarmist," perhaps it is time for alarm. Widespread use of metal detectors in schools harvests large quantities of weapons (N.Y. Times, 5/4/88, 8/13/94).

The failure of the schools to function as an offsetting, stabilizing influence in child-raising, to compensate for the failure of increasing numbers of parents to provide a home life that is conducive to normal social development, is apparent. Conversely, some public school systems have deteriorated to the point where the environment that they offer frustrates the best efforts of "good" parents. In New York City schools alone, 17,000 incidents of vandalism, drug offenses, robbery, assault and rape were reported in 1993. "When I read the list of weapons we have seized, I wonder if we shouldn't start handing out medals for valor instead of report cards" said N.Y. Schools Chancellor Cortines (N.Y. Times, 8/13/94). Later, signaling a major reversal of policy, he called for the reinstitution of special "disciplinary academies" (old Sing Sing High?) for weapon-carrying children (N.Y. Times, 3/8/95).

On the right to education itself, the U.S. Supreme Court has made several pronouncements that are difficult to reconcile. Notable are the ringing words in *Brown,* the basic school integration case of 1954: "[T]oday, education is perhaps the most important function of state and local governments." A more modest view was expressed in *San Antonio* (the 1973 school financing case): "Education, of course, is not among the rights afforded explicit protection under our Federal Constitution. Nor do we find any basis for saying it is implicitly so protected * * *." By 1982 in *Plyler,* involving the illegal alien child right to schooling, the Court wavered back: "Public education is not a 'right' granted to individuals by the Constitution. But neither is it merely some governmental 'benefit' indistinguishable from other forms of social welfare legislation. * * * By denying these children a basic education, we deny them the ability to live within the structure of our civic institutions, and foreclose any realistic possibility that they will contribute in even the smallest way to the progress of our Nation." In the 1994 election, California passed "Proposition 187" that would deny illegal alien children most public services, ranging from schooling to non-emergency medical help. Under *Plyer*, this proposition seems quite unconstitutional—as well as absurd, in the sense that if—as seems to be the fact—illegal aliens are here to stay, *everybody*, not just the children, will be better off if they are not only allowed but required to go to school.

§ 14.10 Medical Care

There are simple cases in which parental neglect fails to provide proper medical care for the child, and the intervention of the juvenile authorities results in providing such care, with or without formal proceedings. More complex are situations in which a court is called upon to balance a parent's assertion of parental authority, often on religious grounds, to deny a child needed medical treatment. Blood transfusion cases involving members of religious sects provide an illustration that has been dealt with more or less summarily. Courts generally appoint a guardian for the child and direct the guardian to consent to necessary blood transfusions and to assure that further necessary care is rendered (*Sampson*). Parents whose child dies after being denied medical care on religious grounds have been prosecuted criminally (*Walker*, but *cf. Twitchell*), and a Minnesota jury awarded a father $9 million in punitive plus 5.2 million in compensatory damages against the Christian Science Church, his child's custodial mother, and her new husband, after his child died in consequence of the mother's refusal to seek medical help, other than through prayer (N.Y. Times, 8/27/94).

Greatly improved medical care capabilities have focused popular and legal interest on the so-called "Baby Doe" cases—cases in which an infant is born alive, but with a serious impairment, and the parents wish to withhold life-sustaining medical treatment (*Custody of a Minor*). Traditionally this was settled in private by physician and parents or, when the issue reached the courts, by accepting the parents' "substituted judgment" to withdraw life support from, for instance, a "comatose or vegetative" child (*Rosebush*). Today, when involving newborns, the issue has been linked with the abortion controversy. An emotional national debate precip-

itated federal involvement through the Child Abuse
Prevention and Treatment Act that defines medical
neglect as a form of child abuse. Except under the
most extreme and hopeless circumstances, (45 CFR
1340.15; *cf.* Bowen), medical treatment is mandated for "disabled" infants, including provision of
nutrition, hydration and medication, and state
agencies must investigate and correct any denial of
treatment. In *Baby K.,* a Virginia court required a
hospital to provide ventilation treatment to an an-
encephalitic baby when the mother, out of her
Christian faith, wished treatment. The court held
that if the hospital refused to treat the baby's next
respiratory crisis it would violate not only the
Americans with Disability Act and other federal
laws, but also the mother's due process rights to
"bring up children" as she saw fit.

Even more perplexing (though less fundamental)
are situations where the treatment is not strictly
necessary in terms of survival, but "merely" highly
desirable. Celebrated cases that did *not* involve
immediate medical emergencies include that of a
fourteen year old boy with a hare-lip whose father
refused him corrective surgery (*Seiferth*) and that
of a sixteen year old boy with a severe case of
curvature of the spine (*Green*). In both cases the
courts refused to intervene, being influenced, however, by the fact that neither child wished the
treatment and both were of an age at which the
judges felt that they should be heard. A variation
on this theme involved 7–year old identical twins,
one of whom faced imminent death from a kidney

ailment. The question was whether to allow the transplant of one of the healthy twin's two kidneys to the other twin. After lengthy deliberation, the court decided that the parents did indeed have authority to decide in favor of the operations, their decision being based on mature consideration, consultation with their minister and physicians, the medical information that a kidney transplant from one identical twin to another is all but assured of success, that there would be psychological benefit to the donor and, conversely, that she might later experience trauma upon learning that her twin could have been saved (*Hart*). In a more complex situation, the unmarried father of 3–year old twins requested that they be blood-tested and, if compatible, that a bone marrow harvesting procedure be performed on them, for the benefit of leukemia-stricken Jean–Pierre, another son of his by another mother. The twins' mother had their sole custody and refused to consent. Giving great weight to the fact that the twins and their half-sibling did not live together in one family unit and barely even knew each other, the Illinois Supreme Court denied the request, fully aware "that, without the transplant, Jean–Pierre will almost certainly die" (*Curran*).

To summarize, parents have substantial powers concerning medical treatment administered to their child. Except in emergencies, their consent continues to be required for nearly all types of medical care. This may include ear-piercing—but where *reproductive rights* are concerned, the U.S. Supreme Court has given minors considerably more independence from state and parents. The related issues of parental consent or notice to parents when a minor seeks an abortion were the subject of so many U.S. Supreme Court cases with abundant dissents, concurrences, or mixed issue pluralities, that they can safely (safely at least for this author) be summarized only in the Court's own words:

"We next consider the parental consent provision. Except in a medical emergency, an unemancipated young woman under 18 may not obtain an abortion unless she and one of her parents (or guardian) provides informed consent * * *. If neither a parent nor a guardian provides consent, a court may authorize the performance of an abortion upon a determination that the young woman is mature and capable of giving informed consent and has in fact given her informed consent, or that an abortion would be in her best interests. * * * Our cases establish, and we reaffirm today, that a State may require a minor seeking an abortion to obtain the consent of a parent or guardian, provided that there is an adequate judicial bypass procedure. See, *e.g., Akron II; Hodgson; Akron I; Bellotti II* (plurality opinion). Under these precedents, in our view, the one-parent consent requirement and judicial bypass procedure are constitutional" (*Casey*).

Approximately the same rule applies to parental *notice* statutes (*Akron II, Hodgson*).

But what standards govern a parent's authority to subject a pregnant, *"immature "* daughter to an abortion? So far, there is no clear answer (*cf. Matter of Smith*). Other cases involving reproductive rights deny parents of mentally incompetent minors the right to have him or her sterilized (*A.L., cf. Stump*), or restrictively define the procedures that must govern any such decision (*Grady*). The parents' authority to commit their child to a psychiatric institution has come under Due Process scrutiny, with the U.S. Supreme Court holding that a full, adversary hearing is *not* required, so long as certain basic safeguards are in place to prevent parents from "railroading their children into asylums" (*Parham*).

CHAPTER 15

THE CHILD SUPPORT OBLIGATION

§ 15.1 Father's and Mother's Obligation

Today, the parental obligation to support their children rests on father *and* mother, to be shared in accordance with their respective abilities to earn and pay, to render services, or other relevant circumstances. Many statutes have been modernized expressly to change the tradition that imposed primary liability on the father. Courts have intervened (*Lepis*), and an "equal rights" based attack on the traditional, discriminatory support duty imposed on the father has succeeded (*Conway*). As a practical matter, however, so long as the tradition of favoring the mother in matters of custody proves resistant to change (§ 18.3), "equality" in terms of support obligations continues to mean that most fathers pay dollars, whereas most mothers fulfill their obligation by rendering personal care. As the incidence of custodial awards to husbands increases along with the ability of divorced wives to earn meaningful incomes, we may one day see financial support obligations imposed on mothers as often as on fathers. In a better future, disincentives to family formation that currently inhere in our tax and welfare structure would be removed. Beyond that and despite the current fashion of opposing outlays that are or may resemble "welfare," the State will have to take a more active role in supporting the rearing of children. The $500 per child tax credit discussed in 1995 would be a start. In European democracies, the duties of providing sustenance and personal care are tempered by "children's allowances" of varying generosity as well as subsidized day care arrangements, and the two financially most burdensome aspects of child support—health and higher education—are accepted as primarily social responsibilities.

Historically, the statutory civil obligation to render support is an outgrowth of the English "poor laws." These were enacted to protect the public from incurring a welfare burden. In the middle of the eighteenth century, Blackstone did not express a civil support liability running from parent to child, but referred instead to a monthly twenty shilling fine which may be imposed on a parent who does not support his child. It may be incorrect to jump from this (as many have) to the conclusion that the common law did not recognize the parental obligation of child support—Blackstone himself assumed it as a matter of course and called it an obligation of "natural law." Instead, this seeming gap in the common law appears to have been due more to lack of remedies (paralleling other immunities concerning litigation between parent and child and husband and wife), than to disregard of the substance of the obligation. Whatever the historical truth, it surely is worth noting that the Supreme Court of New Jersey struggled mightily in 1953 to find a child support obligation in the common law, failed, and then fashioned one from equitable principles, natural law and reference to the laws of "civilized European countries" (*Greenspan*).

§ 15.2   From Discretionary Factors To Presumptive Child Support Guidelines

The child support obligation is a composite of the child's needs and of the obligor's ability to provide. What is deemed "need" increases in relation to the parents' standard of living. In the recent past, the court's discretion regarding the amount of child support still reigned nearly supreme. The Uniform Parentage Act summarized factors that, prior to the state-by-state enactment of guidelines, were commonly used by the courts in the exercise of their broad discretion:

"In determining the amount to be paid by a parent for support of the child and the period during which the duty of support is owed, a court enforcing the obligation of support shall consider all relevant facts, including (1) the needs of the child; (2) the standard of living and circumstances of the parents; (3) the relative financial means of the parents; (4) the earning ability of the parents; (5) the need and capacity of the child for education, including higher education; (6) the age of the child; (7) the financial resources and the earning ability of the child; (8) the responsibility of the parents for the support of others; and (9) the value of services contributed by the custodial parent" (UPA § 15(e)).

The Uniform Marriage and Divorce Act contains a similar listing.

Even before the advent of federally mandated state-wide child support guidelines, the courts did not adhere consistently to these "common-sense" factors which sought to put some ground under their otherwise unbridled discretion. Despite recent U.S. Supreme Court decisions that may seem to require equal treatment of children, whether nonmarital or of married, divorced or separated parents (§ 11.8), there are three or four distinct regimes of child support. One is applicable in the ongoing marriage, quite another applies after divorce and still different *attitudes* apply in the context of reimbursing welfare authorities and in the case of the nonmarital child.

In the case of the intact family, the courts' traditional and actually well-placed reluctance to interfere with "family harmony" subjects support provided to a child to parental discretion—so long as necessaries are provided (*cf.* § 8.3), and a standard of minimum care that is set by neglect and dependency laws is not infringed upon (Ch. 17). In short, married parents in the ongoing family do *not* owe their children a lifestyle that is consistent with their income and station in life. They may choose to rear their children in any *reasonable* way they see fit.

The theory does not remain the same when the parents separate (see *POPS*, § 15.3), and the practicalities change as well. The decision-making power now is exercised by the custodial parent who, more often than not, is not the paying parent. In that situation, the custodial parent's reasonable choice of lifestyle largely controls, so long as it is consistent with the non-custodial parent's ability to provide. The *de facto* duality of standards of child support applicable to children of ongoing and divorced marriages (§ 15.7), may be illustrated by the fact that children of *divorced* parents have often been held to be entitled to higher education, if the *custodial* parent or perhaps even the child so decided—assuming ability to pay on the parent's part and the child's ability to profit from such education. Without custodial, decision-making control, the non-custodial parent may thus find himself (and, in a future that is near, herself) paying amounts well in excess of those the law would require as a minimum if he (or she) had custody of the child or if the marriage had continued. Increasing use of joint custody arrangements (§ 18.14), may help to alleviate the support problem arising from excessively one-sided decision-making.

§ 15.3 Statutory Child Support Guidelines

A principled approach to child support must *fairly* weigh the child's need against the absent parent's ability to pay. What is "fair?" In the past, few judges had looked kindly at any restraint on their wisdom. That was changing (*Melzer*), even before the federal government required the states to legislate "normal" rates of support, depending on a parent's income and other obligations. Discussion of that subject goes as far back as the early drafting stages of the 1975 Federal child support enforcement legislation (§ 16.2). However, it took Congress until 1984 to require that "each State, as a condition for having its State plan approved, must establish guidelines for child support award amounts within the State. The guidelines may be established by law or by judicial or administrative action." The theory behind allowing each state to develop its own guidelines (while detailed recommendations by a federally appointed panel were made available) was to encourage experimentation, the ultimate goal being to find the "best." So far, the guidelines remain state-by-state, although in 1988, the guidelines became presumptive and any deviation must be specifically justified under stated criteria. Patterns have emerged. Some states employ percentage tables based on various definitions of the absent parent's "net" or "gross" income (*Boris*). The "Melson" formula is based on the father's minimal needs and shares the rest (*William R.T.*). So far, no *national* guidelines have been legislated. It may be hoped that, before long, national guidelines (with appropriate adjustments for regional differences) will bring uniformity and predictability—near synonyms for fairness—to this important decision if only because several impatient states have enacted overly simplistic and rigid tax-table-like formulae, but without sophistication in defining "income," or dealing with the problem of multiple families. State approaches range from California's *extremely* complex formula (CA Legis 542 (1991)), to Illinois' relatively simple schedule allotting 20% of the non-custodial parent's net income to one child, 25% to two children, 32% to three, 40% to four, 45% to five, and 50% to six or more (750 ILCS 5/505). Some states specifically "cap" the income level at which the formula is more or less mechanically imposed, others leave that to the courts' discretion. The "problem" of the "rich" father is that he has too much money to sensibly allow a fixed percentage to be allocated to the child (*e.g., White, Estevez*).

Constitutional attack on state guidelines failed in the Ninth Circuit Court of Appeals (*POPS*):

"P.O.P.S. [Parents Opposed to Punitive Support] maintains that the requirements of procedural due process prevent the state from ordering parents to pay support without affording them an opportunity to show that the award does not reflect the 'actual' cost of rearing their child. P.O.P.S. claims that the supreme court has long disfavored irrebuttable presumptions. But not all so-called irrebuttable presumptions are unconstitutional. * * * The economic table does not purport to provide merely for the child's subsistence; rather it is designed to sustain the child at a standard of living concomitant with his or her divorcing parents' income. The measure of that standard is subjective. Washington declares it to be irrelevant whether the non-custodial parent actually spent less than the amount indicated in the economic table to support the children before the divorce; the table tells parents what they ought to spend. To the extent that the presumption is conclusive, it is a substantive rule of law based on a determination by the legislature as a matter of social policy, that divorcing parents will be required to sustain their children at a certain standard of living determined by the parents' income. We reject P.O.P.S.'s procedural due process challenge.   * * * According to P.O.P.S., the financial pressures created by the schedule alienate non-custodial parents from their children, cause divorces between non-custodial parents and their new spouses, deter new marriages, and prevent non-custodial parents from having more children with their new spouses. P.O.P.S. argues that because the schedule impacts family relationships, we should apply strict scrutiny to the schedule. We reject the argument.   * * * The schedule does not discriminate against children of non-custodial households. Courts may deviate from the basic support obligation when either parent has other children. Thus the court can insure that children from non-custodial families are not unduly burdened by the child support award. P.O.P.S. complains that the schedule does not give the court any guidance for deviating from the presumptive amount based on other children. The state need not create a perfect schedule; it need only have a rational basis for the statute."

§ 15.4 Modifiability of Child Support Awards

In contrast to spousal alimony awards (that may be negotiated or be waived or be final), the parents' compromise concerning the child support obligation binds neither the child nor the welfare authorities. True, in their separation agreement, the parents may make a contractual "settlement" regarding that issue, but under the UMDA such a settlement is not binding on the court. It is effective, if at all, only between the parents, in terms of defining their relative shares of the total duty. Even if the contract succeeds in making one parent the primary obligor, the child has recourse to the other parent when that obligor defaults.

Child support awards are modifiable when there is a significant change in circumstances. In an effort to tidy up the resulting confusion—that often leads to unwarranted harassment of the supporting parent by the custodial parent and wasteful use of court facilities—the UMDA requires "a showing of changed circumstances so substantial and continuing as to make the terms [previously set] unconscionable." This language did not produce significantly greater certainty and it is doubtful that it could, given the checkered history of the term "unconscionable" as a legal term of art. Nor do typical statutes define a "significant change in circumstances." Until the advent of support guidelines, judicial discretion reigned uncertainly and unpredictably. Statutory guidelines now are used to modify all awards, even those imposed prior to the enactment of the guidelines.

Support judgments typically are for fixed amounts that need to be modified by specific court order to deal with changing circumstances. This often causes trouble. When losing employment, the typical person does not (or should not) make it the first priority to go back to court to have a child support obligation modified. But if that is not done, arrears will accrue and may soon become an all but insurmountable burden. Too often, it is the overwhelming accumulation of unpaid past support that persuades many a basically willing father to flee from accrued responsibilities that have become unrealistic. Most states allow essentially unlimited enforcement of arrears—such as the Vermont case that held a father liable for ten years of child support arrears (*Lyon*), and the Illinois case holding that a mother's silent acceptance of reduced payments did not estop her from enforcing unpaid support after 22 years (*Ellingwood; contra: Padgett*, involving nine years of nonenforcement and *Davidson*, involving twenty years).

The answer to this dilemma and to several other problems is the imposition of flexible and affordable amounts of child support that are geared directly to fluctuating earnings with which much of our population—though not the judge—has to cope. Increasingly, courts have upheld automatic adjustment clauses. In combination with wage deduction or any other form of timely and regular enforcement, such clauses will prevent the accrual of arrearages that ultimately become impossible to pay.

§ 15.5 New Families, Imputed Income, Earning Capacity, and "Involuntary Servitude"

A very basic question has no satisfactory solution: What effect should be given either parent's creation of a new family? Traditionally, the courts took the position that the non-custodial parent's prior child support obligations have absolute precedence over the needs of any new family. Arguably, the balance of social interest (though not necessarily individual equity) weighs in favor of the father's *current* family because that family might founder if earlier obligations were enforced beyond the father's reasonably available means—with the possible result of two families drawing welfare payments rather than one, and neither being better off than before. On the other hand, ideally, all children should stand on an equal footing and have equal legal claims, and modern equal protection reasoning should make it difficult to defend blanket discrimination in favor of or against the children of one or the other marriage or, for that matter, nonmarital children. However, the current trend again favors the first family. (*See* quotation from *POPS,* § 15.3).

In 1992, a Wisconsin court ordered a non-custodial *mother* to pay support to her children of a prior marriage based on her *capacity* to earn, when she had quit work in order to take care of her child of her new marriage (*Roberts*). Some courts have considered the interests of both families and have suggested a fair apportionment. The Iowa Supreme Court in principle upheld the use of the *one-*

child guideline with respect to a father who had three children in three separate households, but noted that a father of five children in separate households would be required to pay out 85% of his income (*Nicholson; cf. Gilley*).

What freedom does an absent parent have to change his or her occupation or professional status for one less lucrative, or to quit work altogether? May a voluntary change in earnings serve as the basis for a reduction in a child support obligation? (*Cf.* § 25.7 regarding alimony.) May a court issue a "seek work" order? ("Yes", *Dennis*). Holdings have ranged all over the place, but "good faith" has played an important, though not always decisive role (*Ilas*). Reduction in payments was granted a successful, salaried construction worker who became a practitioner of law, whereby his income was reduced by half (*McQuiddy*). Upward modification of his support obligation was resisted unsuccessfully by a machinist who had changed his name to "Krishna Venta" and had founded a religious society which paid all his expenses including child support previously ordered, but which paid him no salary (*Pencovic, accord M.I.*, involving a "Hare Krishna"). A Talmudic scholar who had never held a job was deemed "voluntarily impoverished" when the time came to assess his support obligation for six children—at $4,000 per month based on an imputed income of $60,000 (*Goldberger*). A father was fired from his job because of customer complaints. The court held that the father's unsatisfactory job performance was not beyond his control and was therefore deliberate. He was *not* allowed a reduction in his support obligation to three children (*Imlay*). Mothers have had income imputed to them when they gave up work (*Roberts*, *Brady*, *Abbey*).

§ 15.6 Duration of the Support Obligation— Majority

The parental support obligation ends at emancipation or majority, except when an adult child is incompetent or otherwise in need of support and unable to provide its own livelihood (*e.g., Sininger, McCarthy*). Statutes that discriminated between male and female children in terms of the duration of the support owed have been struck down as violating the Equal Protection Clause (*Stanton I, II*). Typical statutes define the parental support obligation in terms of the child's minority, rather than in terms of specific ages. Ironically, the change in the age of majority from 21 to 18 years of age proved a dubious victory, when it had the (unexpected?) consequence that the support obligation now generally terminates at age 18. Disputes may still arise over support decrees or separation agreements that speak in terms of "minority" and date back to the time when minority extended to 21 years of age. Some courts held that the term "minority" used in the agreement or decree means minority at the time of attempted enforcement of the order, and refused to provide support after age 18. Other courts held that the word "minority" must be understood in the sense that it had when the agreement was entered into or when the support order was made (*Ganschow*).

§ 15.7 Higher Education

Some legislatures and courts have sought to mediate the conflict between (1) the traditional rule that the age of majority terminates the parental support obligation, (2) the increasing recognition that higher education is a "necessary," and (3) the relatively recent lowering of the age of majority to eighteen years of age. Three decades ago, higher education increasingly came to be viewed as "necessary", and a corresponding obligation was imposed up to the age of majority—then twenty-one years of age. At that time, there was little need to deal with education *past* majority, because college would be completed or nearly completed by the time the student reached majority. Today, several states give the courts discretion to order educational support for children past majority age to allow for the continued education of a child who, at eighteen years of age, may not even have completed high school. The child in the ongoing family, on the other hand, has no basis for such a claim. While this duality of standards may make little sense to the child, the Illinois Supreme Court upheld it against constitutional challenge (*Kujawinski*). In Pennsylvania, on the other hand, a lower court held that the imposition of a higher education obligation on divorced parents violated their right of equal protection, the court finding no rational basis for distinguishing between married and divorced parents (*Curtis*).

If a parent does provide his or her *adult* child a college education, whether voluntarily or under order of court, does this confer on the paying parent any decision-making power concerning the choice of institution, curriculum and life style? If the support is voluntary, the answer is obvious—if the parent does not like what he or she sees, the payments can be stopped. If support is rendered under order of court, the answer is more difficult. Cases establish that the choice of college—especially whether private or public—must be "reasonable." Should it be argued that continued acceptance of parental support after reaching the statutory age of majority effectuates a sort of "reverse emancipation" and implies parental authority commensurate with the parental obligation (*cf. Ross*)? In one approach to this question, the Arkansas Supreme Court denied an *adult* daughter's claim for college expenses on the basis of her unwillingness to discuss college plans and expenses with her father. As the daughter felt capable of deciding without her father's advice what school to attend and how to spend the money, the Court held that she could do without his financial help as well (*Riegler*). And a son who spat into his mother's face and pushed her down was held not entitled to college support from her (*Milne*). An important corollary is whether financial grants or loans to adult college students should be conditioned on "need" defined in terms of parental income and resources to which the "adult child" of well-off parents may have no access, or have access only under conditions imposed by the parents, whereas the student who has "poor" parents is not subject to any parental control, *de jure* or *de facto*.

§ 15.8 Duration of the Support Obligation— Death

The parental support obligation ends at the parent's or the child's death. Absent a will, the intestacy laws provide a portion of the parent's estate for each child, nonmarital children being included up to a point (*Labine, Trimble, Lalli*, § 11.8). By *will,* however, a parent has full power to disinherit even a minor, dependent child and leave the child without any means whatever. This remarkable carryover from the common law has not generally been remedied by statute. "Pretermitted heir statutes" provide protection only against *un*intentional disinheritance. Provisions that allow at least the state to claim child support against a parent's estate, if the child is left "chargeable to the county", are rare. By contrast, children of *divorce* increasingly find protection against loss of support upon the obligated parent's death, and this preference over children in ongoing marriages has also been upheld against constitutional challenge, as was the preference in terms of higher education. The difference is rationalized by assuming that the parent in an intact family may be trusted to make a decision in the child's best interest, whereas the absent parent cannot be so trusted (*Kujawinski*).

The civil law stands at the opposite extreme. A parent generally may not deprive a child of inheritance, even if the child has long reached adulthood. Based on French law, Louisiana defines "just causes for which parents may disinherit their children" of any age, as including physical violence towards the parent, refusal to support a parent when in need or insane, refusal "to ransom them, when detained in captivity" or make bail when in prison, "if the son or daughter, being a minor, marries without the consent of his or her parents", and if the child, after majority, has failed to communicate with the parent for a period of two years. To protect the child's rights, donations *inter vivos* are restricted (La.Civ.Code art. 1621).

CHAPTER 16

CHILD SUPPORT ENFORCEMENT

§ 16.1 Civil and Criminal Remedies

In the *ongoing* family, child support is due but not enforced directly (§ 15.2). The courts will interfere only where the default is gross, typically by means of the neglect laws (§ 17.1). Short of that, a merchant or other person or agency may sue for having furnished "necessaries" for the child's support, with some flexibility attending the definition of necessaries (*cf.* § 8.3).

If the parents live apart—whether by reason of divorce or separation, or if they have remained unmarried—various remedies are available. State statutes generally provide criminal misdemeanor penalties for a default on support obligations, but the contempt power of the court is the typical enforcement vehicle. *Civil* contempt is imposed to "encourage" payment by jailing for an indeterminate time an obligor *who is able to pay* and leaving him or her "the key to the cell," which means freedom as soon as payment is made. *Criminal* contempt is imposed as punishment for default, the sentence being for a specific period (*Hicks*).

261

The criminal penalty, either form of "contempt" or all three sanctions may apply in the same circumstances, depending on applicable statutes. Some courts fail to distinguish clearly between civil and criminal contempt, although quite different and stricter procedural safeguards (should) apply in the criminal arena (*Sword*). In any case, the penalty may be a fine or imprisonment or both. In the case of a criminal prosecution, the penalty may be suspended on condition of compliance with the support obligation, thus achieving a "civil" result. Courts have *not* viewed imprisonment resulting from failure to comply with a judicially imposed support obligation as imprisonment for debt—which would of course be prohibited. Similarly, forcing an unwilling, unemployed parent to seek work by threat of jailing has not been viewed as a violation of the Thirteenth (anti-slavery) Amendment (*Pouliot*). Some courts have (*Cox*) and others have not (*Andrews*) extended the right to free counsel to civil contempt defendants.

The Child Support Recovery Act of 1992 makes willful failure to support a child in another state a federal crime (P.L. 102–521, 18 U.S.C.A. § 338 (1992)). Prosecution is available for arrearages exceeding $5,000 or remaining unpaid for longer than one year. Penalties range from imprisonment to fines. First offenses are misdemeanors. Repeat offenses are felonies. Along with that, federal courts may make the payment of spousal and child support a condition of probation.

As a practical matter, the difficulty in child support enforcement has lain less with the unavailability of remedies than with their utilization. After all, if the objective is the procurement of child support, it would usually be counterproductive to *fine* the defaulting parent, thereby making him or her less able to comply with the support obligation that is sought to be enforced. To order *jail*, whether for contempt of court or as a consequence of a criminal prosecution, may be even more destructive of the purpose of support enforcement, because a term in jail may cost the defendant's job. As discussed below, preventive enforcement, as by automatic deduction from paychecks, is the sensible alternative that is being implemented nationally, even while a credible *threat* of criminal prosecution remains a forceful incentive to comply.

§ 16.2 Federal Legislation on Child Support Enforcement

By the 1970's, child support enforcement lay in shambles—especially at the welfare level. Inadequate laws were producing low returns at prohibitive expense. Studies of the problem, whether private or commissioned by the federal government, met with apathy. Ideological dislike of support enforcement aggravated neglect of the issue. At that time, the welfare community widely accepted the notion that the State, rather than absent fathers, should support abandoned children. Feeble attempts to bring deserting fathers to accept responsibility were discounted with the peculiar argument that the funds thus collected would not benefit the children, because collections would only be offset against AFDC entitlements.

In 1975, Congress enacted sweeping legislation to strengthen enforcement of child support obligations across the nation, to reduce the cost of Aid to Families with Dependent Children (AFDC) programs. State authority and state laws remain the primary vehicles for the establishment of paternity and child support collection, but the federal government has become the overseer and financier of state systems. Each state enforcement agency—commonly known as a "IV–D Agency," reflecting its statutory location—must meet standards imposed by the Office of Child Support Enforcement (OCSE) or lose some of its federal AFDC funding. If, on the other hand, the enforcement program meets federal standards, the state receives a considerable portion of the program's cost from Washington.

In brief summary, the federal law requires state AFDC programs to act as intake agencies for child support enforcement. Specific rules include the following: state AFDC agencies must collect data, use the social security numbers of all AFDC applicants as identification, notify the state child support enforcement agency whenever benefits are granted to deserted children, and open its records to support enforcement officials. Applicants must assign their right to uncollected child support to the state and must cooperate in locating the absent parent, establishing paternity, obtaining a support judgment if none is outstanding, and securing payments. In case of an applicant's *unjustified* failure to cooperate, AFDC benefits are withheld from the applicant, but not from children.

The states maintain state parent locator services, equipped to search state and local records for information regarding the whereabouts of absent parents. Enforcement authorities may call upon the sophisticated, computerized federal parent locator service based in Washington with access to Social Security, Internal Revenue and vast other federal information resources. Once the absent (or alleged) parent is located, the state, if necessary, establishes paternity, obtains a support judgment, and enforces the obligation through either in-state or interstate proceedings. All states must cooperate fully with their sister states. Access to the federal courts is provided as a last resort. If other efforts have failed, a state may request that OSCE certify outstanding judgments to the Internal Revenue Service for collection. Past due support is collected from state and federal income tax refunds. A statutory waiver of sovereign immunity allows support obligations to be enforced against federal employees or beneficiaries of income from federal sources. After collection, the state disburses child support payments, keeping detailed records and reporting to OCSE. To encourage local participation in child support enforcement, a portion of the proceeds is turned over to the collecting unit of local government.

It was recognized early that the primary objective to reduce the cost of AFDC programs could be secured more successfully if *potential* recipients were kept "off welfare" by extending the program to them. Accordingly, support enforcement also is available to non-AFDC parents who pay a reasonable fee. Experience has developed rapidly and favorably. In fiscal year 1993, the parent locator service located nearly 4.5 million absent parents, paternity was established in 550,000 cases, and new support orders were established by court order or administrative process in more than one million cases. Total support collections under the federal program reached nearly nine billion dollars in 1993. In a broader study, the Census Bureau reported that, in 1991, custodial parents were owed \$17.7 billion, of which 11.9 billion (67%) was collected (A.P. 5/13/95).

In the years since 1975, broad amendments further strengthened enforcement powers. State laws must require withholding of child support from the paycheck of a parent delinquent for one month. Employers are held responsible if they do not comply. State laws must provide for the imposition of liens against the property of defaulting support obligors, credit companies may be informed of unpaid child support, unpaid support must be deducted from federal and state income tax refunds, expedited hearings—judicial or administrative—in support cases are required, and statutes of limitation for the establishment of paternity up to 18 years after the child's birth are mandated, the latter following and extending the U.S. Supreme Court's decisions in *Mills*, *Pickett*, *Paulussen*, and *Clark*.

To allow welfare families to receive at least some direct benefit from the parent's payment, the first $50 per month are *not* deducted from the welfare check. The states must establish presumptive guidelines for child support awards and make these available to all judges or officials who determine child support awards. Employer group health plans are obligated to comply with the "Qualified Medical Child Support Order" (QMCSO). The custodial parent may enroll the child in the absent parent's health plan and force the latter to pay the applicable premiums (42 U.S.C.A. § 1396g–1).

§ 16.3 Interstate Enforcement Remedies: Full Faith and Credit—New and Old

The general rule accords full faith and credit to valid and final sister state judgments. In the traditional child support enforcement context, this general rule translated as follows: (1) If accrued installments are reduced to a money judgment, full faith and credit is due, as it is due to any other sister state money judgment; (2) if accrued installments have not been reduced to judgment, full faith and credit is due if the accrued installments are final and not modifiable where the judgment was rendered. Under the general rule full faith and credit was usually held not due to modifiable accrued installments and future support (which is always modifiable), simply because such judgments are not final. In 1994 Congress enacted the Full Faith and Credit for Child Support Orders Act which requires just what its name says (28 U.S.C.A. § 1738B). If a sister-state child support order meets the standards of the Act, it must be enforced in any state and may be modified only in very limited circumstances. By and large, the Act sets jurisdictional requirements similar to those of the Parental Kidnapping Prevention Act located directly beside it at 28 U.S.C.A. § 1738A (§ 18.22).

Full faith and credit, of course, does not extend to judgments rendered in a foreign country. However, if basically in accord with American ideas of due process, such judgments may and usually are accorded "comity", which means that they are enforced even in the absence of constitutional compulsion.

§ 16.4 Interstate Enforcement Remedies: The Uniform Interstate Family Support Act Replaces The Uniform Reciprocal Enforcement of Support Act

The great mobility of our population, combined with the legal separatism of fifty states and various associated jurisdictions, produces particularly serious problems in terms of effective, nationwide support enforcement. In the 1950's and 1960's, these enforcement problems led to the universal enactment, in one form or another, of the Uniform Reciprocal Enforcement of Support Act ("URESA"). In its time, URESA provided the principal tool for out-of-state enforcement of support obligations, whether reduced to judgment or not. Where enacted, the Uniform Recognition of Foreign Judgments Act (allowing the "domestication" of out-of-state judgments) provided additional help.

Briefly, URESA allows a support action to be initiated in a court at the dependent's place of residence. After the complaint is forwarded to the court where the obligor is located, the case is tried there. This avoids the expense and inconvenience of travel. Defenses are heard and a judgment is rendered and enforced where the obligor is located. The support obligation is determined under "the laws of any state in which the obligor was present during the period for which support is sought." The amounts collected are sent back to the initiating court for disbursement to the dependents. URESA also may be used in the context of nonmarital paternity, when there has been a prior adjudication of paternity. Failing that, the 1968 version of the Act specifically provides that the responding court may decide the issue of paternity.

In 1992, the National Conference of Commissioners on Uniform State Laws—heeding calls from Congress to develop such an Act—approved the Interstate Family Support Act (UIFSA) that will replace URESA as it is enacted state by state. In the Uniform Law Commissioners' own summary, UIFSA

"is designed to improve the interstate establishment and enforcement of spousal and child support awards, and to eliminate the possibility of multiple exercises of jurisdiction over support awards with attendant multiple, conflicting support awards from more than one state. Jurisdiction to modify an award is meant to be held by one and only one state at a time. This is accomplished by providing comprehensive long-arm provisions so that a state can take jurisdiction over a party to a child or spousal support dispute, who is outside of the state, but who has a significant connection with the state and the dispute. A state that has taken jurisdiction, and which is the state of residence for any party, retains continuing exclusive jurisdiction as long as residency of a party continues. Continuing exclusive jurisdiction prevents other states from establishing a competing award or modifying the existing award. If simultaneous proceedings are initiated in more than one state with a basis for taking jurisdiction, the state that is the home state of the child takes priority over the other states in adjudicating the dispute and establishing an award. If a state initiates an enforcement action that is transmitted to another state, there are limitations upon the modification jurisdiction of the state that is the responding state. States have the capacity to bring and to transport actions pertaining to establishing or modifying support awards, including proceedings for initially determining parentage" (ULC, Short Summaries, 1992).

By mid–1995, about one half of the states had enacted UIFSA. Given the strong federal endorsement, UIFSA will soon have replaced URESA.

§ 16.5 The Future of Child Support Enforcement

The federal child support collection initiative has injected federal authority more deeply than ever before in matters that traditionally had been viewed as the states'.   Congress signalled this decisive change in attitude in 1984, when it passed a "Sense of Congress Resolution" to the effect "that state and local governments should focus on the problems of child custody, child support, and related domestic issues":

"(1) State and local governments must focus on the vital issues of child support, child custody, visitation rights, and other related domestic issues that are properly within the jurisdictions of such governments; (2) all individuals involved in the domestic relations process should recognize the seriousness of these matters to the health and welfare of our Nation's children and assign them the highest priority; and (3) a mutual recognition of the needs of all parties involved in divorce actions will greatly enhance the health and welfare of America's children and families."

Increasingly, Washington will define standards for acceptable state law on these questions.   One objective has been achieved: Less counterproductive methods of support enforcement are now employed than have been the rule—perhaps most importantly, wage deduction *to avoid default,* rather than jail and loss of job *after default.*   In 1992, the U.S. Commission on Child Support issued its final report to Congress, proposing further federalization and tightening of existing state and federal enforcement processes.   The Commission recommended:

"Speeding up support collection by enhancing access to parent-locate and income information through development of an integrated, automated computer network linking all the states. The network would draw from an array of more than 15 data bases, and from a new base containing information from expanded W–4 forms. It also would connect to new state registries of support orders. Enhancing support collection across state lines through income withholding and sending support to a child or the child's state directly from an obligor's income source, such as an employer, in another state. Improving uniformity and thus simplicity in processing by requiring identical enactment by states of the Uniform Interstate Family Support Act, the improved proposed replacement for the Uniform Reciprocal Enforcement Act (URESA). UIFSA would provide for one-state control of a case and for a clear, efficient method of interstate case processing. Streamlining the establishment of support responsibility by creating a system for early, voluntary parentage determination for children born out of wedlock, and for uniform evidentiary rules in contested cases. Expanding healthcare for children by requiring universal access to healthcare insurance for children of separated or divorced parents. Ensuring that all cases can be processed as quickly and attentively as needed by requiring states to provide all the staff and other resources needed and by improving the training of staff. Ensuring common direction and focus by the states by mandating vigorous leadership by the federal government."

On the proposal that child support enforcement be federalized *completely*, a

"vast majority of Commission members is not convinced that the federal government would do a better job than the states in establishing and enforcing support. And this majority is concerned about the potential economic, political and social costs of federalization: 1) the undermining of creativity and commitment at the state and local level; 2) detached treatment of one aspect of family law that often must be addressed in the context of other family issues; 3) adding to the already heavy backlog in federal courts; 4) proceeding without * * * an effective federal administration model; 5) improper identification and distribution of payments; 6) replicating at unknown cost a system that already exists at the state level; and 7) taking such a major step prior to evaluating the value of automation and other reforms that are improving or could significantly enhance the states' abilities to effectively process cases".

CHAPTER 17

CHILD NEGLECT AND ABUSE, DEPENDENCY, TERMINATION OF PARENTAL RIGHTS

§ 17.1 Neglect, Dependency, Abuse

State laws on neglect, dependency and abuse are the principal limitation on parental authority over children. "Neglect" is a composite of many factors and requires a highly individualized judgment on all the circumstances of each case. Given the varied nature of the situations sought to be covered, statutes *need* to be flexible to provide broad discretion to the courts, but they have been criticized for not being sufficiently specific to give parents notice of unsatisfactory conduct or, indeed, being unconstitutionally vague (§ 17.6). Typical statutory language runs in terms of neglect "as to proper or necessary support, education as required by law, or as to medical or other remedial care recognized under state law or other care necessary for his well-being."

In defining "dependency," statutes may refer to a child "who is abandoned by his parents, guardian or custodian or whose environment is injurious to his welfare or whose behavior is injurious to his own welfare or that of others." The factual circumstances of "dependency" are roughly the same as those covered in "neglect." What difference there is between the two concepts lies mainly in the element of parental fault that is present in a neglect adjudication but absent in dependency. In view of this small distinction and the frequent confusion created by the dichotomy, attempts have been made to unify the standards. It may be, however, that a standard that avoids the stigma of "neglect" increases parental willingness to request help when in need. On the negative side of the argument, if there is no finding of parental *fault* when the child is taken into custody initially, a subsequent disposition against the parent's will may present unnecessary difficulty, especially if it is ultimately decided that it would benefit the child to terminate parental rights (§ 17.4).

Child *abuse* ranks high among specific causes for intervention by juvenile court authorities and poses few problems of definition. While a mother was arrested, handcuffed, jailed and charged with a felony potentially carrying 1–20 years in prison for slapping her unruly 9–year-old son in a grocery store in Georgia "for picking on his 12–year-old sister" (N.Y. Times, 6/26/94), we generally have little difficulty agreeing when it is that parents cross the line between legitimate discipline and forbidden violence, or between friendly caresses and sexual abuse—even if a father who had taken nude photos of his 6–year-old daughter for an art class was handcuffed, jailed and banned from his home and any contact with his daughter (N.Y. Times,

1/30/95). Notwithstanding the excessive zeal of some store clerks or photo processors, much abuse goes undetected. In all states, laws require or encourage physicians, nurses, teachers, social workers or other professionals to report cases of suspected child abuse, but some reporting statutes may be too timid. Many simply provide the informant immunity from tort suits (unless the report was made maliciously) and thus do little more than restate pre-existing common law tort privilege. Few statutes carry sanctions for failure to make a "required" report and those that do are rarely enforced.

§ 17.2 "Cultural Relativity"?

The child of poor parents may not be neglected in any meaningful sense when it lives in exactly the same physical circumstances that would spell a *prima facie* case of neglect if the parents were rich. Is "neglect" thus of necessity a relative concept? Beyond poverty, in cases involving minority children, counsel have argued that "what might be considered abusive in one social milieu is the norm in another" (*F.N.J.*). Does this argument have merit? Judge Polier gave a lawyer's answer:

"Respondents urge that the court should take into consideration that their failure to maintain contact with their children must be weighed in the light of the 'class mores of poor, black, and unschooled persons', and the 'impossible barriers' created by requirements that they comply 'with the customs of bourgeois urban existence'. * * *

This plea must be rejected. To accept it would constitute regression to the period when the rights of parents were treated as absolute, and would negate the rights of children as developed by the legislature and courts of the State of New York. It would require courts to sanction less protection for the children of poor, black and uneducated than for children of more privileged parents thus violating their constitutional right to equal protection under the law" (*In re P.*).

Some have complained of discrimination in the close association between the receipt of welfare benefits and scrutiny by juvenile authorities. In 1971 a welfare mother attacked an AFDC home visit (that apparently brought to light that the child had a skull fracture, a dent in the head and possible rat bite) on the basis of the Fourth Amendment, alleging an unreasonable search (*Wyman*). The U.S. Supreme Court upheld the home visit, noting specifically that this case involved a "reasonable" intrusion, not "the early morning mass raid upon homes of welfare recipients". In 1990, Justice O'Connor's majority opinion rejected a mother's invocation of the Fifth Amendment privilege against self-incrimination in her attempt to avoid a court order to produce her abused child in court (*Bouknight*). Justices Marshall and Brennan dissented, being "disturbed by the Court's willingness to * * * deny Bouknight her constitutional right against self-incrimination, especially in light of the serious allegations of homicide that accompany this civil proceeding", but they took "some comfort in the Court's recognition that the State may be prohibited from using any testimony given by Bouknight in subsequent criminal proceedings".

§ 17.3 Dispositional Powers of the Juvenile Court

After an adjudication of neglect, abuse or dependency—typically in a confidential hearing, closed to public and press (*T.R.*)—the court may appoint a temporary or permanent guardian who may be an individual, a State agency or a private institution. The guardian takes control over the child's well-being, but guardianship does not necessarily involve the termination of the natural parent's rights, nor even transfer of custody. A common disposition is to "remand" the child into the custody of the natural parent, but under the guardian's supervision. Alternatives are foster care or institutional care in a state home or private institution.

Where the guardian takes custody of the child, but parental rights are not terminated, guardianship leaves intact all "residual" parental rights and duties that are not encompassed by custody. Most importantly these include the right to visitation, the right to consent (or refuse to consent) to the adoption of the child, and the duty of rendering support. The chief purpose of striving to maintain the parent and child relationship is, of course, that in many cases of neglect and dependency the parents' difficulty is temporary, and appropriate assistance through social services may improve the home situation to the point where the child can safely be returned to the parents' custody.

§ 17.4   Termination of Parental Rights

Our law deeply respects the parent and child relationship (§ 14.1). This is reflected in innumerable court decisions dealing with, and often denying, the termination of parental rights. The statutory standards that *theoretically* govern a judicial declaration of parental "unfitness" sufficient to terminate parental rights may be more detailed, but often are not much stricter or less vague than those required for a finding of "neglect". A rather detailed statute speaks in terms of "abandonment of the child," "failure to maintain a reasonable degree of interest, concern or responsibility as to the child's welfare", "desertion of the child for more than 3 months", "substantial neglect of the child if continuous or repeated", "extreme or repeated cruelty to the child", "two or more findings of abuse to any children", "failure to protect the child from conditions within his environment injurious to the child's welfare", "other neglect of, or misconduct toward the child", parental "depravity", "open and notorious adultery or fornication", "habitual drunkenness or addiction to drugs * * * for at least one year", "failure to demonstrate a reasonable degree of interest, concern or responsibility as to the welfare of a new born child during the first 30 days after its birth" (this being a first attempt to cut off claims of unwed fathers, see § 11.17), "failure by a parent to make reasonable efforts to correct the conditions which were the basis for the removal of the child from the parent, or to make reasonable progress toward the return of the child to the parent within 12 months after an adjudication of [neglect or abuse or dependency] * * *, evidence of intent to forego his or her parental rights, (1) as manifested by his or her failure for a period of 12 months: (i) to visit the child, (ii) to communicate with the child or agency, although able to do so and not prevented from doing so by an agency or by court order, or (iii) to maintain contact with or plan for the future of the child, although physically able to do so, or (2) as manifested by the father's failure, where he and the mother of the child were unmarried to each other at the time of the child's birth, (i) to commence legal proceedings to establish his paternity * * * within 30 days of being informed * * * that he is the father or the likely father of the child or, after being so informed where the child is not yet born, within 30 days of the child's birth, or (ii) to make a good faith effort to pay a reasonable amount of the expenses related to the birth of the child and to provide a reasonable amount for the financial support of the child, the court to consider in its determination all relevant circumstances, including the financial condition of both parents; provided that the ground for termination provided in this subparagraph * * * shall only be available where the petition is brought by the mother or the husband of the mother" (this being a second attempt to cut off the unmarried father, see § 11.17), "repeated or continuous failure by the parents, although physically and financially able, to provide the child with adequate food, clothing, or shelter", and finally, "inability to discharge parental responsibilities supported by * * * a psychiatrist [or other mental health professional]" (752 ILCS § 50/1).

Except in unusual circumstances, nothing is gained by terminating parental rights *and obligations* where no effective, permanent parental substitute can be provided by way of adoption. Accordingly, many social workers are reluctant to seek termination of parental rights, unless there is no hope for reconstituting the family unit and the child is "highly adoptable" (§§ 12.1, 2). Courts may be even more reluctant to terminate parental rights, since the child's *immediate* welfare usually can be protected by a neglect disposition. Accordingly, neglect (or dependency) adjudications are the typical first step. A "Catch 22" difficulty often results: Evidence that originally might have supported termination of parental rights, is "lost" in the neglect or dependency adjudication and, after the child is taken out of the neglecting parent's custody, no new grounds can accrue, other than "parental abandonment" or an equivalent. For that reason, abandonment or desertion tend to be the grounds most frequently relied upon in termination proceedings. However, "abandonment" of a child who is in good foster care will not seem as damning as might have been the evidence of serious neglect that originally led to the removal of the child from the parent's custody. Accordingly, many courts, cognizant of the extremely serious nature of terminating parental rights, require very strong evidence of complete abandonment (17.8). Even a slight indication of continuing parental interest has kept many children in the custodial and legal limbo of a neglect disposition, past the point where they were readily adoptable.

§ 17.5 Can a Child Divorce Its Parents?

Considerable, but misleading, publicity surrounded the case of Gregory, the 11–year-old Florida boy who "divorced" his parents. The trial judge's turn in the media (*e.g.*, Trial, June 1993) ended when the appellate court held that the boy had no standing on his own to bring an action for termination of parental rights or to seek to be adopted by his foster parents. The appellate court also held, however, that this was "harmless error", inasmuch as the foster parents, the state, and his guardian ad litem had also filed petitions on the child's behalf (*Kingsley*).

§ 17.6 Constitutionality of "Vague" Statutory Standards and Due Process

The "termination cases", even more poignantly than the neglect cases, pose the often irresolvable dilemma of choosing between the welfare of the child and the rights of the parents. Both interests have constitutional dimensions and have come under scrutiny at three levels: Are the imprecise standards provided by the neglect and dependency laws unconstitutionally vague? What is the constitutionally required standard of proof in termination cases? Do indigent parents have the right to free counsel?

In the main, the statutes have been upheld against challenge for "vagueness" (*McMaster*). In a few cases they have been struck down by courts seemingly confusing the civil adjudication of neglect, the objective of which is the welfare of the child, with a punishment meted out to the parent. A prime example in the latter category is *Alsager I,* in which the court seemed very much concerned with the constitutional rights of parents *to* their children—a "fundamental right to family integrity, protected by the Due Process Clause". Against that stringent test, statutory language referring to "necessary parental care and protection" and to behavior "detrimental to the physical or mental health or morals of the child" did not stand up. The Court invalidated the challenged provisions both "on their face and as applied". On appeal, the holding "as applied" was upheld, but the Court reserved the question whether the statute was void on its face (*Alsager II*).

As *applied* in *Alsager,* the statutory standard may well have been abused—the case did *not* involve "shocking" facts. However, the possibility that such a statute may be held unconstitutional *on its face* raises the problem of how (or indeed whether) a workable neglect standard can be defined with abstract precision. The spectator may readily agree with the trial court that the standards involved in *Alsager* "(1) do not, and did not here, give fair warning of what parental conduct is proscribed, (2) they permit, and permitted here, arbitrary and discriminatory terminations, (3) they inhibit, and inhibited here, the exercise of the fundamental right to family integrity." But what about real life? It should not be overlooked that, in the first instance, much broader, wholly unsupervised and potentially much more detrimental (to the child) discretion may be exercised by the investigating social worker who determines *not* to intervene! Consider *DeShaney*, in which Joshua and his mother sued the state social welfare agency under 42 U.S.C.A. § 1983 for failure "to intervene to protect him against a risk of violence at his father's hands of which they knew or should have known." (After repeated and reported instances of prior abuse, Joshua's father had been convicted of beating him into a coma. Resulting brain damage will require Joshua's institutionalization for life). The U.S. Supreme Court held:

> "Judges and lawyers, like other humans, are moved by natural sympathy in a case like this to find a way for Joshua and his mother to receive adequate compensation for the grievous harm inflicted upon them. But before yielding to that impulse, it is well to remember once again that the harm was inflicted not by the State of Wisconsin, but by Joshua's father. The most that can be said of the state functionaries in this case is that they stood by and did nothing when suspicious circumstances dictated a more active role for them. In defense of them it must also be said that had they moved too soon to take custody of

the son away from the father, they would likely have been met with charges of improperly intruding into the parent-child relationship, charges based on the same Due Process Clause that forms that basis for the present charge of failure to provide adequate protection. The people of Wisconsin may well prefer a system of liability which would place upon the State and its officials the responsibility for failure to act in situations such as the present one. They may create such a system, if they do not have it already, by changing the tort law of the State in accordance with the regular law-making process."

In *Suter*, children sought but failed to obtain declaratory and injunctive relief on their allegation that the director and the guardianship administrator of the Illinois child abuse and neglect agency had failed to make reasonable efforts to preserve and reunite families in contravention of the Adoption Assistance Act which provides that "reasonable efforts will be made" to prevent removal of children from their homes and to facilitate reunification of families where removal has occurred. The U.S. Supreme Court held that the Adoption Assistance and Child Welfare Act of 1980 (providing that a state will be reimbursed by the federal government for certain expenses it incurs in administering foster care and adoption services) does *not* confer on the Act's intended beneficiaries a private right that is enforceable in a 42 U.S.C.A. § 1983 action. However, the Fourth Circuit Court of Appeals has held that the removal from the home of a "home alone", "latchkey" child by child welfare authorities "entitled" the parents "to proceed at least to the summary judgment stage" of a § 1983 claim (*Jordan*).

In the main, the child welfare workers' professionalism must be relied upon as the principal safeguard against abuse of "vague" standards. Another safeguard comes as an unintended benign consequence of the heavy workloads of under-financed child protective agencies: State intervention in the family typically is possible only in circumstances in which reasonable men and women would have little difficulty agreeing that the intervention is justified. And when there is a case of severe child abuse or failure to provide acutely necessary medical care or food or other essential tangibles, the concreteness of the factual situation overcomes the vagueness of the statutory standard.

§ 17.7 Right to Counsel and Standard of Proof in Termination Proceedings

In 1981 and 1982, the U.S. Supreme Court ruled on two related questions: Do indigent parents have a right to counsel in termination cases, and what is the required standard of proof in termination proceedings? In *Lassiter,* a divided Court decided that parents do *not* have a constitutionally guaranteed right to free counsel, continuing its long hesitation to extend the right to counsel to cases in which the physical liberty of the indigent is not threatened. The Court, however, was evidently troubled by the importance of the right at stake and noted that thirty-three states do provide counsel in termination cases. While it seemed pleased with North Carolina's rather careful procedures in termination cases, the Court decided to leave the door a crack open:

> "If, in a given case, the parent's interest were at their strongest, the State's interests were at their weakest, and the risks of error were at their peak, it could not be said that the *Eldridge* factors did not overcome the presumption against the right to appointed counsel, and that due process did not therefore require the appointment of counsel. But since the *Eldridge* factors will not always be so distributed, and since 'due process is not so rigid as to require that the significant interests in informality, flexibility and economy must always be sacrificed', neither can we say that the Constitution requires the appointment of counsel in every parental termination proceeding."

In *Santosky,* the Court decided that the parent and child relationship is so important that evidence to terminate it must be "clear and convincing", citing many state laws that already so require. The Court could

> "not agree with [the New York Court's] conclusion that a preponderance standard fairly distributes the risk of error between parent and child. Use of that standard reflects the judgment that society is nearly neutral between erroneous termination of parental rights and erroneous failure to terminate those rights. For the child, the

likely consequence of an erroneous failure to terminate is preservation of an uneasy status quo. For the natural parents, however, the consequence of an erroneous termination is the unnecessary destruction of their natural family. A standard that allocates the risk of error nearly equally between those two outcomes does not reflect properly their relative severity."

Four dissenters in *Santosky* argued that

"when, in the context of a permanent neglect termination proceeding, the interests of the child and the State in a stable, nurturing homelife are balanced against the interest of the parents in the rearing of their child, it cannot be said that either set of interests is so clearly paramount as to require that the risk of error be allocated to one side or the other. Accordingly, a State constitutionally may conclude that the risk of error should be borne in roughly equal fashion by use of the preponderance of the evidence standard of proof."

If reduction of risk of error is the overriding goal, that goal might have been achieved more efficiently if *Lassiter* and *Santosky* had reached results opposite from those they reached; specifically, by striking an equal evidentiary balance between child and parents and by assuring the accuracy of that balance by requiring counsel in termination cases.

§ 17.8 Criminal Prosecution

Not to be confused with the *civil* adjudication under the neglect or termination of parental rights statute, is a *criminal* prosecution of parents or custodians for child neglect, abandonment, abuse or for a whole host of offenses especially relating to minors, in addition to possible prosecution under general statutes relating to assault and battery. However, prosecutions of parents in these situations are rare, except in very serious cases, typically life-threatening or involving sex-abuse. The State's chief interest—safeguarding the welfare of the child—usually is satisfied in the civil proceeding.

Increased concern with sex-abuse cases has led to a variety of court decisions, statutes and (in Illinois) even a (state) constitutional referendum involving the abused child's testimony: Must it be "live" in court, face-to-face with the accused abuser (yes: *Fitzpatrick*), or may it be recorded and televised (yes: 1994 Illinois Referendum)? In *White*, the U.S. Supreme Court allowed juries in child abuse cases to consider some hearsay evidence—such as a spontaneous declaration made while the child was receiving medical care—where the child was excused from testifying in court.

In several states, belief in the phenomenon of "repressed memory" of sex abuse has rolled statutes of limitations far back. Prosecution is allowed of alleged sex-abusers decades after the alleged deed. Some argue that "[r]epressed memory is not a fantasy of the victim, but rather a vivid memory of a criminal action that should not go unpunished. No persuasive argument exists for closing courts to adult survivors or in protecting pedophiles who clearly rape and molest more than one child in a short period of time. Actually, adult survivors are at a much better place to name their perpetrators and seek justice than are child victims." Others respond: "We live in a strange and precarious time that resembles at its heart the hysteria and superstitious fervor of the witch trials of the 16th and 17th centuries. Men and women are being accused, tried and convicted with no proof or evidence of guilt other than the word of the accuser. * * * What decades of memory research have shown, however is that the techniques in question can seriously contaminate memories, and even create false memories in vulnerable minds. * * * Suggestion is insidious—no one knows the extent to which it operates beneath the cover of authentic therapy". This is why the American Medical Association issued a policy statement saying "the use of recovered memory is fraught with problems of potential misapplications" (1994 A.B.A.J. at 42–43).

In response to a flood of so-called "cocaine babies" being born at great damage to the children and cost to the taxpayer, drug-abusing mothers-to-be have come under scrutiny for harm done to their viable, but unborn, fetuses. Attempts to remedy the situation have ranged from criminal prosecution of the mother for involuntary manslaughter or delivery of a controlled substance (C.U. News Gazette, 5/9/89, 8/26/89) to neglect or abuse proceedings (*Felicia B.; Ruiz*), to termination of her parental rights (*Gray*). Agreeable—and constitutionally acceptable—answers are difficult to find. (See Field, Controlling the Woman, 17 L., Med. & Health Care 114

(1989)).   Aside from the *illegality* of cocaine (which is *not* relevant to harm done to the child), where is the line that divides cocaine abuse from a pregnant woman's alcohol abuse (resulting in fetal alcohol syndrome) or poor nutrition or other potentially harmful behavior (jogging)?

§ 17.9   Use and Abuse of Child Abuse Reporting Laws

Despite the universal acceptance of laws most of which require and the rest of which encourage physicians and often other professionals, such as nurses, teachers, social workers, to report cases of suspected child abuse, much abuse goes undetected. The greater number of these reporting statutes simply provide immunity from tort suits (unless the report was made maliciously) and really do little more than restate pre-existing common law tort "privilege".   Many do not carry sanctions for failure to report.   For a variety of reasons, these statutes have not been wholly effective.   Many physicians, in their own conception of the patient-physician relationship, prefer to retain friendly contact with the parents of the child and, in some cases, that may even work to the benefit of the child. (This remains so despite specific abrogation of the physician-patient privilege in most of the reporting laws.)   Many others shy away from the often inordinate amount of time required by typical juvenile court proceedings which stumble from continuance to continuance with scant regard for the value of time of anyone concerned, whether they be witnesses, jurors, judges, or even lawyers.

The question of sanctions for failure to report suspected abuse forces a dubious choice. If there are no sanctions, many reports that should be made no doubt will not be made. On the other hand, if there are sanctions and parents have to count on the certainty of being reported and having their child brought under the control of the juvenile court and perhaps being prosecuted criminally, they may become more hesitant than they are now in seeking medical aid for a child they have abused. Moreover, the enforcement of sanctions against non-reporting teachers, physicians, nurses, and social workers raises other questions, both on the level of policy and in terms of the unlikelihood of obtaining the proof necessary for a conviction. Child abuse cases usually develop from mere suspicion on the part of the observer, and one may safely assume that it could be established only in extremely flagrant situations that a person should have had "suspicion".

Very serious questions regarding the reporting statutes may be raised from the standpoint of the right to family privacy and basic notions of due process. In its very nature, the typical reporting procedure is anonymous, and many reporting laws require the name of the original "reporter" to be kept in confidence. The result is that many complaints from non-professionals turn out to be groundless and that these laws may be abused. For instance, an ex-husband who wants to harass his wife who obtained custody of their child—or *vice versa*—or a spiteful neighbor may telephone in a report.

Central registries of cases of suspected child abuse are operated in many states and have been suggested for national use. They seek to deal with the problem of the abusing parent who, in successive cases of abuse, goes from hospital to hospital to avoid seeing the same professionals more than once—in the justified belief that, the *first* time, many physicians will give a suspected parent the benefit of the doubt. They may believe the standard explanation that the child fell off the diaper table, or in severe cases, down the stairs. They may even judge that an isolated instance of abuse does not merit the possibly destructive involvement of the juvenile authorities.

The theory of these registers is wholly beneficial. The practice, however, of necessity involves the storing of rumors and suspicions concerning possibly innocent parents who neither have opportunity to confront their accusers nor to correct or expunge the record. Indeed, usually they would not even know that such a record exists. This is not to belittle the value of the reporting laws or to discount the menace of child abuse. The recent flood of publicity concerning child abuse, however, may have caused uncritical acceptance of dubious or inadequately "fail-safed" remedies for this important social problem. *Sims* faced the problem head-on:

"Of course, the state may maintain investigative files. However, to the extent that [a computerized system designed to collect and store the confidential information gathered by the state from the inception of an investigation through final disposition] purports in any way to be a clearinghouse of child-abuse information without a judicial determination thereof, it is an unconstitutional infringement on the rights of the parents."

CHAPTER 18

CHILD CUSTODY ON DIVORCE

§ 18.1 Introduction

There are four types of custody cases, all of them bad. The "best" are those in which both parents want their children, but care enough not to fight over them. Then there are cases where only one parent wants the children, and the other does not interfere. Next are the cases in which both parents want the children and fight over them. Truly sad are those cases in which neither parent wants the children. Disputed child custody thus is the next to most intractable dilemma attending divorce, and divorce is not good for children. Dr. Wallerstein notes: "The earlier view of divorce as a shortlived crisis understood within the familiar paradigm of crisis theory has given way to a more sober appraisal, accompanied by rising concern that a significant number of children suffer long-term, perhaps permanent detrimental effects from divorce, and that others experience submerged effects that may appear years later." (J. Child Adolescence & Psychiatry 30:3, p. 358 (1991)).

§ 18.2   The Child's "Best Interests" and Own Preference

If we (or at least our judges and experts) only knew what that is! Whatever it is, it is the modern test for child custody. Despite many attempts to spell out criteria for custody awards, we have not come far since ancient King Solomon offered to settle a custody dispute between two women by slicing the child in two, one-half for each of the disputants. (When she offered to forego her claim, the true mother demonstrated her greater love, and Solomon awarded the child to her). Three thousand years later, a Michigan judge ordered the deceased child of divorced parents cremated and the ashes divided equally among them, unless they agreed who would have the body (Chi. Daily L. Bull., 7/27/78).

UMDA § 402 defines the child's best interest as a composite of the following factors:

"(1) the wishes of the child's parent or parents as to his custody; (2) the wishes of the child as to his custodian; (3) the interaction and interrelationship of the child with his parent or parents, his siblings and any other person who may significantly affect the child's best interest; (4) the child's adjustment to his home, school and community; (5) the mental and physical health of all individuals involved. The court shall not consider conduct of a present or proposed custodian that does not affect his relationship to the child."

Even applying the UMDA's stated criteria, the judge retains nearly total discretion and, for all practical purposes, may award custody as he or she sees fit. The trial judge's power is all the greater because appellate courts are most reluctant to upset trial court decisions that are based on facts and impressions that cannot easily be captured in written records.

Good intentions abound. Two important books failed to center on the best interests of the child and went "Beyond" and "Before" (Goldstein, Freud, Solnit, 1973, 1979). The paramount virtue most experts currently perceive is *continuity* in the child's environment and *permanence* in its psychological attachments. This necessarily involves a substantial devaluation of the claim of at least one of the natural parents (*cf.* § 18.11). Even assuming that "continuity" is psychiatric "truth" and even if, psychiatrically, the blood tie is a myth, the myth of blood is such a basic cultural truth that more caution seems in order than a few courts have shown when they have rushed to embrace the new "findings" in favor of biological strangers (*Hoy*). Moreover, the courts should (but do not always seem to) be aware that they are not just balancing psychiatry against culture, but that they are balancing psychiatry against constitutional law. For better or for worse, *both* parents' *rights* have constitutional dimensions, *as should the rights of the child* (§§ 12.7, 14.1, 17.6, *cf. McGaffin*).

On the latter point, what weight is to be accorded the child's own *preference*? The answer varies and typically has *not* been put in constitutional terms. Given a child with a reasonable level of maturity, however, courts generally accord considerable weight to its wishes (*Knock*). The child's preference typically is ascertained by the judge in a private, in-chambers interview rather than in the formal hearing, so that the child is not forced to side openly against one parent (UMDA § 404). Independent representation of the child by an attorney (as guardian ad litem) in custody questions is increasing and, where useful, encouraged by UMDA § 310. In practice it remains the exception. In such cases, the attorney bears a great responsibility (*Veazy*), and faces a potential conflict between the role of "attorney" (in the sense of representing the client's wishes) and the role of "guardian" (in the sense of advocating what is "best" for the child).

§ 18.3 Parent's Gender, the "Tender Years Doctrine", and the "Primary Caretaker"

Not long ago, sometimes by statute, elsewhere by common law or judicial custom, rather definite rules governed the disposition of children on divorce. A basic factor was the sex of the parent claiming custody. At common law the father all but "owned" his children and had the primary custodial claim—but then divorce was rare (*Devine*). Paternal preference gave way to the perception that children (at least those of "tender years") need "mothering" and that women are better suited to provide that. Another prime factor was the parent's sexual morality, especially if that figured as the ground for divorce, and still another was religion. There also was a culturally conditioned reluctance of fathers to claim custody of their children, and a corresponding feeling of obligation on the part of mothers to fulfill their "natural" responsibility—whether they really wanted their children or not, or actually were the "better" parent. For many good reasons, all this is breaking down today.

Desirable as these developments are from many perspectives, they also are causing an increase in the incidence of disputes. When rigid and predictable factors applied to custody decisions, many potential disputes did not arise, simply because there was no point in bringing them to court. Given the near certainty that seriously adverse parental positions on custody harm their children, it is not altogether clear that the new openness (and consequent unpredictability) of custody decisions does quite as much good as it does harm—if we are looking solely at the children's best interests.

A California statute (repealed in 1970) summed up the lost national consensus in terms of "other things being equal, if the child is of tender years, custody should be given to the mother; if the child is of an age to require education and preparation for labor and business, then custody should be given to the father." In 1973, the Supreme Court of Pennsylvania still said "that the best interest of children of tender years will be best served under a mother's guidance and control is one of the strongest presumptions in the law" (*Kreischer*). Past the "tender years" (which, as any parent will confirm, end at about the beginning of teenage), the rule of thumb was that—other things being equal—boys would go with the father and girls with the mother. Reluctance to separate siblings was an important additional factor.

Many states have amended their statutes along the lines of Colorado's to the effect that "no party shall be presumed to be able to serve the best interest of the child better than any other party because of sex." In some states, the courts have struck down the "tender years presumption" on the basis of the constitutional requirement of equality of sexes (*Devine*, *Watts*, but *cf. Cox*). Does this mean that it really always is in the best interest of the child to disregard the parent's sex in awarding custody? Since psychiatry lays claim to scientific validity, the next question is whether science can be unconstitutional. Or is traditional psychiatry itself the product of a "sexist" society and culture? But has there ever been another? Or is this precisely the wrong question to provide useful answers for the future?

"[C]hildren must have adult models with whom to identify. Which parent they need most will vary according to age and, of course, according to the sex of the child. It has become traditional for mothers to be the parent of first choice for children below the age of adolescence. This is psychologically sound provided that the mother is emotionally capable. With the onset of adolescence, however, the like-sexed parent becomes more important since learning to become male or female is the principal psychological task for that age group. This means that with boys there should be a higher incidence of placement with fathers if the needs of male children are to be met" (Watson, 21 Syracuse L.Rev. 55 (1969)).

On rational balance, it appears that the sex of parent and child *should* remain an important *circumstance* to be considered in the overall picture, though not the sole factor. And it remains just that in many courts, overtly or covertly. The "primary caretaker rule" has emerged from West Virginia as a thinly disguised variant of the maternal preference rule (Neely, 3 Yale L. & Pol. Rev. 167 (1984)), and is gaining ground. In 1992, the Reporter's preliminary draft of the American Law Institute's "Principles of the Law of Family Dissolution," elaborated on the new rule:

"§ 7.08 (1) Where the parents do not [agree], the court shall [award] parental authority and physical custody to the parent the court determines, after a hearing, had performed the principal responsibilities for the care and supervision of the child during the family relationship, unless the court finds under subsection (3) that the other parent is the more appropriate caretaker.

"(2) Parent who had performed the principal responsibilities for the care and supervision of the child during the family relationship means (a) the parent who has stayed home to care for the child full time, or (b) the parent who has worked out of the home but has done so only part time to have time to care for the child, or (c) in the case where both parents worked out of the home full time, the parent who has had the most social interaction with the child and has carried the primary responsibility for child care arrangements, for medical, dental and other care for the child, for school and other activities, and for counseling and emotional support of the child.

"(3) The court may enter an order awarding parental authority and physical custody to the secondary caretaker parent during the family relationship if it finds (a) the primary caretaker parent is unfit, or (b) by clear and convincing evidence, the secondary caretaker parent is the more appropriate caretaker * * * or the parental bonds between the secondary caretaker and the child are greater than those between the child and the primary caretaker; or the child is of sufficient age to form an independent opinion and has expressed a preference for the secondary caretaker parent; or the primary caretaker parent is unwilling or unable to cooperate in fostering the child's relationship with the other parent."

Some feminist scholars advocate an unvarnished return to a "maternal deference standard": "I assess custody standards against their ability to protect the greater emotional commitments of women to children. I reject the best interest standard, joint custody, and deference to the mature child because they do not protect adequately the strong emotional bonds between children and their mothers. * * * At divorce, judges should defer to the fit mother's decision with respect to custody" (Becker, 1 So. Cal. Rev. of L. & Women's Studies at 223–24 (1992)). And outrage greeted a Michigan judge's decision giving custody to a (fit) father who would have his mother care for the child while he was at work, when the mother had put their child into care for 35 hours per week while attending the University of Michigan. Ms. Steingold, a board member of NOW, commented: "It illustrates an attitude toward women about where they should be—the bedroom, kitchen and those kind of places, not at college" (N.Y. Times, 7/27/94). In a District of Columbia court, Judge Harriet Taylor, herself a mother, described Sharon Prost, counsel to Senator Hatch, as a "tightly wound," "driven workaholic" and gave the child to its low key father who, after nearly two years of unemployment, held a flex-time job. The mother also was ordered to pay $23,010 in child support per year. The judge wrote: "A woman is as entitled as defendant, or any other man, to put her work and career ahead of the other demands in her life" (N.Y. Times, 9/20/94). Marcia Clark, of O.J. prosecuting fame (earning about $100,000 a year), was faced with her ex-husband's (earning about half that) petition for their two children's custody when she presented him with a *child* support claim for additional clothing, hairdressing and baby-sitting costs she was incurring during the 16 hour workdays she was keeping (Wash. Post, 3/3/95, Newsweek 3/13/95). Columnist

Ellen Goodman commented: "What better moment for a man to tell a woman in full view of the world that she can't have it all" (Boston Globe, 3/5/95).

While these celebrated cases have caught the public's eye, an important analysis of 1,100 divorcing California families found that mothers still outscore fathers in custody settlements by 7 to 1, and that a mere 1.5 percent of divorces involving children require the judge's decision on custody (Maccoby & Mnookin, Dividing the Child (1992)).

§ 18.4 Parent's Race

In many interracial custody cases, race had been held to be a legitimate consideration to the extent there was an effect on the best interest of the child (*but cf. Kreischer*), though race could not be the *sole* or *determinative* factor (*Beazley, Drummond*). In 1984, the U.S. Supreme Court decided *Palmore I,* holding as follows:

"It would ignore reality to suggest that racial and ethnic prejudices do not exist or that all manifestations of those prejudices have been eliminated. There is a risk that a child living with a step-parent of a different race may be subject to a variety of pressures and stresses not present if the child were living with parents of the same racial or ethnic origin. The question, however, is whether the reality of private biases and the possible injury they might inflict are permissible considerations for removal of an infant child from the custody of its natural mother. We have little difficulty concluding that they are not. The Constitution cannot control such prejudices but neither can it tolerate them. Private biases may be outside the reach of the law, but the law cannot, directly or indirectly, give them effect. * * * Whatever problems racially-mixed households may pose for children in 1984 can no more support a denial of constitutional rights than could the stresses that residential integration was thought to entail in 1917. The effects of racial prejudice, however real, cannot justify a racial classification removing an infant child from the custody of its natural mother found to be an appropriate person to have such custody."

On remand, the Florida Appellate Court resolved the case by leaving the final decision to the Texas court where the child had resided with its father and his new wife for more than two years (*Palmore II*).

Read restrictively, *Palmore* may be interpreted not to have changed the law at all, since the Supreme Court found expressly that the lower "court was entirely candid and made no effort to place its holding on any ground other than race." As the *sole* factor, race has not passed muster on *any* recent appeal. Read expansively, however, the U.S. Supreme Court's opinion casts doubt on whether race may be considered *at all* and in *any* circumstances. Ironically, it escaped the Supreme Court that the original award to the mother may well

have been the result of pro-mother gender prejudice.

§ 18.5 Religion

In deciding on the "better" parent, religion has
played a significant, but not always convincing role.
Constitutional considerations under the First
Amendment loom large (*Osteraas*), but not so large
as to overcome the child's best interests, as when "a
belief system's secular effects are likely to cause
physical or emotional harm to children" (*Leppert*).
This applies with particular force when provision of
medical care is at issue (*Osier*). Many arguments
for and against factoring religion into the custody
determination process resemble those involved in
the decision on the suitability of prospective adoptive parents (§§ 12.4). During marriage, parental
autonomy in deciding the *child's* religion is subject
to few restrictions (*cf. Yoder*). After divorce, that
autonomy may come to be exercised by the custodial
parent alone. While the separation agreement may
prescribe the religious upbringing of the child and
such a stipulation may be enforceable (*Perlstein*),
the Colorado Supreme Court has held that even in
the presence of a separation agreement requiring
joint decisions regarding their child's schooling, the
mother—who had physical custody—had the exclusive power to make any such decision. In that case
she wished to send the child to a Buddhist school
which the father feared would remove the child
from the American mainstream. Their agreement,
viewed as merely an "agreement to agree," was
deemed unenforceable (*Griffin*).

§ 18.6 "Morality"

Not long ago, if the *mother's* adultery was the ground for divorce, she had hardly a chance of winning a disputed custody proceeding. Courts almost routinely held that "immorality" either during marriage or thereafter, *ipso facto* rendered the mother unfit to have custody, regardless of whether her conduct had a direct effect on the well-being of the children. The UMDA § 402 specifically guards against this outcome by providing "the court shall not consider conduct of a proposed custodian that does not affect his relationship to the child". Even where the UMDA does not govern, the significance of the custody-seeking parent's sexual (im)morality is now being restricted to cases where the court perceives a direct effect on the well-being of the child. More of this will be brought out in connection with the discussion of modification of custody (§ 18.19).

§ 18.7 Allegations of Sexual Abuse

Increasingly courts have had to grapple with the dilemma of either believing more or less unsubstantiated allegations of a parent's sexual abuse of a child to avoid any risk of such abuse occurring in the future, or insisting on actual proof to safeguard the parent's rights and reputation. Practitioners have called an allegation of child sexual abuse the "atom bomb" of child custody litigation. The use of the child's testimony may often be as worrisome as the testimony of some "experts" (§ 17.7). The epic saga of Drs. Morgan and Foretich left most underlying questions in the air, but spawned multi-faceted litigation, vast publicity (more than 500 articles in the news media, books, TV specials and soundbites), world-crossing child abduction (ultimately "down under" to New Zealand, then not party to the Hague Convention, § 18.22), years in jail for the mother, Congressional legislation to get her out, and, of course, very large lawyers' fees (*Morgan*). Another headline case involved a family lawyer who, in the words of a friend, saved her daughter "from a fate worse than death" by murdering the child and killing herself in violation of a court order granting the father visitation. First the district attorney, then the family court had found the mother's sex abuse allegations unsubstantiated. Gloria Steinem commented on this case: "The court system is the real abuser of children" (Nat. L.J. 7/26/93, N.Y. Times, 6/26/93). In the celebrity custody case of 1993, 57–year-old Woody Allen disputed Mia Farrow's sex-abuse charges involving their 7–year-old adopted daughter Dylan—but there was no doubt about his affair with his 21–year-old stepdaughter Soon–Yi, nor the pictures Woody had taken of her, he said, as a consenting adult. He called the pictures erotic, the Court thought them pornographic and "totally unacceptable". The custody case ended with limited, supervised visitation with his son, Satchel, and, preferring to "err on the side of caution", no visitation with Dylan, although the sex abuse findings were inconclusive (*Allen.*) Woody was ordered to pay Mia's $1.2 million legal fees (N.Y. Times 5/13/94).

§ 18.8 Gay Lifestyles

Beyond "conventional" adultery, a rather more relaxed attitude has expanded to include gay lifestyles: What the child does not see does not hurt it. Nevertheless, a Virginia trial court awarded custody of a child to its maternal *grandmother* when it found that the *mother's* admitted lesbian activity was illegal under Virginia law and thus rendered her unfit. The child had spent most of the time since the mother's divorce with the grandmother. The latter had filed for custody when the mother objected to the grandmother's male live-in companion who, the mother charged, had sexually abused the mother 800 times. The trial court's ruling was reversed on appeal, the mother arguing that no sexual activity between her and her lover had taken place in her son's presence—although she admitted "hugging, kissing or patting one another on the bottom", in the child's presence (*Bottoms I*). In 1995, Virginia's Supreme Court upheld the trial court and gave custody to the grandmother (*Bottoms II*).

The issue of custodial or visitation rights for same-sex, *de-facto* co-parents has met with mixed results. The Wisconsin Supreme Court simply held that the companion did not qualify as a parent and denied her standing (*Z.J.H.*).

Another scenario involves allegations of HIV infection or AIDS. While the fact is provable, the chief issue here goes to relevance—how likely is transmitting the virus to the child and what about

the carrier's life expectancy? A Georgia appellate
court concluded in a change-of custody case that,
while his homosexuality as such did not matter, a
father's failure to disclose his positive HIV test
until the day of the hearing reflected adversely on
his credibility "regarding his views toward promis-
cuity, the gay lifestyle and his fears of danger
attending each," and changed custody to the mother (*H.J.B.*). A Maryland appellate court reversed
an order that had allowed a gay, HIV-positive father
unsupervised daytime visitation while denying him
overnight visitation (*North*).

§ 18.9 Domestic Violence

Proof of violence directed at the child is the
strongest indicator of unfitness for custody. However, the relevance of *spousal* abuse in *child* custody
adjudications has increased sharply. Congress, the
National Council of Juvenile and Family Court
Judges, and the great majority of states have taken
the affirmative view. In the presence of corroborat-
ing police and medical reports, the Connecticut Supreme Court allowed the "battered *spouse* syndrome" (§ 9.11) as evidence in a *child* custody case
(*Knock*).

§ 18.10 Smoking—and Feeding?

In today's ranking of immorality, smoking may be
the worst (or last) remaining sin. Courts have
taken a wheezing child from her mother, a smoking
registered nurse (N.Y. Times, 10/16/93), awarded a
child's custody to its grandparents and restricted a

smoking mother's visitation with an asthmatic son (*Bacon*), and ordered a custodial mother not to smoke in her children's presence or take the children into a house or car in which she had smoked within the last ten hours (*Unger*). Some legal commentators would rank secondary smoke exposure as child neglect (Time, 10/25/93). Should "junk food" be next? Ominously, Virginia Hudgins of Norfolk was charged in 1994 with (animal) neglect for overfeeding Pinky Starlight, her Vietnamese potbellied pig, and faced a year in jail (Vero Beach P.J., 11/10/94). Ultimately a judge dropped the cruelty charge on the condition that Pinky be put on a court-approved diet (Virginian–Pilot 12/29/94).

§ 18.11   Natural Parent vs. Third Party

A typical scenario involving a third party in a custody dispute is the situation in which the parent who obtained custody of children upon divorce remarries, integrates the children into her or his new family—with the new spouse acting as a kindly stepparent—and then dies. If the stepparent has adopted the children, there is no question (*Ivey*). If the stepparent's custody is informal, however, the natural parent may now reassert parental rights. Again, the older law provided a clear rule: On the death of the custodial parent, custody was transferred to the surviving parent more or less automatically (*Simpson*). More recently, such disputes have had varying results, depending as much on the circumstances of the case as on the judge. Some courts now give a shade less credence to the blanket presumption that it is always in the best interest of the child to be with a natural parent. More consideration is given to "sociological" parenthood and a little less to biological parenthood (*Hoy*). Similar conflicts often arise between relatives such as grandparents or an aunt and a surviving parent, and these disputes have not always been resolved in favor of the parent (*Painter, McGaffin, McLendon*). Emphasis is put on the emotional and physical circumstances in which the child finds itself. If, however, an actual bond exists with the natural parent, the latter will typically win out (*Simons*).

§ 18.12 The Role of Experts

In the mid 1960's, a *cause célèbre* arose in Iowa. Upon the death of his wife, a father had placed his son with his wife's parents who, after the father had remarried and thought himself able to reassume custody, refused to return the child. Based on a pessimistic assessment of the father's sense of responsibility, the Iowa Supreme Court favored the grandparents. The Court praised the grandparents' farm home as "stable, dependable, conventional, middle class, middle west," admitted that the father's home would be "more exciting and challenging in many respects, but romantic, impractical and unstable," noted that the father was "a political liberal and had gotten into difficulty in a job at the University of Washington for his support of the activities of the American Civil Liberties Union" and decided to deny him custody in the belief that the home he would offer "would be unstable, unconventional, arty, bohemian and probably intellectually stimulating" (*Painter*). The story does not end here. The father wrote a book ("Mark, I Love You"), the grandparents ultimately permitted Mark to visit his father, on which occasion a California court awarded custody of the child to the father (*cf.* § 18.21).

A fascinating facet of that case was the Iowa Court's heavy reliance on a child psychologist's testimony who speculated that "the chances are very high (Mark) will go wrong if he is returned to his father." What indeed should be the role of the psychological or psychiatric expert in such cases? Professor (of psychiatry and law) Watson admits that behavioral scientists lack "scientific certainty", but hastens to note that this kind of information is considerably more "hard" than the alternatives—the "hunches of philosophers" or the "theoretical predilections of judges." He suggests an elaborate interview and testing program for each case to determine the optimal disposition, admitting, however, that experts are scarce, costs would be high, and quantification of results would be difficult. All too often, he suggests, "experts" are inadequate, and he "would say categorically that those psychiatrists who are capable only of pasting diagnostic labels on their cases, and who do not have the ability to delineate and formulate the psychodynamic patterns of behavior of the parents and the child, have no utility whatsoever for the court. The parties would do better to save their money than to embark upon that kind of examination." (*Cf.* Watson, § 18.3).

The role of mental health professionals testifying as experts in child custody cases must be sharply distinguished from the situation of a psychiatrist who has treated either of the parents or the child being called as a witness. In the latter context, the professional may refuse to testify on the ground of privilege. For example, in her proceeding to void Woody Allen's adoption of her children, Mia Farrow was not allowed to depose the psychiatrist of her adopted daughter Soon–Yi (*Farrow*). In some circumstances, the professional may testify and be immune to a tort claim (*Searcy*; *Bird*) or, depending on the context, become subject to tort liability (*Renzi*).

§ 18.13 The Role of Judges

When a court delegated the decision on visitation to a psychiatrist, this was held improper (*Shapiro v. S.*). The experienced judge must balance many factors in addition to psychiatric profiles, ranging from the economics of the case to legal rights of constitutional significance. Years ago, the Family Court of Milwaukee County adapted the following "Bill of Rights of Children in Divorce Actions" from decisions of the Wisconsin Supreme Court:

"I. The right to be treated as an interested and affected person and not as a pawn, possession or chattel of either or both parents. II. The right to grow to maturity in that home environment which will best guarantee an opportunity for the child to grow to mature and responsible citizenship. III. The right to the day by day love, care, discipline and protection of the parent having custody of the child. IV. The right to know the non-custodial parent and to have the benefit of such parent and to have the benefit of such parent's love and guidance through adequate visitations. V. The right to a positive and constructive relationship with both parents, with neither parent to be permitted to degrade or downgrade the other in the mind of the child. VI. The right to have moral and ethical values developed by precept and practices and to have limits set for behavior so that the child early in life may develop self-discipline and self-control. VII. The right to the most adequate level of economic support that can be provided by the best efforts of both parents. VIII. The right to the same opportunities for education that the child would have had if the family unit had not been broken. IX. The right to periodic review of custodial arrangements and child support orders as the circumstances of the parents and the benefit of the child may require. X. The right to recognition that children involved in a divorce are always disadvantaged parties and that the law must take affirmative steps to protect their welfare, including, where indicated, a social investigation to determine, and the appointment of a guardian ad item to protect their interests.''

While not suitable as law, this is good food for thought. Awareness of the dilemmas of child custody after divorce is the beginning of help for the child that finds itself in these unfortunate circumstances. The depth of the difficulty is apparent from the fact that the statement could hardly have been written much more precisely. There are few clear answers.

§ 18.14 Joint Custody

The custodial rights exercised by *both* parents in the ongoing marriage (*i.e.,* full decision-making power over all aspects of upbringing, religion and education, short of the neglect, abuse and dependency laws) traditionally went solely to the *one* parent who obtained custody upon divorce. The visitation rights given to the non-custodial parent may be analogized to a mere "possessory" interest—unhappy fathers derisively call visitation "entertainment time". This marks the custody decision upon divorce as a very basic *legal*, not only factual, change in the noncustodial parent's relationship with his or her child. It might very nearly be compared with termination of parental rights regarding which strict constitutional limits apply (§ 17.4)—with the important difference that termination of parental rights ends the child support obligation whereas divorce reinforces it!

However, real social change is obvious in the rapid decline of marital role division. Many fathers have assumed an active parental role in the ongoing family, and there has been an increased willingness of fathers to claim custody and of courts to grant fathers custody on divorce. It is fair neither to the father nor to the child to terminate his active participation on divorce. Yet the "tender years presumption" is dying a slow death, and the "primary caretaker rule" is giving it a new lease on life. The great majority of custody dispositions—7:1, according to Maccoby and Mnookin (§ 18.3)—still go to the mother.

Since the mid–1970s, the concept of "joint custody" has striven to solve the dilemma just outlined. Joint custody, briefly, means that *legal* custody, *i.e.,* decision-making power over the child's life-style, remains in both parents, with physical custody going to one or the other, or being shared. The idea has been hailed as much as condemned. Obviously, if both parents are able to share the decisions of parenting after divorce, the unfairness implicit in traditional practice and law—all but terminating the noncustodial parent's rights and nevertheless asking for full support—would be avoided or alleviated. Equally obviously, joint custody will be harmful if, after the divorce, the parents continue to play out their lingering animosity, or confuse the child with conflicting directions, or are simply unwilling to agree on basic issues involving the child.

Some states presume that it is in the child's best interests to be in the divorced parents' joint custody, but others limit joint custody to exceptional cases. The unresolved question is how to resolve disputes that the parents cannot resolve themselves. Continuous recourse to the courts is neither in the child's nor in the courts' best interests, even if a Michigan appellate court has held that "a court must determine the best interests of the child in resolving disputes concerning 'important decisions affecting the welfare of the child' that arise between joint custodial parents" (*Lombardo*). Arbitration may provide a better answer, or less formally, a "deciding vote" may be given to a person whose judgment both parents trust and are willing to follow. The alternative is to award sole custody either to the "more reasonable" parent, or to the parent who has had more day-to-day physical "possession" of the child. The first alternative may encourage *other* parents to be more reasonable—but should *this* child pay the price? If the latter course is taken, the initial adjudication of joint custody potentially becomes a mere placebo (*cf. Gordon*), with physical "possession" remaining the key to long-run rights over the child (*Griffin*).

To conclude, the problems joint custody raises seem to equal the solutions it offers. The appropriate attitude may be a careful case-by-case approach with no presumption for or against joint custody, until reliable empirical data support a strong preference for one or the other disposition. The key undisputed principles remain that the best interests of the child involve continuity and stability, but equally extend to a mutually responsible relationship with *both* parents.

§ 18.15 Visitation Rights

Visitation is only a partial answer to an award of sole custody to one parent. Visitation poses additional dilemmas in practical and legal terms, starting with its very name. In an attempt to get away from the word "visitation" (according to Webster's Collegiate, a "special dispensation of divine favor or wrath", "a severe trial"), the ALI's 1992 draft Principles speak in terms of the "Secondary Caretaker Parent's Parent–Child Contact Time." Not much help there! The basic dilemma is that while the grant of meaningful visitation rights to the non-custodial parent softens the impact of a custody decision and helps preserve for child and parent a continuing social relationship, coerced visitation, when parents "hate" each other, may prolong the child's trauma. Unfortunately, there *are* cases in which visitation rights are exercised as much to harass (or attempt to keep up a relationship with) the former spouse as to retain closeness to the child—and there are cases in which the custodial parent intentionally interferes with visitation. In "Beyond the Best Interests of the Child", Goldstein, Freud and Solnit go as far as to advocate *abolition* of enforceable visitation rights on the theory that "once it is determined who will be the custodial parent * * * it is that parent, not the court who must decide under what conditions he or she wishes to raise the child". Whatever may be said against brutal enforcement of visitation rights in situations of great conflict and tension, this extreme position is as unfair to the child (who is entitled to know two parents) as it is to the non-custodial parent (who remains a parent, divorced or not). The very *possibility* of enforcement will in many cases evoke voluntary and peaceful compliance, and blanket denial of visitation rights is apt to exacerbate initial custody disputes. In any event, courts and statutes generally speak of the non-custodial parent's *right* to visitation (*J.S. & C.*). And they should, especially where the non-custodial parent bears the burden of paying child support. UMDA § 407 strengthens preexisting law by allowing a *denial* of visitation *only* if visitation would "endanger seriously the child's physical, mental, moral, or emotional health". Other statutes give the court power to deny visitation rights simply if visitation is deemed not to be in the best interest of the child.

§ 18.16 Enforcement of Visitation and Custodial Rights

Judicial sanctions prominently include contempt, with fine or jail, indefinitely or until there is compliance, (in November 1994, the Illinois Supreme Court upheld jailing a recalcitrant father for seven years—so far (*Sanders*), or, in D.C., until Congress passes a law (*Morgan*, § 18.7)). Alternatively, custody may be turned over to the other parent (*Quirk-Edwards*).

What other remedies are there? "Kidnapping" of the disputed child, not long ago widely practiced by frustrated parents as a form of "self help", is definitely *not* recommended. Through a special exception, the federal "Lindbergh" kidnapping law does not apply, even when the abducting parent's rights have been terminated (*Sheek*), but this immunity does not extend to a stepparent, such as the mother's new husband (*Sheek*). However, the federal

Parental Kidnapping Prevention Act and severe state statutes, imposing up to felony charges, do apply specifically (§ 18.22).

May a parent simply stop paying alimony or child support when visitation rights are thwarted in one way or another by the custodial parent? While alimony payments may possibly be stopped (*Herrera*), child support payments must go on. (Otherwise in *Damico* where the child had been concealed). In *any* such case, the only sensible course is to apply to the court whose visitation order is in question and accept that court's guidance. While some courts allow the suspension of child support (*P.K.*)., it is more useful to order the funds paid into court until the custodial parent complies with the other's visitation rights.

In Florida's Supreme Court, a mother unsuccessfully invoked her right to free speech when she had been specifically ordered "to do everything in her power to create in the [children's] minds a living, caring feeling toward the father * * * and to convince the children that it is the mother's desire that they see and love their father" (*Schutz*). As the Court put it, "the cause of the blind, brainwashed, bigoted belligerence of the children toward the father grew from the soil nurtured and tilled by the mother". The Iowa Supreme Court has allowed a tort action for money damages (potentially including punitive damages) for wrongful interference with one parent's custody of a child by the other (*Wood*). That may be a suitable remedy in the atypical case where the defendant has money. Due to its "deep pockets", the U.S. government has found itself a defendant in such cases. A father won a $100,000 settlement ($95,000 for himself and $2,500 for each of the children), because he had been deprived of his two children while their mother was being protected as a federal witness after agreeing to testify against the "Hell's Angels" (N.Y. Times, 3/9/85). A mother was awarded $17,000 damages under the Tort Claims Act while her child was in the witness protection program with the father (*Ruffalo, cf. Franz*).

The parents' extended reconciliation without enforcing their separation or interlocutory divorce decree may override a custody disposition and therefore immunize a parent from prosecution if he or she later takes "possession" of a child in derogation of the earlier decree (*Howard*).

§ 18.17 Grandparents' Visitation Rights

In 1983, the House of Representatives passed a resolution calling on the states to enact generous laws allowing visitation to grandparents (H. Con. Res. 45, 4/9/83), and by 1995 the Uniform Law Commissioners were drafting an Interstate Child Visitation Act. President Clinton proclaimed 1995 the "Year of the Grandparent" (Presidential Proclamation 6766). This comes after grandparents gained substantial legal recognition as interested parties in custody proceedings. In one form or another, nearly all states now grant grandparents potential visitation rights. The content of these laws varies greatly. Several states limit visitation to cases where the parent is deceased, others specifically extend the right to the case of divorce, annulment or separation. Remarkably, a few states allow grandparental visitation even over the objections of both parents in an ongoing family (*King KY*), and even against the argument that parents have the constitutional right to raise their child as they see fit (*Herndon MO*). Most states, however, hold by statute or court decision that the ongoing family is not subject to enforced intrusion by grandparents, if both parents are fit and object (*Hawk*). A few states allow that adoption by a stepparent does not bar visitation by grandparents (*C.G.F.*), but the majority continues to hold that any adoption preempts visitation (*Bronstein*). Moreover, grandparents generally have no right to intervene in an adoption proceeding involving their grandchild (*Suster, cf. B.B.M.*).

§ 18.18 The Unwed Father's Visitation Rights

In many states, the fit though unwed father has been expressly granted visitation rights by statute. *Lehr* and related U.S. Supreme Court cases (*e.g. Vanderlaan*) should be read to hold that where the father, the mother and the child have lived in a *de facto* family setting, the fit father has standing to assert appropriate visitation rights (§§ 11.17, 18).

§ 18.19 Change in Custody—Modification

Custody awards are *not* final orders and remain modifiable if there is a material change in circumstances. Since the stability of the child's environment is in itself a major consideration in custodial decisions, courts are reluctant to modify awards. A trial judge in Oregon expressed this poignantly: "I find that the chances of (children) developing emotional problems as they grow up increases in direct proportion to the thickness of the file involved in a divorce case. You two people remember that" (*King OR*). In short, the original award often turns out to be the final award, *de facto* if not *de jure*. In an attempt to reduce post-divorce custody litigation, UMDA § 409 provides that a child custody order may not be modified for two years unless the child's environment seriously endangers the child's "physical, mental, moral or emotional health". The catch is that after two years, nearly the same criteria must be met, unless the custodial parent consents. This has had the unintended result of exacerbating the initial custody decision and may have led to the spread of joint custody. Still, vexatious custody litigation is not extinct, and remedies are not always available. A California court *denied* a custodial father an action for malicious prosecution where the mother had filed a series of custody motions that had cost the father $200,000 in lawyer's fees. A dissenting judge would have allowed the father to proceed against "the wicked former mother-in-law" who had financed her daughter's effort to bankrupt her ex-husband (*Bidna*).

Even absent the UMDA, solid proof of a serious change in circumstances is necessary to change

custody.   Traditionally, sexual mores—especially
the mother's—were emphasized.   This still echoed
in 1979 in the Supreme Court of Illinois when that
court upheld a change of custody of three children
from a "cohabiting" mother to an "equally caring
and affectionate" father "whose conduct did not
contravene" the "statutorily expressed moral standards of the State " (*Jarrett*).   In New York on the
other hand, as far back as in 1974, a transfer of
custody of children to the father was held *not* proper on a mere showing that the mother socialized
with a married man, advertised in a "swingers"
magazine and was interested in sexually oriented
literature, where the children were emotionally and
physically well provided for (*Feldman N.Y.*).   As
discussed above, today it is generally held that a
parent's sexual orientation, so long as the child is
not brought into contact with it too directly, is *not* a
disabling factor in terms of custody or visitation
(§ 18.6).

§ 18.20   The Custodial Parent's Right (?) to Relocate or Travel—Interstate and Abroad

Geographic mobility and eagerness to move after
divorce produce practical difficulties with visitation.
A typical part of a custody award is an order of the
court that the custodial parent is not to leave the
jurisdiction of the court without specific permission.
Violation is punishable as contempt.   The chief
purpose of such orders is as much to protect the
non-custodial parent's visitation rights as it is to

preserve the court's jurisdiction. Aside from the conflicts problems this tends to spawn (§§ 18.21, 22), some have asked whether such orders violate the custodial parent's constitutionally guaranteed right to interstate travel (*Shapiro, cf. Sosna*). The Minnesota Supreme Court fumbled an opportunity to deal with this issue in 1983 (*Ryan*), but held in 1992 that there is a case law presumption that the custodial parent may relocate with his or her child (*Ayers*). In 1984, the Idaho Court of Appeals held that a 100–mile-radius travel restriction did *not* violate a custodial mother's constitutional right to travel, emphasizing that there was no flat prohibition, but only a requirement for prior court permission for more extensive travel (*Ziegler*). Intelligent analysis would balance the non-custodial parent's constitutional right to visitation (*J.S. & C.*) against the custodial parent's constitutional right to travel, all in the light of the best interest of the child.

So much for theory—in practice courts are inclined to grant the custodial parent's request to remove a child from the court's jurisdiction, if the parent has a legitimate reason (not just a desire to start a new life after divorce) and the move is not harmful to the child (*Cooper*). A higher standard is sometimes applied in cases involving *joint custody* (*McDole*). In the interest of custodial continuity— if the alternative is a change of custody to the "nonpossessory" joint custodian—several state supreme courts have favored the "possessory" parent who decides to move elsewhere, some going as far as to invoke a presumption in favor of the "possessory" parent (*Gordon, Hill, Mize*).

More difficult are cases involving the proposed removal of children to foreign countries. South Dakota's Supreme Court allowed a mother to take her five-year-old daughter to her native Scotland, with generous (though recognized to be impractical) summer visitation privileges to the father and the sanction of withholding support payments should the mother not comply (*Bolenbaugh*). A New York court, on the other hand, denied a mother permission to take her five year old daughter to Australia, holding that " 'nowhere in the world today is the right of citizenship of greater worth to an individual than it is in this country. It would be difficult to exaggerate its value and importance'. This court will jealously guard this treasured birthright of the child" (*O'Shea*). In *Frey,* the Supreme Court of Oklahoma let two girls move to live with an aunt in France (after their father had murdered their mother) when a French official testified that, in France, the children would have "free education to the Ph.D. level; a monetary family and orphan's allocation of approximately $150 per month for each child; and free medical and hospitalization care." In *Schleiffer,* a ten-year-old American citizen was denied a civil rights action (under 42 U.S.C.A. § 1983), when he sought to enjoin enforcement of a Swedish decree awarding his custody to his mother. During the Cold War, the Illinois Supreme Court disapproved, but could not change the outcome, of a political drama that had been played out with U.S.

State Department involvement. In derogation of
the wishes and custodial claims of his fit and suitable immigrant parents who were returning to the
Ukraine (then part of the Soviet Union), a twelve-
year-old Soviet citizen had been processed in juvenile court as a "minor in need of supervision" with
the ultimate outcome that he became a U.S. citizen
in 1985 (*Polovchak*). (The "kidnapping" of a child
to a foreign country in violation of a custody decree
is discussed in § 18.22).

§ 18.21 Interstate Custody Problems

Much mischief came from the indispensable rule
that custody determinations remain modifiable to
safeguard the child's best interests, when combined
with the rule that "Full Faith and Credit", *i.e.,*
nationwide recognition and enforcement, is *not* due
judgments that are not final (and *modifiable* judgments are not final). The U.S. Supreme Court
declined to settle the question (*Ford*). Given that
state of the law, parents dissatisfied with custody
awards went "forum shopping". Seizing on the
basic jurisdictional fact of the child's presence,
courts would take jurisdiction over basically out-of-
state custody disputes and impose their own ideas
of the appropriateness of earlier custodial decisions,
usually with lip service to an alleged change in
circumstances that would justify modification. This
tempting prospect encouraged dissatisfied parents
to "kidnap" their own children from the legal custodian, take them to another jurisdiction, and seek
modification of the original award. Some custody-

seeking parents would drag a child from forum to forum until a "friendly" court was found. In their heyday, an estimate of parental abductions ranged between 300,000 to 600,000 cases per year (N.Y. Times, 10/23/83).

The Uniform Law Commissioners' Child Custody Jurisdiction Act seeks to "avoid jurisdictional competition in conflict with courts of other states in matters of child custody which have in the past resulted in the shifting of children from state to state with harmful effect on their well-being." Since 1984, the Act has been in effect in all states and has changed the picture radically for the better. Now only the state with the closest connection to a child may provide the forum for adjudication of its custody, and sister-state courts may interfere with out-of-state custodial arrangements only if the case presents a serious emergency. Along similar lines, UMDA § 401(b) provides that, except in a case of abandonment or other emergency or if no other state has a better base for jurisdiction, "physical presence * * * of the child * * * is not alone sufficient to confer jurisdiction on a court * * * to make a child custody determination."

§ 18.22 The Federal Parental Kidnapping Prevention Act, the Hague Convention and the International Parental Kidnapping Crime Act

Even as the states—by adopting the UCCJA— were accepting their long-neglected responsibility in this area, Congress moved into the picture in 1980.

The "Parental Kidnapping Prevention Act" parallels, but does not wholly coincide with the UCCJA's jurisdictional criteria. This has led to unnecessary uncertainty and occasional confusion (*Erler*).

By 1995, drafting efforts were under way to conform the UCCJA to the PKPA. Substantively, the PKPA provides that a custodial adjudication—if the rendering state had jurisdiction as defined in the federal law—now carries "Full Faith and Credit" and *must* be enforced by all other states. Federal courts are given jurisdiction, where previously they would have declined such cases on the basis of the "domestic relation exception" (*DiRuggiero, Flood,* § 1.5). The federal parent locator service that was set up for the enforcement of child support (§ 16.4) is available to aid in locating an abducting parent. If parental child-snatching is a felony in the state where it occurred, the abducting parent is brought under the sweep of the "Federal Fugitive Felon Act". Given that incentive, the majority of the states have enacted felony statutes in order to invoke this portion of the PKPA.

The PKPA has further strengthened the hand of the custodial parent, although some commentators have regretted the considerable, and to the child potentially harmful, inflexibility brought along by the invocation of Full Faith and Credit. No longer is a court in another state with "significant connection" to the child allowed to modify an existing court order, and the court that originally rendered the decree remains the exclusive arbiter (*cf. Arbogast, Heartfield*). As Professor Foster put it with just a trace of value judgment, "certainty and stability are given priority under the PKPA; the UCCJA provides flexibility and accords the best interests of the child top priority."

In 1985, the U.S. Senate ratified the Hague Convention on the Civil Aspects of International Child Abduction. The Convention facilitates the return of abducted children and the exercise of visitation rights across international boundaries. The Hague Convention, along with U.S. implementing legislation (International Child Abduction Remedies Act, 42 U.S.C.A. § 11601), are powerful weapons in the orderly resolution of international child custody disputes; even while many practitioners may still perceive the new remedy as slightly exotic. Numerous court decisions have been rendered world-wide, and U.S. courts have not hesitated to return even U.S.-born children abroad, where an American parent had brought his or her child to the United States in violation of a foreign custody order (*Prevot* (France); *Grimer* (U.K.); *Friedrich*, (Germany)). By 1995, the treaty was in effect between the United States and nearly thirty countries. While the civil mechanism of the Hague Convention should remain the first choice, the "International Parental Kidnapping Crime Act" (18 U.S.C.A. § 1204) adds criminal clout to the Convention's civil sanctions.

*

PART VI

TERMINATION OF MARITAL STATUS

CHAPTER 19
DIVORCE, TRADITIONAL STYLE

§ 19.1 History—From No Divorce to Unilateral Divorce In One Long Century

Lasting marriage is the goal and, even as divorce statistics signal trouble, remains the norm. For lawyers who rarely deal with the "normal," divorce is the essence of family law. So far we have seen how people get married and what substantive and formal prerequisites apply. We have concerned ourselves with the limited involvement of the law in the ongoing marriage, and we may have been left wondering whether the law has struck that balance between involvement and non-involvement that maximizes the parties' potential for a good relationship. Now we shall see what happens when the relationship has irrevocably turned sour: Divorce.

So long as there has been marriage, there has been a need for divorce. Greater today, perhaps, than ever. Longer life expectancies have dramatically increased the time partners may expect to spend together in the "bonds of matrimony." Availability of birth control and prenatal health care has drastically decreased the number of marriages that are terminated by the wife's death in childbirth. Unprecedented employment opportunities for women have reduced the number of marriages that stay together for economic motives. Finally, the philosophy has changed. Many see lasting marriage not as a virtue *per se,* and divorce has become a socially accepted, in some circles a fashionable, event.

Books have been written on the history of divorce—only a few words fit here. Contrary to common misconception, it should be noted that history cannot be divided neatly into an early period without divorce and our modern, liberal times, starting perhaps when England enacted a secular divorce statute in the 1850's. Divorce has had ups and downs for centuries. Periods of liberality have alternated with periods of difficult divorce, from Roman times through the Middle Ages and since then. To illustrate, the Prussian Code of 1794 not only permitted childless partners to divorce by consent, but "irreparable breakdown" of marriage, now the vogue here, may also be found there. Divorce followed if one party could prove "the existence of so violent and deeply rooted an aversion that no hope remains for a reconciliation and the achievement of the ends of the marital state." Even during periods supposedly without divorce, such as some periods of ecclesiastical dominance, a substitute was relatively readily available because myriad types of impediments or technical defects allowed annulment of marriages (Ch. 21).

In England, the ecclesiastical courts had exclusive jurisdiction over actions relating to marriage until 1857. They could grant annulments, then called "divorce a vinculo," that retroactively voided a defective marriage. Other than annulment, these courts would decree divorce only from bed and board ("a mensa et thoro"), that freed the parties from each other, but did *not* free them to remarry. Blackstone wrote a century earlier that "divorces * * * for adultery have of late years been frequently granted by act of parliament", but only the privileged were in a position to avail themselves of such a difficult and expensive process. Even after matrimonial jurisdiction was handed to the civil courts, and a statute permitting full divorce (with right to remarry) was enacted, the break with the past was not complete. Without giving the matter much thought, the secular courts took over the ecclesiastical jurisprudence all but unchanged, persevering in the concept that divorce was a remedy for "wrong", available only to an "innocent" party, against a "guilty" party. Few questioned whether the Church's view of matrimonial rights and wrongs should remain applicable in a secular society or, more fundamentally, whether it made sense to carry forward a set of rules developed for incomplete divorce that did not permit remarriage, into an era in which remarriage after divorce was to be permitted. Developments in the United States differed from state to state, but followed the English model in broad outline.

When the only issue was whether people should be allowed to *separate*, common sense had dictated a retrospective inquiry into the quality of their relationship. Accordingly, grounds and defenses dealt with divorce from that perspective, although the excessive application of the concept of fault, especially through the doctrine of recrimination (§ 19.9), played unnecessary tricks. But the questions asked, *i.e.*, the grounds and defenses, went to the point at issue: Should the parties be allowed to *separate*?

The same inquiry had much less relevance, if any, when the result of divorce was that the parties would be allowed to *remarry*. Confronted with *that* question, common sense would have dictated a prospective inquiry, the investigation going to the parties' fitness for remarriage. Some early divorce courts and laws saw and applied this logic by forbidding guilty parties to remarry for a specified period of time, during the life of the innocent party, or to the paramour if the divorce was for adultery. For better, this overreaction has not survived. For worse, however, most legislatures and courts stayed with the traditional approach and dwelt solely on the previous failure. That failure had limited predictive value as to fitness to remarry. Often as not, the outcome was quite the opposite from what a rational observer might have expected: The worse the previous failure, the more readily would divorce and thereby remarriage be allowed. The analogy to a law that allows renewal of a driver's license only on proof of a crash—the worse, the better—is not altogether far-fetched.

In view of the logical inapplicability of grounds and defenses justifying separation from a present spouse, to eligibility for a "license to marry" a new one, it is not surprising that tensions developed which soon tore the illogical law of divorce to shreds. First there was evasion (perjury and collusion on the primary or only divorce grounds of adultery or physical cruelty), then avoidance (through legislative enactment of "fuzzier" grounds, such as "mental cruelty" and their judicial redefinition as encompassing more or less normal, daily, "post-honeymoon" marital behavior). This uneasy compromise between "Puritans" and "Libertines" gave way to no-fault divorce by various criteria, such as "incompatibility" (a sort of low-key, mutual mental cruelty) and ultimately to the "true" test: "irretrievable breakdown of marriage," usually shown by "living apart" for a specified period.

But this does not really describe what has happened. Actually, we have moved from restrictive divorce (to be granted only in a few objectively intolerable situations), past consent divorce (which we have long had by collusion not only between the parties but also with the courts), to unilateral divorce (divorce on demand of one party, regardless of fault on either side). The situation has taken a serious turn in terms of greatly increasing the potential cost of marriage for those who value stability, while decreasing it for those who don't. This in turn, has accelerated the destabilization of marriage. It is rather an open question whether some aspects of modern reforms are themselves an over-reaction and have exchanged one bad situation for one about as bad at the other extreme. Before we evaluate the future, however, we must familiarize ourselves with the past—especially when it remains alive in the majority of states.

All states have abandoned the pure fault-based system. In the mid–1980's, Illinois and South Dakota were last to fall in line. (Even in these bastions of "traditional values", the delay had been politically acceptable only because consent divorce was liberally available through collusion on fault grounds). Did this make the United States a no-fault divorce country? Not so fast—only about one third of the states opted for pure no-fault divorce. Significantly, some thirty states mixed the old with the new by adding no-fault grounds to a more or less traditional fault-based system. At least as an alternative to a no-fault ground, divorce for fault thus remains available in the majority of states and requires explanation. Much of what follows remains "face-value law" somewhere in the United States, even if much of it makes little sense today.

§ 19.2 Fault Grounds for Divorce

Over the last century, fault grounds for divorce expanded slowly from the early grounds of adultery and physical cruelty. Toward the end of the reign of fault in divorce law, there were about one dozen other grounds, such as willful desertion for a specific period of time (typically one, three or five years), habitual drunkenness or use of drugs (sometimes "gross" or for a specific period), mental cruelty, conviction of a felony (sometimes with a specific prison sentence), venereal disease and so forth.

Modern Delaware, a mixed fault and no-fault jurisdiction, now speaks broadly in terms of "misconduct" instead of defined, specific grounds for divorce, as follows:

" 'Misconduct' means conduct so destructive of the marriage relation that petitioner cannot reasonably be expected to continue in that relation; and 'misconduct' includes, *as examples*, adultery, bigamy, conviction of a crime the sentence for which might be incarceration for one or more years, repeated physical or oral abuse directed against petitioner or children living in the home, desertion, homosexuality, lesbianism, willful refusal to perform marriage obligations, contracting venereal disease, habitual intemperance, habitual use of illegal drugs or other incapacitating substances, and/or other serious offenses destructive of the marriage relation" (Delaware, § 1503(4). Emphasis added.)

§ 19.3   Adultery

This most traditional of grounds for divorce is named sufficiently descriptively to explain itself. Only a few more words are in order. Adultery is often difficult to prove. That is overcome by the rule that the complainant has to show no more than an "adulterous disposition" or "inclination" on the part of his or her spouse and the alleged paramour, and that there has been opportunity to succumb. Opportunity *and* inclination may be established by a motel registration as husband and wife, and if someone keeps a diary, so much the better (*Leonard*). Times are changing, however, and in 1992 in Mississippi, a photo of the alleged paramour, clad only in shorts and lying on the parties' bed, "does not rise above mere suspicion" and shows no more than friendship and "horse-play" between the wife and her alleged paramour (*McAdory*). More exotically, several early cases discussed the question whether a wife's artificial insemination, without (or even with) her husband's consent, amounts to adultery (*Sorensen, Dornboos*). One argument is that there can be no adultery without sexual intercourse; on the other hand, the worse aspect of adultery was the risk to the husband that a "false" heir might be produced and that, by operation of the "presumption of legitimacy" (§ 11.4), he would have difficulty escaping a child-support obligation that should not be his (*cf.* § 13.2). Even direct testimony may not always be reliable. Judge Buchmeyer recalls the wife's reply when asked why she thought her husband unfaithful: "First of all, I don't believe he's the father of my child" (ABAJ, 10/93).

§ 19.4 Desertion

To serve as a fault ground for divorce, desertion must be willful and against the deserted spouse's wishes and it must have continued for a specified period. Even when parties are already separated, the period is held to run from the time the *intent* to desert permanently was formed. The line may sometimes be fine, but desertion must be distinguished from the no-fault ground of "living apart" for a specified period which may be, but need not be, consensual (§ 24.5). In the context of divorce for fault, the party who walks out physically is not always the "deserter." If Spouse A's conduct makes it reasonable for Spouse B to leave, Spouse A will be deemed the "deserter" or "constructive deserter", and Spouse B will be entitled to the divorce (*Mancuso*). It is not even always necessary that one party physically leave the home. Some courts hold that, for instance, the *unjustified* refusal of one party to have sexual relations with the other amounts to "constructive desertion" (*cf. Aichner*). In 1993, a New York man was denied a divorce after his wife refused to visit him in prison, the court holding that she had not voluntarily separated from him and that her intent not to resume cohabitation was not unjustified (*Defeo*). Traditionally, an offer to resume cohabitation, refused by the "deserter" without justification, provided the best proof of desertion. In 1993, however, New York refused another husband a divorce for "constructive abandonment" when he had last asked his wife in 1990, been refused, and since then had silently acquiesced in their lifestyle of sexual abstention (*Brian D.*).

§ 19.5 Physical Cruelty

In older days, physical cruelty had to involve danger to "life, limb or health." The courts allowed early that a spouse need not wait until actual harm was done. A reasonable apprehension of serious harm was deemed sufficient. Even today, however, many jurisdictions require "cruelty" to be repeated (*i.e.,* at least twice) or intolerable (*Capps*). For procuring the standard collusive consent divorce, physical cruelty long was favored over any other ground. Remarkably, cruelty was then considered less socially objectionable than adultery (§ 19.14).

§ 19.6 Mental Cruelty

States that clung to divorce for fault, but nevertheless wished to liberalize divorce, invented "mental cruelty". Legislation typically provides no clear (or even unclear) definition of mental cruelty, perhaps intentionally. Many statutes garnish mental cruelty with adjectives such as "extreme and repeated", and some courts require evidence of injury to physical or emotional health, but these qualifications neither help nor hurt much (*Farnbach*). Mental cruelty remains a vague notion which leaves the decision as to whether or not a divorce should be granted to the court's discretion, or in practice, to the parties' imaginativeness in presenting their collusive case. The very flexibility of the ground made it the ideal vehicle for *de facto* consent (collusive) divorces, with the beneficial side effect of at least reducing the unpleasantness of rampant perjury that had been previously routine (§ 19.14). In *any* marriage, mental cruelty is where you look for it and depends on how you look at it. Moreover, mental cruelty is usually understood to be a subjective concept: "What might be acceptable and even commonplace in the relationship between rather stolid individuals could well be extraordinary and highly unacceptable in the lives of more sensitive or high-strung husbands and wives. Family traditions, ethnic and religious backgrounds, local customs and standards and other cultural differences all come into play when trying to determine what should fall within the parameters of a workable marital relationship and what will not" (*Pochop*). When the divorce is contested, however, many courts have applied quite stringent rules, and pleas of mental cruelty have been refused in very unhappy situations (*Palmer*).

§ 19.7 Insanity

If very extreme, of course, mental cruelty or "indignities" may reach the level of insanity. How to define and what to do with "insanity" has baffled the courts and legislatures. If the condition antedates the marriage, an annulment may be the proper remedy (Ch. 21). In many states, insanity is a ground for divorce, in others its manifestations may be implicit in other grounds, such as incompatibility, indignities, and mental or physical cruelty. The traditional rule, on the other hand, considers insanity to be a *defense* to a ground for divorce. The reasoning is that as divorce is based on fault, there can be no divorce for insane behavior, since insanity negates fault. In 1992, the South Carolina Supreme Court held that even adultery, if committed

in the throes of insanity, would not allow divorce
(*Rutherford*).

There is no agreement as to what constitutes
insanity, either as a ground for or as a defense to
divorce. At one point, North Dakota's statute attempted to put some order into mental disorder by
defining the requisite insanity in terms of "para-
noia, paresis, dementia praecox, Huntington's cho-
rea, or epileptic insanity". Several states achieved
certainty by requiring the party to be divorced for
insanity to have been confined in a mental institution for a stated period. Even in the same jurisdiction, however, different criteria may apply to "defense" and "offense." For instance, one and the
same mental condition may not measure up to a
ground for divorce, although it may suffice as a
defense, or *vice versa* (*Steinke*).

§ 19.8 Bars and Defenses to Divorce

As were the grounds for divorce, a network of
fault-related defenses was taken over nearly intact
from ecclesiastical antecedents, without serious regard for their applicability in the civil context or
concern with the fact that absolute divorce with the
right to remarriage had become possible. In accordance with the thesis that divorce was available
only for the other party's fault, equitable notions of
"clean hands" played an important role. The traditional defenses to divorce sprang from the strong
interest of the Church in maintaining marriage at
(almost) any cost. When remarriage was not permitted, when social customs made sexual relation-

ships outside of marriage difficult and the law punished them, this was, perhaps, a not unreasonable objective.

To make certain that parties truly had an approved ground for divorce, the courts themselves saw to it that each cause of divorce was fully proved and that applicable bars were raised. In contrast to the normal civil suit in which the defendant may choose to defend, compromise or give in, a current Illinois statute, (re)enacted in 1985, continues to insist that, in divorce, "No admission * * * shall be taken as evidence unless the court shall be satisfied that such admission was made in sincerity and without fraud or collusion". Moreover, if the evidence indicates collusion between the parties or assent of the petitioner to the "injury complained of," the statute still says that no divorce may be adjudged. Needless to say, if the courts would actually enforce that statute, it would be repealed. As it actually "plays in Peoria", most fault divorces are obtained through collusion between the parties and, indeed, the court (§ 19.14).

§ 19.9 Recrimination

Most states now have abandoned or at least restricted the doctrine of "recrimination." It pushes the idea of divorce for fault to the breaking point. The fault approach comprehends that there is a guilty party and, borrowing from equity, that only an innocent party is entitled to relief. Once in that frame of reference, the conclusion logically follows that if both parties are guilty, the court is barred from giving a divorce to either party. The alternative, *i.e.,* to grant the divorce to *both* parties, was tried out by enterprising courts and succeeded in some cases (*De Burgh*). Other courts held that, like it or not, the legislature must decide whether to abandon recrimination (*Mogged*). In the early stages of divorce reform, recrimination became an affirmative defense, instead of a bar, to divorce.

Ironically, the addition of liberalized grounds for divorce increased the importance of recrimination. When adultery or well-proved and repeated physical cruelty were the only grounds, the establishment of a recriminatory defense required some doing. But when mental cruelty became the prime ground for divorce, setting up a "counterclaim" of mental cruelty became relatively easy. The effect was to make it more difficult to win a contested divorce, at least in jurisdictions that allowed the reach of recrimination to grow along with the grounds for divorce. Other jurisdictions limited recrimination to the original grounds, or to adultery alone, and still others employed a balancing process (descriptively titled "comparative rectitude"), allowing only grounds of "equal magnitude" to be offset in recrimination (*Chastain*), or under a Nevada statute, granting the divorce to the party "least in fault."

§ 19.10 Provocation

If the divorce-seeking spouse was not guilty of marital misconduct constituting a ground for divorce, recrimination would not apply as a bar or as a defense. However, a divorce action may yet be defended successfully by proving that the plaintiff's conduct "provoked" the defendant's marital offense (*Capps*). The defendant's retaliation, however, must have been appropriate to the provocation. Thus, a wife's extra-marital affair, terminated years before and subsequently "condoned" (§ 19.11) by the husband, was held not to be adequate provocation for the husband's later conduct which included frequent intoxication, sleeping on the front lawn, vomiting throughout the house, provoking frequent arguments, calling the wife "trash" and "whore" and mistrusting her to the extent of examining her clothes for evidence of seminal discharge, threatening her life with a gun and seeking to have her submit to unnatural sexual practices (*Griffie*). On the other hand, a husband's withdrawal from the marriage relationship was held based on adequate provocation where his wife maintained up to seventy-five dogs and cats in the home, the parties' adopted child was allergic to the animals, the doctor had recommended that the animals be removed, and "testimony tended to show that animal excretions, hair and cages were to be found throughout the house, leaving a permanent odor" (*Therrell*).

§ 19.11   Condonation

"Condonation" involves forgiveness of a prior marital offense, thus eliminating it as a ground for divorce. Questions often concern proof. While any satisfactory proof will do, it is generally accepted that sexual intercourse with knowledge of the offense implies condonation. A second question goes to the extent of forgiveness. Once condoned, is a marital offense forgiven forever? Courts have divided on whether condonation can be or always is conditional. Some hold the reasonable view that, once forgiven, a marital offense should not remain a "blackmail" weapon in the hands of the "offended" spouse. Most courts, however, consider that condonation is conditional and that the original offense is revived if the "conditions" are breached. This approach has in its favor that it encourages reconciliation. If forgiveness were unconditional and the price of reconciliation were loss of the ground for divorce, the offended spouse might be reluctant to try to reconcile. Some states clarified that situation by permitting reconciliation to be attempted pursuant to court order which, if the attempt failed, assured the survival of the ground for divorce.

A defendant's conduct that revives his or her prior marital offense is not necessarily conduct that in and of itself amounts to a ground for divorce. In the latter case, of course, a divorce could be procured on the new ground. However, that may or may not be advantageous. Even today it may be of financial interest in some states to procure a divorce on the ground of an earlier, condoned adultery, revived by, for instance, subsequent mental cruelty.

§ 19.12 Connivance

This defense derives from equitable maxims and is both more and less than consent. "Connivance" involves the participation of the spouse seeking the divorce in developing the grounds for divorce. The typical fact situation involves one spouse actively creating an opportunity for the other to commit adultery, as by hiring a private detective or persuading a friend to seduce his or her spouse (*Greene*). The defense does not arise if a known opportunity to commit adultery is simply allowed to proceed or if the other spouse (or a detective) merely stands by to assemble evidence. The line may be fine: in 1993, a Virginia court denied a wife a divorce for her husband's adultery when she had urged him to fall in love with a particular woman (because she did not want him to marry "some bimbo"), and she had sent flowers when the husband and the women first had sexual relations (*Hollis*).

§ 19.13 Collusion

Because it negates fault or makes it difficult for the court to ascertain whether misconduct has in fact occurred, "collusion" traditionally has been fatal to divorce for fault. Precisely what amounts to collusion varies. The strict traditional view holds that, if *any* agreement between the parties to divorce is shown, even actual proof of a marital offense will not be accepted. The theory is that, in the presence of collusion, the court cannot trust evidence brought before it. Other jurisdictions have limited the bar of "collusion" to the case where, pursuant to an agreement between the parties, one spouse goes out and commits a marital offense to enable the other to bring the divorce action. Still others have applied "collusion" as a bar to divorce only where the alleged marital offense did not occur at all.

§ 19.14 The Negotiated Fault Divorce

In the past, the significant—often overriding—stimulus to keeping as much of the divorce as possible out of the court was the fact that a *contested* divorce was difficult to obtain under the fault system. True, grounds for divorce had proliferated, theoretically making divorce easier to obtain, but so had defenses, with the opposite effect. Indeed, in many circumstances a *contested* divorce was impossible to obtain; specifically, where the "guilty" spouse sought the divorce, or where there was no technical ground, or where a defense applied. Moreover, there was the unspoken, but observable, tendency of courts to apply in contested cases more stringent standards not only to proof, but even to the very circumstances alleged as a ground for divorce, especially when "soft" grounds were at issue, such as "mental cruelty" (*cf. Farnbach*). Finally, even winning a contested fault divorce was at best a mess and typically a quite destructive exercise.

These factors put a premium on obtaining the partner's agreement to the divorce, to avoid contest. And for a long time, the typical fault divorce (percentage estimates went to the mid-nineties) had been uncontested, *i.e.,* consensual. How was it possible that, in their most vital disagreement, the vast majority of aspiring ex-partners were in agreement? Put brutally, the capability or even the possibility of successfully contesting a divorce, thereby preventing the divorce-seeking spouse's remarriage, permitted the party less eager to be divorced to "sell" the divorce for concessions involving money or child custody. Accordingly, one should not believe for a moment that the widespread practice of collusive consent divorce really overcame the divorce-for-fault laws. On the contrary, those laws were the decisive background in the divorce negotiations regarding divorce consequences, *i.e.,* property, alimony and child custody.

But did we not just learn that "collusion" was a bar to fault-divorce (§§ 19.8, 13)? As a practical matter, the courts all but made themselves party to the collusion by simply not worrying about it. Unless the judge's nose was rubbed in the attendant lies and perjuries, the maxim "what I don't know won't hurt me" seems to have assuaged the typical judge's conscience. In practice, the typical uncontested divorce barely surfaced in court, and collusion became the basis for *winning* rather than losing the divorce action. The parties were carefully briefed by their attorneys to answer leading questions regarding physical or mental cruelty, depending on the applicable law, their personal preferences and (possibly) the facts (*cf. Stein and Turndorf, Hesse*). The typical court routinely accepted the most perfunctory allegations and, within minutes, declared the parties divorced. Since the consequences of divorce usually had been negotiated in advance in exchange for the consent, little occurred in court regarding alimony, property or child custody—the parties' agreement was usually accepted.

CHAPTER 20

"LIMITED DIVORCE" AND "SEPARATE MAINTENANCE"

§ 20.1 Evolution of the Remedies

Short of complete divorce, the law permits partial liquidation of the marital status. When full divorce became available, many states simply continued the traditional jurisdiction that had permitted courts to grant divorces *a mensa et thoro*—limited divorces without the right to remarry (§ 19.1). Grounds for and defenses against divorce from bed and board often remained the same as in the case of full divorce, although some variance developed here and there. Other states abolished divorce from bed and board, but soon found the gulf too wide between full divorce and complete non-interference in the marital relationship. "Separate maintenance" statutes were then enacted, compelling provision for the support of a spouse living separately. Some of these statutes require specific grounds for the separation. More typically, access is limited to the "innocent" spouse, but "innocence" is not necessarily determined in accordance with traditional grounds for divorce. To illustrate, in 1993 a persistently "nagging" wife was denied separate maintenance (*Lynch*), but in 1994 one married to a "cross-

353

dresser" was granted support (*McKolanis*). In a third group of states, divorce from bed and board (requiring grounds) remained on the books and separate maintenance (without grounds) was added as a new option. Several states, finally, abolished limited divorce but did not provide separate maintenance by statute. Some courts then fashioned an equitable remedy permitting marital support obligations to be enforced when the parties live separately, but not while they live together (§ 8.1).

§ 20.2 Legal and Practical Consequences

Technically, divorce from bed and board directs the parties to live apart, legitimizes their living apart, and "nullifies the marital obligation of cohabitation, whereas separate maintenance exists to enforce the husband's obligation of support, and favors a resumption of cohabitation" (*Capodanno*). In the not-so-distant past, statutes allowing divorce from bed and board had earned a bad name. They often served as a tool for "blackmail", in that a counterclaim for limited divorce would be threatened or brought in a suit for full divorce and, if won, would bar full divorce, thereby freezing the parties in a not-married and not-quite-unmarried limbo, and effectively thwarting any remarriage plans (*Hesse, cf.* § 19.9, 14). This is no longer a problem because—given the no-fault option—a marital tie cannot long be maintained against the will of one party.

§ 20.3 The UMDA

In sum, if *both* parties wish to go that route, no policy opposes limited divorce, and there is no cost in providing both alternatives. Commendably, UMDA § 302(b) provides: "If a party requests a decree of legal separation rather than a decree of dissolution of marriage, the court shall grant the decree in that form unless the other party objects". No-fault divorce on the ground of living apart, or in some states specific "conversion" statutes that permit either party to convert a limited into a full divorce, protect both parties if there is a later change of mind. To guard against possible injustice resulting from the conversion of a pre-no-fault, limited divorce into a full divorce against the will (and to the disadvantage of) one of the parties (*Gleason*), New York enacted a specific statute that allows recovery in such cases of "an amount equivalent to the value of any economic and property rights of which the spouse was deprived" by the later full divorce.

§ 20.4 Choosing Limited Divorce or Separate Maintenance

Important distinctions appear between limited divorce and separate maintenance. Under decrees of divorce from bed and board, the court may settle the property interests of the parties. This is not the case in a separate maintenance action where marital property rights may continue to accrue during the separation (*Anglin*). Divorce from bed and board thus provides a potentially valuable alternative to full divorce where the parties (1) want to settle the full range of their economic affairs, (2) do not intend to remarry and (3) want to preserve entitlements available to spouses under public or private benefit plans, such as social security insurance, survivors' benefits or state or private pensions, worker's compensation or health care plans or (4) are religiously or emotionally opposed to full divorce. Under these circumstances, a simple separate maintenance statute dealing only with support would not offer enough flexibility.

§ 20.5 Tax Consequences

For federal income tax purposes, separate maintenance is interpreted as maintaining marital status, both to *allow* filing joint returns (*Capodanno*) and to enable one party to *require* the other to participate in filing a joint return (*Weinkrantz*). Separate maintenance also does not allow filing separately under the "singles" tax tables, nor is the payor entitled to deduct support paid as alimony. While the Internal Revenue Code (Sec. 143(a), *cf.* Sec. 71) says an individual "shall not be considered as married" if "legally separated from his spouse under a decree of divorce or of separate maintenance," court decisions have read this as referring to the traditional distinction that the decree must *require,* not just allow, the parties to live apart (*Capodanno, Muracca*). If marital status is to terminate for tax purposes, the parties need more than merely a decree for separate support. Instead, a decree on the order of traditional divorce from bed and board is required.

CHAPTER 21

ANNULMENT

§ 21.1 To Be or Not to Be Married

In the strict sense, annulment is a judicial declaration that, by reason of a defect in its inception, a purported marriage does not exist and never has existed. Facts are stubborn, however, and something usually did exist. Accordingly, annulment also may be viewed as the legal termination of a *de facto* arrangement resembling marriage. From this perspective, annulment is an alternative to divorce.

Substantial confusion surrounds the difficulty of reconciling the legal theory of non-contract with the actuality that a relationship did in fact exist. Our earlier concern was with what limited legal consequences a defective marriage may produce under various circumstances (Ch. 5). The concern now turns to the opposite: How may a defective marriage be prevented from having legal consequences?

§ 21.2 History of Annulment

Annulment stems from the same canonical roots that gave us divorce and separate maintenance. Annulment long was the only form of divorce which permitted remarriage, and this is continued in present day Roman Catholic doctrine. But even when

357

annulment was exclusively the subject of ecclesiastical jurisdiction, the canon law definition of impediments shifted with the moral climate of the time. During liberal periods, an annulment could be obtained on as simple a representation as that, at the time of marriage, either or both parties had had a secret reservation concerning the marriage relationship. This would vitiate consent, allow annulment and make subsequent remarriage possible. Blackstone discusses canonical and civil impediments at length, with more subtleties than can be accommodated here (Commentaries, Ch. XV).

When, along with jurisdiction over divorce, annulment passed to the civil courts, the impediments, defenses and procedures existing at the time were taken over as well. The basic reference is to marriage prohibitions. Common grounds thus include incest, bigamy, non-age, mental incapacity, and insanity. Marriage resulting from fraud, dare, or jest may lack necessary consent (§ 4.1). The important point to remember is that the ground for annulment must have existed at the time of marriage. For instance, impotence, insanity or mental incapacity developed later is not ground for annulment, though it might be a ground for divorce. In the absence of an applicable annulment statute (Illinois, for instance, did not have one until 1977), courts have asserted their equitable power to declare nonexistent what by virtue of the laws regulating marriage may not exist and fashioned remedies to protect what does exist.

§ 21.3 Defenses

Equitable doctrines, including variants of the clean hands doctrine, estoppel, ratification and laches, often apply as defenses in annulment actions, especially where the defect is primarily of interest to the partner, *e.g.,* fraud or non-age. For instance, the "defrauder" or the over-age partner may be estopped from attacking the marriage, and the "victim" may be held to have ratified the marriage (but only after obtaining knowledge of the fraud or after the proper age for marriage has been reached). Of course, the partners may not ratify a marriage that offends an important policy, such as the prohibition on incest. In the case of bigamy, however, UMDA § 207(b), where adopted, validates a void marriage upon divorce from or the death of the "surplus" spouse, but only as of the time the impediment is removed.

§ 21.4 Annulment for Fraud

To permit annulment of a marriage, "fraud" generally must go to the "essentials of marriage." It is less clear, however, just what is essential to marriage. Meeting the basic reliance test applied in contract cases, whether *but for* the fraud the other party would not have entered into the contract, usually does not suffice. Many jurisdictions have developed detailed, objective definitions of what is essential to marriage. Others give more or less regard to the parties' subjective perception of the gravity of the matter. A failure to communicate inability (*Kshaiboon*), or a false representation of

willingness to consummate the marriage is sufficient for annulment, but *not* where the husband
had agreed to marry the wife despite her psychological inability to consummate, on condition that she
seek psychiatric help (*Naguit*). A false representation that the wife is not pregnant at the time of
marriage, whereas in fact she is pregnant by another man, has universally been held to go to the
essentials of marriage. Some courts have hesitated
when the representation as to pregnancy was accurate and only(?) the representation as to paternity
was false. When the representation as to pregnancy was false, a husband thereby induced to marry
his wife was not entitled to an annulment, because
"the wife is not prevented from bearing only the
children of her spouse" (*Hill*). Premarital representations as to intent to have children, combined
with subsequent refusal to have uncontracepted intercourse, have been accepted as going to the essentials of marriage. The case is less clear when false
representations go to intent *not* to have children,
combined with subsequent insistence on uncontracepted intercourse. The difference seems to be the
notion that having children is the essence of marriage, whereas not having children contradicts an
important purpose of marriage. Misrepresentations
as to wealth or position or character generally have
not met the test for annulment, but a state correc-
tions officer was allowed an annulment of her marriage to a convicted felon (*Haacke*).

It should be noted that a substantial liberaliza-
tion in the test for fraud took place in states in

which the grounds for divorce were narrowly limited (especially New York, New Jersey). Some cases even seem to espouse a subjective, simple reliance test: If the matter in question was essential to the specific party, the marriage will be annulled (*Bilowit*). A final factor of note is that some courts may still adhere to the traditional notion (developed before premarital sex, the decline in the importance of virginity, the advent of the "pill" and pregnancy tests) that a marriage that has not been consummated may be annulled more readily.

§ 21.5 Choosing Divorce or Annulment

A given fact situation may offer the litigant a choice between annulment and divorce. Depending upon the parties' circumstances and applicable state law, advantages may lie with either choice. Annulment traditionally does not permit the granting of alimony or property rights. Instead, the annulment of a second marriage may revive the alimony obligation of an earlier marriage, where it "clearly and persuasively" appears that reinstatement is "necessary to rectify serious inequity or injustice" (*Ferguson*). More typically today, alimony is *not* revived after the nullification of any attempted later marriage, voidable or void, especially if the state permits alimony to be provided in the annulment action, whether or not the second "husband" is in fact able to render support (*McConkey,* § 25.11). More liberal revival rules seem to be applied to pension or government benefits relating to earlier marriages (*Skagen, Harris*). Tax conse-

quences also may be interesting: The basic rule is
that joint income tax returns filed during a voidable
marriage survive an annulment, but this is *not* so in
the case of a void marriage.

§ 21.6 Retroactivity of Annulment

Consistently with the logic of annulment that
there never was a marriage, the court's declaration
of nullity with respect to void and voidable marriages is retroactive to the inception of the relationship. In many cases this rule produces sound results, in others it does not. Children may have
been born to the parties who, with strict application
of the retroactivity doctrine, would become illegitimate. The relationship may have continued so long
that there are questions as to ownership of property
and it may seem reasonable to impose a near-
marital property regime or even a continuing duty
of support. Assuming "clean hands," concepts of
equitable distribution have been applied (*Rance*,
Splawn, *Lane*). In short, many courts have hesitated to apply retroactivity strictly. In some jurisdictions, annulment thus has evolved into an action
nearly akin to divorce (§§ 5.3, 21.7). Further protection for the innocent part to the invalid marriage
has come from the putative spouse doctrine (§ 5.5)
and from the "cohabitation cases" (Ch. 6).

§ 21.7 The UMDA Narrows the Gap Between
Divorce and Void and Voidable Mar-
riages

The UMDA treats void and voidable marriages
similarly, (1) in terms of legal consequences, (2) in

terms of limiting the circle of persons permitted to attack a defective marriage, and (3) in terms of allowing or requiring a formal "declaration of invalidity." With respect to *voidable* marriage, of course, the rule has long been that only the parties themselves and few others could attack the validity of the marriage and that the marriage was valid until it was voided. With respect to the *void* marriage, however, a declaration of nullity was merely a reassurance that the marriage did not exist and never had existed. UMDA § 208(c) suggests that even a void marriage (including a prohibited marriage, whether incestuous or bigamous) may be effective until attacked by the parties or, in the case of a bigamous marriage, the legal spouse, or a child of either party or the "appropriate state official", before either partner's death (Alternative A) or within five years thereof (Alternative B).

The UMDA also provides flexibility on the question of retroactivity. Declarations of invalidity are retroactive "unless the court finds, after a consideration of all relevant circumstances, including the effect of a retroactive decree on third parties, that the interests of justice would be served by making the decree not retroactive". In that case, "the provisions * * * relating to property rights of the spouses, maintenance, support, and custody of children on dissolution of marriage are applicable" (UMDA § 208(e)). In terms of outcome, the non-retroactive declaration of invalidity turns into the equivalent of divorce.

CHAPTER 22

THE ADVERSARY PROCESS, FAMILY LAWYERS, FAMILY COURTS, CONCILIATION, MEDIATION, ARBITRATION

§ 22.1 The Adversary Process Near Its Worst—"Bombers" and Harassment Tactics

A New York Times headline (9/5/93) asks "Are Divorce Lawyers Really the Sleaziest?"

"Describing horror stories that make Arnie Becker, the sleazy divorce lawyer on television's 'L.A. Law' look like a nice guy, the New York City Department of Consumer Affairs today judged the state's divorce system guilty of being 'an expensive and costly failure.' * * * The report, which * * * was based on 107 interviews with lawyers and judges, lambasted lawyers for foreclosing on client's houses, garnisheeing their wages and attaching their Individual Retirement Accounts—all in the name of collecting fees. * * * The chairwoman of the matrimonial lawyers committee of the City Bar Association, * * * declined to discuss the report after saying, 'I've already shouted at too many people about it.' A spokeswoman for the bar association, said the group would send it to 'the appropriate committees for review' when a copy came in" (N.Y. Times, 3/13/92).

"A committee issued a report today that sharply criticized divorce lawyers, asserting that some of them rely on pressure tactics to secure fees, overbill their clients and keep them uninformed about their cases. * * * Among its major recommendations, the committee called for restricting lawyers' abilities to obtain liens on clients' properties, prohibiting lawyers from withholding files from clients who have discharged them, requiring lawyers to sign agreements stating their fees at the beginning of a case and prohibiting sex between lawyers and their clients." (N.Y. Times, 5/15/93).

In response to the criticism, New York's courts issued rules to govern matrimonial lawyers and to help end misconduct (N.Y. Judiciary Law, § 90[2]; see also 212 N.Y.L.J. Nov. 30, 1994, "reporting some mixed successes and a great deal of lingering resentment among lawyers").

The UMDA provides broad powers to perpetuate harmful practices by outlining a veritable catalogue of "harassment" opportunities in connection with divorce. Under UMDA § 304(b) the court may issue injunctive relief

"(1) restraining any person from transferring, encumbering, concealing, or otherwise disposing of any property except in the usual course of business or for the necessities of life, and, if so restrained, requiring him to notify the moving party of any proposed extraordinary expenditures made after the order is issued; (2) enjoining a party from molesting or disturbing the peace of the other party or of any child; (3) excluding a party from the family home or from the home of the other party upon a showing that physical or emotional harm would otherwise result; (4) enjoining a party from removing a child from the jurisdiction of the court; and (5) other injunctive relief proper in the circumstances."

In view of the perfunctory approach taken to the issuance of orders that can so vitally affect a person's life, the lawyer acting for a vindictive spouse retains a frightening capability for the equivalent of legalized blackmail. More often than one likes to think, such orders are so used. In a feeble attempt to reduce abuse, the UMDA allows the court to issue a temporary restraining order *without requiring notice* to the other party "only if it finds on the basis of the moving affidavit or other evidence that irreparable injury will result to the moving party if no order is issued until the time for responding has elapsed" (UMDA § 304(c)). In short, the threat or reality of pre-trial harassment provides an incentive for coming to terms with the ex-partner that is reminiscent of the older style of legalized blackmail that produced "voluntary" settlements in the context of traditional divorce-for-fault. An Illinois statute, originally based on the UMDA, provided for an *automatic* restraint against transferring, encumbering or disposing of *any* property, including nonmarital property, but was held unconstitutional in 1993 (*Messenger*).

§ 22.2 Professional Ethics and Discipline

During decades of "fault practice" in the majority of jurisdictions, the practitioner who sought for a client what not only the client but society perceived as justice, *i.e.*, divorce, was forced to resort to practices that skimmed close to, and too often overstepped, the line of officially proscribed conduct. Much perjured testimony regarding residence, divorce grounds or defenses was produced and tolerated in court. Prosecutions or disbarment proceedings directed against lawyers, or impeachment proceedings against judges who allowed this sort of thing to go on in their courts, were rare (*Stein*). The bar associations' disciplinary procedures have lately been of some help, but, in the view of many family lawyers, have not provided sufficiently explicit guidance. In 1991, the American Association of Matrimonial Lawyers (AAML) developed its own, very detailed, code of conduct, and aptly named it "The Bounds of Advocacy." These standards are essential, eye-opening reading for anyone concerned with the practice of family law. It is fair to speculate that if our lawyers and judges had earlier refused to prostitute the law and themselves in their effort to satisfy the popular demand for divorce (§ 24.1) the practice of family law would not have earned so much scorn. More importantly, the lid would have blown off the old law long ago. Divorce reform would have come much sooner.

§ 22.3 The Lawyer and Divorce Reform

Divorce law still produces much of the public distrust of lawyers and the legal system. While the criminal process has suffered a black eye in the public perception that many criminals are set free on "technicalities", this image may be a fair price to pay for the constitutional safeguards extended to defendants in criminal trials. No such "redeeming social value" appears in the area of divorce.

It should be recognized that as a group, lawyers have *not* stood in the way of change in family law— many prominent lawyers in the American Bar Association and state and city bar associations as well as the Uniform Law Commissioners have worked toward reform actively, selflessly and without compensation. Nevertheless, the public seems to believe that lawyers' fees and lawyers' attitudes are tied into the *status quo*. This image is reinforced by the organized bar's sometimes heavy-handed attacks on "do-it-yourself" firms that offer "divorce kits". Generally, when such firms overstep the thin line between selling information and giving advice, they are barred from the "unauthorized practice of law" (*e.g., Oregon State Bar*). Ideally, this will protect the public, but the legal profession has not yet met the challenge to draw the proper line between (1) giving needed advice concerning property, support and custodial rights that only a trained lawyer can fully assess and evaluate and (2) exploiting its legal monopoly that permits only a lawyer to complete and file forms even for a routine divorce—essentially a clerical service that in practice is often performed by the lawyer's secretary or a paralegal. An ex-secretary who "practiced law" on her own garnered national attention when she was sentenced to 120 days (90 suspended) in jail for criminal contempt (*Furman*, N.Y. Times, 8/12/84), and in 1995 the Massachusetts Bar was investigating whether a new breed of paralegals known as "document processors" was practicing law without a license when helping people prepare divorce papers and other legal documents (N.Y. Times, 2/3/95).

§ 22.4 Right to Counsel

Should *Boddie's* insistence that indigents must be given access to the courts to "adjust their fundamental human relationships" (§§ 24.2, 3) be extended to the right to counsel? It seems difficult *not* to answer "yes." Depending on the complexity of the case, counsel may be a more serious "precondition" to obtaining a divorce than were the nominal court fees involved in *Boddie*. However, most courts continue to resist extending *Boddie* to the right to counsel in divorce cases (*Smiley,* but see *Flores*). Importantly, the U.S. Supreme Court has held that even the involuntary termination of the parent and child relationship is *not* an event calling for extension of the *constitutional* right to counsel *Lassiter*. That right remains home-based in the criminal law (*e.g., Gideon, Argersinger*).

§ 22.5 Family Courts

In the 1960s, the family court movement was optimistic that this important subject matter—constituting perhaps one-third of the total judicial load—would be brought under the jurisdiction of specialized courts. These courts would be staffed with interested and specially qualified judges, social workers and other appropriate professionals, be subject to more flexible and less adversary rules of procedure than apply in the "regular" courts, provide professional help and be more than an unconcerned forum to settle disputes. This ambitious goal certainly was not reached everywhere, or perhaps, anywhere. In about one dozen states, separate family court systems now handle all family law matters, but the systems are far from uniform and not necessarily close to the ideal. In addition many states and cities assign family matters to separate divisions of the state's regular courts.

A major stumbling block is the question of what subject matter should be brought under the jurisdiction of the family court. Candidates include marriage eligibility (and dispensation from requirements, especially age), divorce, annulment, separation, status questions (legitimacy, presumptive paternity, acknowledgment of paternity, validity of marriage), support problems in the ongoing family or incident to divorce or a paternity judgment or acknowledgment, paternity proceedings, child custody on divorce, child raising issues in the ongoing family or after divorce, adoptions, guardianship, juvenile delinquency, child abuse, neglect and dependency, termination of parental rights, intra-family crimes, including spousal rape and assaults and child abuse, and more—the shopping list being the

Table of Contents of this book. Perhaps the task the reformers set for themselves was too large and the change envisioned too revolutionary. Accordingly, some new "family courts" are little more than renamed juvenile courts. In others, as basic a subject as divorce remains outside of the jurisdiction of the "family court". In 1993, the American Bar Association's "Presidential Working Group on the Unmet Legal Needs of Children and their Families" recommended reforms based on the following principles:

"Jurisdiction over all matters involving families and children should be consolidated into one court system of the highest court of the general trial division; Courts responsible for cases involving children should coordinate or monitor all of the services and assistance those children and their families need; Courts should have adequate resources—both financial and staff—to perform this function; Judges in family courts should hear only those cases that require judicial expertise, most often those best adjudicated through the adversarial process."

§ 22.6 Conciliation and Divorce Counseling

The constitutionality of *required* conciliation may be questioned in terms of the right to marital privacy *(Griswold* and related cases), as well as under provisions of state constitutions. As far back as 1954, the Illinois constitution's guaranty of prompt and effective legal remedies served to invalidate a conciliation statute *(Christiansen*). Equally

serious practical questions arise as to the value of
conciliation. Conciliation is expensive. It is worth
its cost only when there is a reasonable chance of
success. If parties have reached the divorce court
and do not wish conciliation, what good can come
out of a forced session? For these reasons and
others (such as lack of trained personnel), conciliation is not practiced widely.

While the value even of *bona fide* divorce counseling remains in dispute, the field is not free of
quackery. To deal with that, several states have
enacted licensing laws that specify educational standards and practical qualifications for marriage
counselors and conciliators. In many states, however, no qualifications are prescribed. This raises
the worrisome question whether a divorce or marriage counselor may be called as a witness in an
ensuing divorce or whether a privilege protects any
communications (*Yaron*).

§ 22.7 Arbitration

The American Arbitration Association offers its
services, especially involving the interpretation of
disputed agreements or other issues arising in or
out of divorce. The New Jersey Supreme Court has
upheld the enforceability of an arbitration clause,
calling it "a favored remedy", and cited reduced
court congestion, the opportunity for resolving sensitive matters in a private and informal forum,
reduced trauma and anxiety of marital litigation,
minimized polarization of the parties, and the parties' freedom to choose the arbitrator. While the

Court reserved its role as *parens patriae* insofar as children are affected, even an arbitration award involving children must be paid considerable respect, unless it runs against the best interests of the child (*Faherty*). Most states now regulate arbitration, either generally or with specific application in the context of divorce.

§ 22.8 Mediation

Conciliation and arbitration are being eclipsed by *mediation*. Mediation proposes to achieve a non-adversary dissolution of marriage. Much remains unsettled, however. While non-financial issues, especially child custody, lend themselves more readily to mediation, financial questions such as property division, alimony, and child support need to be resolved with full knowledge of the law, *i.e.*, by lawyers.

To be distinguished are mediation by a lawyer and mediation by a non-lawyer mediator. In the former case, conflicts of interest may be insurmountable, especially when the lawyer-mediator purports to act for both parties to the divorce. Most bar associations thus strongly discourage (and may view as an ethical violation) the representation by one lawyer of both sides to a "friendly" divorce. They insist that *if* only one lawyer is involved that he or she must choose sides and make that choice perfectly clear to the unrepresented spouse.

With respect to non-lawyer mediators, the problem is that a non-specialist should not be trusted to (and under "unauthorized practice" laws is not permitted to) give advice regarding the potentially complex and inevitably *legal* issues of property, alimony, child support, custody and taxation that, beside all human drama, most divorces involve. Even if a particular divorce is not "complex", it may require a lawyer to make sure of that. Defining broad categories of "simple" divorces that do *not* need professional help, California's "summary divorce" statute (§ 24.10) sets a good example.

There is a simple solution to the lawyer's ethical problems and the non-lawyer's lack of legal competence in their roles as mediators. Why not require each party to be represented by his or her own lawyer before the mediator? Indeed, that is what the 1984 "Lawyer Mediation" and the 1983 "Divorce Mediator Standards" suggest or require (18 Fam.L.Q. 363 (1984); Fair Share (Jan. 1985)). But if that is the remedy, what magic of mediation justifies the additional expense of interposing still another professional in the divorce process?

CHAPTER 23

DIVORCE JURISDICTION AND RECOGNITION OF OUT–OF– STATE DIVORCES

§ 23.1 Residence Requirements

In order to limit access to their courts to residents, to discourage transient divorce traffic and to assure their courts of jurisdiction that enjoys the protection of the "Full Faith and Credit Clause", most states have long required specific periods of residence that must be met before divorce may be granted. These periods of residence ranged from one to three years and came under constitutional attack based on the theory that denial of divorce to persons not meeting residence requirement infringes on the constitutional guarantee of unimpeded interstate travel (*Shapiro*). Some cases went so far as to hold all residence requirements constitutionally unsound and left intact only the basic jurisdictional factor of "domicile" (*Larsen*). Other cases sought to balance the importance of the claimed interest (divorce was seen as less important than the welfare benefits involved in *Shapiro*) against the reasonableness of the restriction, specifically the length of the residence requirements. Under the latter approach, two year residence requirements had fallen, but shorter requirements

such as six months or one year had been left intact
(*e.g.*, *Davis MN*).

In 1975, the U.S. Supreme Court settled the
matter by upholding Iowa's one-year residence requirement in view of "the state interest in requiring that those who seek a divorce from its courts be
genuinely attached to the State, as well as a desire
to insulate divorce decrees from the likelihood of
collateral attack" (*Sosna*).

§ 23.2 Full Faith and Credit for Migratory Divorce

The "collateral attack" against which *Sosna*
sought to "insulate divorce decrees" could succeed
if "those who seek a divorce" are not "genuinely
attached to the State". In such a case a resulting
judgment would not be protected by "Full Faith
and Credit". Detailed analysis of this complex area
cannot be provided here. Suffice it to say that if at
least one party is "domiciled" within a state, that
state has jurisdiction to adjudicate his or her marital status, even if the other party is not subject to
jurisdiction. Through the operation of the "Full
Faith and Credit Clause," the status proclaimed in
such an *ex parte* divorce decree involving a domiciliary is valid in all sister states (*Williams I, II*).
However, the interstate effect of such a divorce does
not extend to alimony, property and other incidents
of the relationship (*Estin, Vanderbilt*).

Even if neither party has a true domicile in the
state granting the divorce, a "migratory divorce"
obtains a measure of validity through a form of *res*

judicata, if both parties have participated in the divorce action, if they have had the opportunity to contest the jurisdictional question, and if the decree is not susceptible to collateral attack where rendered (*Sherrer*). While the parties to such a divorce are barred from attacking it—and even third parties may be (*Johnson*)—the bar may not extend to the state's attorney who might be able to prosecute for bigamy a party thus remarried. However, not a single such prosecution appears to have occurred during the many decades in which transients obtained divorces in Nevada, Alabama and other divorce havens.

To be distinguished are divorces obtained *abroad* by Americans in evasion of their state's law. No Full Faith and Credit is due a foreign divorce, and the domiciliary court is free to ignore or recognize it on the basis of "comity", as its own policies may dictate (*e.g., Steffke,* but *cf. Rosenstiel*). A frequently litigated fact situation has one spouse, in defense against a divorce action brought by a "new" spouse, alleging the invalidity of either spouse's prior Mexican, Haitian or Dominican divorce from an earlier marriage, *i.e.,* that the current "marriage" was bigamous and invalid from the beginning. In such cases, estoppel theories may bar attack on an invalid divorce by a spouse who was in any way involved in the procurement of the "divorce" now being attacked (*Kazin, Mayer, Poor*).

In the past, the issue in migratory divorce cases had all too often been to what extent the Full Faith and Credit Clause may be stretched to validate a divorce that evaded the often strict limitations on divorce of the divorcing parties' true home and thus violated the home state's public policy. With the advent of no-fault divorce in all jurisdictions, the future incidence of *evasionary* migratory divorce may be expected to be negligible. Accordingly, the practical importance of the conflicts rules that developed in this area will ultimately be reduced greatly. For a time, however, even while *new* migratory divorces have all but disappeared in the wake of divorce reform, the validity of old migratory divorces will continue to have to be determined, particularly in the settlement of estates.

§ 23.3   Annulment Jurisdiction

A valid annulment may be obtained if the court has personal jurisdiction over both parties. In the absence of personal jurisdiction, the jurisdictional criteria for divorce apply to annulment. The choice of law, however, is more complex than in the case of divorce, and the modern view favors application of the law of the jurisdiction where the "marriage" was contracted. Valid annulment decrees are entitled to Full Faith and Credit, no significant difference appearing between them and decrees of divorce.

§ 23.4   Personal Jurisdiction

Sosna decided the question when a court *must* accept divorce jurisdiction involving litigants with less than "Mayflower" credentials connecting them to the forum. The *Williams* cases decided under what circumstances State A *must* respect State B's judgment involving the marital status of a person whom State A would prefer to claim as its own "subject". *Estin* and *Vanderbilt* made clear that while the adjudication of *status* is entitled to full faith and credit under the *Williams* cases, this does *not* carry with it power to decide the incidents of divorce, unless *Sherrer* applies. *Sherrer,* however, requires the parties' consent. Still another question needs an answer: How may personal jurisdiction be obtained over an out-of-state spouse or ex-spouse *without* his or her consent?

The answer lies in so-called "long arm statutes" which may provide the needed jurisdictional reach, either in terms specifically applicable to matrimonial actions (a typical jurisdictional factor is "matrimonial domicile") or in general terms. California provides broadly *and* cautiously: "A court of this state may exercise jurisdiction on any basis not inconsistent with the Constitution of this state or of the United States" (Code Civ. Proc. § 410.10). Indeed, that is the problem with "long arm" statutes. All too often, the assertion of long arm jurisdiction is subject to challenge as not meeting the requirements of "due process". In *Lieb,* for instance, New York's long arm statute was held not to apply in a support action to an ex-husband now residing in France when the following facts were shown: The plaintiff and defendant had been married in New York and lived there for 14 years. The parties then moved to Virginia where they lived for 12 years. Defendant then abandoned his wife and the latter

returned to New York where she brought her action
still another 7 years later. The Court held that
statutory language referring to "the matrimonial
domicile of the parties before their separation"

"means that jurisdiction may constitutionally at-
tach when the matrimonial domicile was in the
state 'where the parties when last together made
their home', and that the phrase 'before their
separation' is to be read as meaning a separation
which took place in this State 'at least within the
recent past' and not, as here, some 12 years prior
to the time of the separation."

The New York Court further summarized selected sister state long-arm statutes as follows:

"California, by judicial interpretation of its
statute, requires that the marital domicile must
have been in California at the time the defendant
left the plaintiff. Idaho and Illinois require the
maintenance within the State of a matrimonial
domicile at the time of the commission of any act
which gives rise to the cause of action for divorce
or separate maintenance. Kansas requires the
parties to have been living in a marital relationship within the State as to all obligations arising
from alimony, child support or property settlement, plus the added proviso that the other party
to the marital relationship '*continues* to reside in
this state'. Oklahoma requires that the defendant be shown to be 'maintaining any other relation to this state or to persons or property including support for minor children, who are residents

of this state which affords a basis for the exercise of personal jurisdiction by this state consistently with the Constitution of the United States'. * * * Wisconsin, the State which established the least restrictive test, requires not merely that the defendant have resided in the State in marital relationship with the plaintiff, but also that the marital residence within the State have lasted not less than six consecutive months within the six years next preceding the commencement of the action."

In *Kulko,* the U.S. Supreme Court *denied* California jurisdiction in a child support action when the New York father had allowed his daughter to visit her mother in California. The matrimonial domicile had been New York. The Court held:

"We cannot accept the proposition that appellant's acquiescence in Ilsa's desire to live with her mother conferred jurisdiction over appellant in the California courts in this action. A father who agrees, in the interests of family harmony and his children's preferences, to allow them to spend more time in California than was required under a separation agreement can hardly be said to have 'purposefully availed himself' of the 'benefits and protection' of California's laws. * * * The circumstances in this case clearly render 'unreasonable' California's assertion of personal jurisdiction."

The Court succinctly explained the difference between contacts legitimating choice of law and those allowing assertion of jurisdiction:

"In seeking to justify the burden that would be imposed on appellant were the exercise of *in personam* jurisdiction in California sustained, appellee argues that California has substantial interests in protecting the welfare of its minor residents and in promoting to the fullest extent possible a healthy and supportive family environment in which the children of the State are to be raised. These interests are unquestionably important. But while the presence of the children and one parent in California arguably might favor application of California law in a lawsuit in New York, the fact that California may be the 'center of gravity' for choice of law purposes does not mean that California has personal jurisdiction over the defendant. And California has not attempted to assert any particularized interest in trying such cases in its courts by *e.g.*, enacting a special jurisdictional statute."

Note, however, that even if California enacted such a "particularized", "special jurisdictional statute", the statute would be subject to due process scrutiny and might not pass muster (*cf. Lieb*).

At the other end of the jurisdictional spectrum, the question arose whether personal service suffices to confer jurisdiction in family law cases. In 1990, the U.S. Supreme Court reaffirmed the traditional position:

"The short of the matter is that jurisdiction based on physical presence alone constitutes due process because it is one of the continuing traditions of our legal system that define the due process standard of 'traditional notions of fair play and substantial justice.' * * * It goes too far to say, as petitioner contends, that *Shaffer* compels the conclusion that a State lacks jurisdiction over an individual unless the litigation arises out of his activities in the State. *Shaffer*, like *International Shoe*, involved jurisdiction over an *absent defendant*, and it stands for nothing more than the proposition that when the 'minimum contact' that is a substitute for physical presence consists of property ownership it must, like other minimum contacts, be related to the litigation" (*Burnham*).

§ 23.5 Service by Publication

If a party to an action cannot be found and jurisdiction thus cannot be obtained by personal service, "constructive service" may be accomplished by publication. The court may grant a valid judgment, if its assertion of jurisdiction based on publication passes muster under the Due Process Clause. As held in the classic U.S. Supreme Court case: "Process which is a mere gesture is not due process. The means employed must be such as one desirous of actually informing the absentee might reasonably adopt to accomplish it" (*Mullane*).

The District of Columbia Court of Appeals endorsed the following criteria for constructive service in *divorce* actions:

"[P]laintiff in a divorce action [should] furnish the court with the following information before an order authorizing constructive notice is entered: (1) the time and place at which the parties last resided together as spouses; (2) the last time the parties were in contact with each other; (3) the name and address of the last employer of the defendant either during the time the parties resided together or at a later time if known to the plaintiff; (4) the names and addresses of those relatives known to be close to the defendant; and (5) any other information which could furnish a fruitful basis for further inquiry by one truly bent on learning the present whereabouts of the defendant. From such basic information, the plaintiff should then detail for the court the particular efforts which have been made in the effort to ascertain the defendant's present address. Armed with such a showing, the trial judge will be in a position to make an informed determination of the diligent efforts issue and, in an appropriate case, to tailor an order for the giving of notice to the facts of a given situation. Alternatively, if the court is not satisfied from the plaintiff's initial papers, the court may aid the plaintiff, using its process if necessary, in whatever further efforts may be called for by the circumstances of particular cases" (*Bearstop*).

CHAPTER 24

DIVORCE REFORM—MISSION OVERACHIEVED?

§ 24.1 Introduction

Law and social reality had come to differ so widely that, to serve the popular demand and need for divorce, the parties, lawyers and, indeed, the judges conspired to violate the law in the majority of instances in which a divorce was granted. That situation should not have lasted as long as it did. For many observers, the corruption of the legal process almost transcended substantive arguments, such as whether a reformed divorce law should be strict or liberal, what or whether there should be grounds for divorce or, indeed, whether there should be marriage. *Any* change seemed to represent an improvement. It thus is no surprise that divorce reform has triumphed; it is surprising only that it did not come earlier. One hundred and fifty years ago, Judge Hitchcock of the Ohio Supreme Court observed that "perhaps there is no statute in Ohio more abused than the statute concerning 'divorce and alimony.' Perhaps there is no statute under which greater imposition is practiced upon the court and more injustice done to individuals. The hearings are generally *ex parte*. Witnesses are examined, friendly to the applicant, and it is almost, if not utterly impossible, for the court in most instances to arrive at the real truths of the case" (*Harter*).

§ 24.2   Is Divorce a Constitutional Right?

In terms of constitutional law, the right to marry "is of fundamental importance" and "is a central part of the liberty protected by the Due Process Clause" (*Loving, Zablocki*). *Griswold* and other cases affirm that the ongoing marriage relationship is equally worthy of constitutional recognition. The right to marry affirmed in *Loving* and *Zablocki* mildly supports the argument that the courts should recognize a constitutional right to divorce. The issue is whether the right to marry is a one-time thing or whether it revives, once a relationship has failed. It is legitimate to argue that all claimants should be allowed an opportunity to adjust their "fundamental human relationship" (*cf. Boddie*, § 24.3), unless the State has a good reason to refuse such an adjustment. It may be argued that the State should have the right to deny a divorce only if it has a compelling and rational reason to do so, *i.e.,* where an overriding State interest demands that the marriage be continued. Instead of requiring the parties to show a ground for divorce, the State might be asked to show rational grounds why they should *not* be freed to remarry if that is what they want—or what one of them wants. Rational grounds for denial of remarriage after divorce might be financial responsibility for children of the marriage or inability to make adequate provision for pronounced economic discrepancies that have resulted from a long-term marriage (*cf.* § 24.4).

An English law holds that "if the court is of opinion that the dissolution of the marriage will result in grave financial or other hardship [hardship shall include the loss of the chance of acquiring any benefit which the respondent might acquire if the marriage were not dissolved] to the respondent and that it would in all the circumstances be wrong to dissolve the marriage it shall dismiss the petition." But this clause has *not* been applied in a significant number of cases. Even if *rational* grounds for denying the right to remarry relate to the financial capabilities of the divorcing spouses, politically and as a matter of constitutional law (*e.g., Zablocki*), such a condition would not be acceptable here. In *Zablocki* (§ 2.1), the U.S. Supreme Court struck down Wisconsin's "financial responsibility law" that denied marriage licenses to persons in default on support obligations. While economic status is not in and of itself a constitutionally impermissible criterion (*e.g., San Antonio*), the Court perceived the right to marry as a "part of the fundamental right of privacy implicit in the Fourteenth Amendment's Due Process Clause" (*Griswold*), and found that the statute failed the constitutional test. While *Zablocki* may not be wholly conclusive, since plaintiff wanted to enter his *first* marriage (he had defaulted under a *paternity* support judgment), it is instructive that the political process took over while the litigation was pending. The Wisconsin legislature quickly repealed the financial responsibility statute.

Intriguing as these lines of inquiry may be, it is unlikely that the U.S. Supreme Court will ever be asked to find a constitutional right to divorce. Rapid and comprehensive divorce reform has rendered the point essentially moot. Divorce is available so easily that the "discovery" of a constitutional "right" is not a pressing need, nor, in view of the change in the Court's composition since *Boddie*, would it be likely to happen.

§ 24.3 Court Fees

In 1971, the U.S. Supreme Court *did* decide that indigents cannot be denied access to the courts in divorce cases by a requirement for payment of court fees and costs for service of process (*Boddie*). On due process grounds, Justice Harlan explained that "marriage involves interests of basic importance in our society" and noted that the marriage contract differs from a commercial contract especially in the sense that it may not be rescinded without invoking the State's judicial machinery. He then concluded that resort to the judicial process by the divorce plaintiff hardly is more voluntary than that of a defendant in a criminal case and that divorce is "the exclusive precondition to the adjustment of a fundamental human relationship." Limiting the holding, he added "we hold only that a State may not * * * pre-empt the right to dissolve this legal relationship without affording all citizens access to the means it has prescribed for doing so."

Justice Douglas concurred but indicated that he would have preferred to see the case decided on the ground that "affluence does not pass muster under the Equal Protection Clause for determining who must remain married and who shall be allowed to separate." Justice Black dissented on the basis of his long-standing conviction that "[n]either due process nor equal protection permits state laws to be invalidated on any such nonconstitutional standard as a judge's personal view of fairness. The people and their elected representatives, not judges, are constitutionally vested with the power to amend the Constitution. Judges should not usurp that power in order to put over their own views."

§ 24.4 Is there a Constitutional Right to Stay Married?

The claim of a wife that her and her husband's religious beliefs would allow divorce only for adultery and that, accordingly, the no-fault divorce granted her husband on the ground of incompatibility "contravenes the religious oaths and vows taken by the parties and the authority of God, the Bible and Jesus Christ", was rejected by the Oklahoma Supreme Court. The Court held neatly that "the trial court only dissolved the civil contract of marriage between the parties. No attempt was made to dissolve it ecclesiastically. Therefore there is no infringement upon her constitutional right of freedom of religion" (*Williams*).

On a more serious plane, it has been argued that legislation liberalizing the availability of divorce should not be allowed "retroactively" to affect marriages contracted in more stable times. Put in simple terms, the argument has been made that a wife who, for an extended period of time, has faithfully discharged her marital duties and who, under the law under which she entered into the marriage, could be divorced only for her fault, should not suddenly become subject to being "terminated" at the husband's will and thereby lose not only a socially valuable married status, but also its economic incidents that range from support, property and inheritance rights to numerous and varied eligibilities under public and private insurance or benefit arrangements. So far, *all* courts that have faced this issue have rejected the claim that the no-fault divorce legislation amounted to a deprivation of property without due process or was an interference with contract rights (*Walton, Gleason, Hopkins, cf.* §§ 24.8, 9).

Whatever their constitutional aspects, these cases do not lack common-sense appeal. *Gleason* involved an earlier separation decree being converted into an absolute divorce under a newly enacted no-fault ground. The court refused the wife's complaint, but New York's legislature subsequently dealt with the issue by giving spouses in these circumstances the right to recover the "value of any economic and property rights of which the spouse was deprived by virtue of such decree."

§ 24.5 Divorce   Reform—"Irretrievable Breakdown"

Divorce reform proposals were numerous and varied. Critics started from the premise that, *taken seriously,* the fault system is too restrictive and too arbitrary in terms of marital realities, long-standing social needs and current norms, that the "airing" in open court of the "dirty linen" of a marriage unjustifiably invades the parties' privacy and that, in any event, "fault" is all but impossible to allocate in a relationship as complex and two-sided as marriage. Since collusive consent divorces based on varying degrees of perjury had long been available quite freely, the substantive thrust of modern divorce reform thus went less to the availability of divorce than to the integrity of the legal process (§ 19.14), and to the most important question whether divorce should be available on *one* party's demand, *i.e.,* unilaterally (§ 24.8). When the latter question received a positive answer, radical redefinition of the economic consequences of divorce became necessary (Chs. 25–28).

The reform proposition was that the true test for divorce must be whether the marriage relationship has broken down "irretrievably" or "irremediably". This test is considered to reflect actualities more faithfully than do fault grounds, inasmuch as a marriage may be "dead" in the absence of a traditional statutory ground for divorce and, conversely, some marriage relationships may prosper even in the presence of technical "fault". What, however, is marriage "breakdown" and how should it be proved? Should the court hold an "inquest", to determine whether a marriage really is "dead"? Most observers deemed the inquest approach (prominently espoused by the Archbishop of Canterbury in the English reform discussion) worse than divorce by statutorily defined fault. A full inquest might produce even "messier" divorces than did the fault system. Moreover, with *serious* inquests, the availability of divorce might have to be restricted far below accustomed rates. Finally, there is the practical argument against bringing an already overburdened court system to the breaking point. Accordingly, the inquest approach never had a chance. The remaining reform choice thus was "breakdown *without* inquest." Three alternatives regarding proof remained: (1) the unequivocal assertion of *both* parties that their marriage is "dead" (consent divorce); (2) the unequivocal assertion of *one* party that he or she considers the marriage "dead" (unilateral divorce); (3) proof of an *objective criterion* that is deemed to show that the marriage is "dead."

Strong legislative opposition to admitting that divorce may be obtained by consent or on unilateral demand made the third alternative most appealing to legislators. Substantively, of course, that alternative may encompass *consensual* divorce, *unilateral* divorce or, indeed, *fault* divorce. Ironically, most objective criteria for "breakdown" come perilously close to traditional fault grounds. They were rejected as landing too soon too near the starting point. The criterion that has found most favor is proof of a specific period of time during which the parties have lived apart. This offers the incidental advantage of preventing overly hasty divorces. On the other hand, reformers saw quickly that any long period of required separation, if that were the sole basis, actually would make divorce significantly less easily available than it had been when a negotiated fault divorce (§ 19.14) was decreed as soon as the parties could get their case into court. To illustrate, when New York liberalized its law in 1967 by providing a new "living-apart-for-two-years" ground as an alternative to "adultery", the two-year period did not meet public approval. It was promptly reduced to one year. Consumer conscious reformers advocated a minimal separation period of six months, and so does the UMDA. In 1984, Illinois adopted a nuanced no-fault option allowing an uncontested divorce after six months' separation, and divorce against the will of the other party after two years.

§ 24.6 The Uniform Marriage and Divorce Act

The UMDA was promulgated in the early 1970's. Originally it provided for divorce if "the court finds that the marriage is irretrievably broken", a finding of irretrievable breakdown being "a determination that there is no reasonable prospect of reconciliation". This approach came under fire from the American Bar Association's Section on Family Law. In response, the UMDA was changed to provide that divorce will be decreed if "the court finds that the marriage is irretrievably broken, if the finding is supported by evidence that (i) the parties have lived separate and apart for a period of more than 180 days next preceding the commencement of the

proceeding, or (ii) there is serious marital discord
adversely affecting the attitude of one or both of the
parties towards the marriage". The definition of
breakdown in terms of there being no prospect for
reconciliation remained unchanged. Obviously, the
change was primarily cosmetic: The 180–day period
is so short as to render the "living apart" requirement not burdensome, and the "marital discord"
ground is phrased so broadly that almost anything
will do.

§ 24.7 The Status of Divorce Reform

In 1985, South Dakota was the last state to
abandon *exclusive* reliance on fault divorce. At the
other extreme, only one third of the states have
swung exclusively to "irretrievable breakdown".
The majority of states have chosen the middle
ground of adding no-fault grounds, such as "breakdown" or "incompatibility" or "living separate and
apart", to their traditional or a modernized set of
fault grounds. Many legislators remain persuaded
that fault grounds should continue to provide immediate relief in severe cases. And, in the popular
mind, there *does* remain a "right" and "wrong" in
marriage and divorce—even if the social scientist
sees adultery as a symptom, not as the cause of
marriage breakdown.

Fault grounds thus remain of some importance:
Divorce for fault still offers an immediate "out" in
states with waiting periods for no-fault divorce. In
many states, depending on which basis the divorce
is obtained, marital fault may affect the economic

consequences of divorce (§§ 25.4, 5). Even where fault grounds were retained, however, the traditional defenses and bars (§§ 19.8–13) were often—but not everywhere—weakened or eliminated.

§ 24.8 The Substance of Divorce Reform

Stripping away the window dressing, what is the substance of our divorce reform legislation? First, it is obvious that consensual divorce—in practice long available through collusion on fault grounds— has been legalized, though not in specific terms. Less obviously, divorce reform has changed the *basis* for consent to divorce. Previously, the need for collusion on fault grounds and the availability of defenses that might preclude divorce provided bargaining chips to the party who wanted the divorce less than did the other. The resulting financial concessions helped make up for the failure of traditional law to provide fair or clear economic ground rules for marriage and its termination (Chs. 8, 25– 29). Note, however, that this opportunity for bargaining was available only to an "innocent" spouse or where both spouses were equally "guilty". More ominously, modern divorce law has made divorce available upon *unilateral* demand. Either (even the "guilty") spouse's assertion that the marriage is "dead" will do. This may not be an unmitigated blessing. Economic aspects will be discussed later, but it may be advanced here that divorce reform has made marriage (or more specifically, child-bearing and child-rearing with resultant role division) a less secure economic and legal status and thus a less acceptable risk for the economically weaker party.

Interestingly, if—as many advocates of reform believed—"cleaning up" the perjury-ridden law of divorce was the chief objective of divorce reform, no state has left it at that. That result could have been accomplished by providing for divorce by (1) consent of the parties (without concern over grounds) *and* (2) a modernized catalogue of fault grounds, corresponding to current perceptions as to what is and what is not acceptable conduct within marriage. Instead, in the moralistic fog regarding supposed policies against divorce by consent, the mark of consent was overshot, in many states perhaps by accident. In the guise of "breakdown", divorce has become a unilateral decision, and marriage a form of "employment at will", typically without a "golden parachute".

Today it sounds absurd that a marriage might be continued as a legal status when the personal relationship is obviously "dead," and thereby to deny the parties the right(?) to legal remarriage. On more thoughtful consideration, however, especially of role-divided marriage of long standing, it appears that unilateral divorce can produce literally incompensable financial hardship for the economically weaker party. Social security benefits, tax concessions, pension eligibilities and a host of legal rights available to a spouse or widow(er) may (or will) be lost by an ex-spouse. These rights often will be lost in circumstances where the divorce-seeking spouse is quite unable to make fair compensation. In many specifics, remarriage allows, indeed requires, a new party to step into the legal shoes of the first partner. In some circumstances, remarriage thus may be compared with giving a second mortgage legal priority over a first mortgage. Potentially incompensable economic hardships have not been weighed against the fact of modern life that few (if any) obstacles hinder *un*married personal relationships (Ch. 6). In identifiable cases, we are unwilling to balance the "equity" of transferring an economically significant legal status from someone who may fairly be considered to have earned it, to an "interloper" for whom the acquisition of this economically valuable status may be a windfall. In short, there is a fair argument that at least in some circumstances one spouse's interest in *re*marriage should be ranked as less important than the other spouse's interest in retaining the status of legal marriage and thereby preserving inchoate and incompensable economic rights. Alas, an atavistic preoccupation with "propriety" has remained with us, and we favor marriage, with no distinction between marriage and remarriage, or even multiple remarriages.

Another tribute to hypocrisy comes from the same source: All states have retained for themselves at least a nominal role in the status decision—should the divorce be granted? Many legislatures still do not admit that divorce may be obtained on the parties' consent or, worse, on a "guilty" party's unilateral demand, even when as a practical matter, the state has abdicated its role in

the status decision. No-fault divorce is almost never denied (*cf. Hagerty, Roberts, Marlenee*). Forth-
right reform would have conceded the *status* decision, and made clear that the State reserves only
the power to participate in the regulation of the
consequences of divorce. The reform movement of
the 1960's and early 1970's thus missed its proper
mark.

Divorce reform was premised on two major mis-
understandings: First, that divorce was hard to get
and, second, that people should not be forced to stay
together when they are emotionally out of tune. In
fact divorce had long been available quite freely in
most jurisdictions (§ 19.14), and the vision that the
law kept seriously quarrelling couples together in
their homes, was fiction. Certainly, whether married, divorced or unmarried, no one is or was forced
to live together or apart, despite the laws prohibiting fornication and adultery that many states retain
but rarely enforce. Parties who merely want to *live
apart* do not need divorce. For them an action to
sort out the economic and child custody aspects of
their relationship suffices (Ch. 20). Conversely, to
live in a relationship with a person of the other (or
for that matter, the same) sex, one does not need
not to be married (or unmarried)! The critical
meaning of modern divorce thus is not the right to
separate, but the right to substitute a new legal
relationship for a prior one.

In this light, divorce should have been divided
into two components: (1) The legal settlement of
economic and custodial rights arising out of an

emotionally intolerable interpersonal relationship, and (2) the grant of a "license" to invest a new, emotionally alive, interpersonal relationship with legally enforceable obligations. If the subject had been approached in this manner, the intelligent answer would have been that, as to (1) nothing more than the satisfactory settlement of all economic obligations incident to that relationship will be required, and as to (2) nothing less than the satisfactory settlement of all economic obligations incident to the preceding relationship will do.

§ 24.9 No–Fault Brings New Economic Rules for Divorce

The optimistic prediction that divorce reform would bring a decrease in divorce litigation (or bitterness) has not been borne out by developments. Instead, no-fault-divorce has brought an *increase* in complicated litigation. In retrospect, this stands to reason: If the divorce-resisting partner's consent must no longer be "purchased," less may be expected from negotiated settlements. Accordingly, the courts are called upon more frequently than before to delve into the parties' financial or custodial arrangements, or to make such arrangements for them.

Little was lost with the failure of Wisconsin's attempt to impose a "means test" on marriage (*Zablocki*). More was lost by the disregard legislators showed in the early stages of divorce reform for the reasonable protection of the dependent spouse's legitimate economic interests. Specific legislation needed to govern financial arrangements upon divorce was enacted. But the remorseful rush toward community property (instant or deferred) that became the essence of financial reform has not provided all the answers, (§§ 8.10–11, 25.15, 26.5). Reform on the economic level should have been consistent with the contemporary concept of marriage as a partnership of equals, yet the "no fault, equal property, rarely alimony" approach has produced much new inequity, though less than did the tradition of fault-dependent permanent alimony and zero-property.

§ 24.10 Summary Divorce

Another new idea had its start in California and is spreading east: "Summary Divorce" provides for very much facilitated dissolution of marriages that, by definition, offer scant potential for serious controversy. The California model provides that a childless marriage of not more than five years may be dissolved when irreconcilable differences have caused irremediable breakdown, where neither party has any interest in real property, where their debts (excluding car loans) do not exceed four thousand dollars, where community property (excluding encumbrances and cars) totals less than 25 thousand dollars, and where neither party has separate property (excluding encumbrances and cars) in excess of 25 thousand dollars, and the parties have agreed on a division of assets and waive spousal support as well as a right to appeal (West's Ann. Cal. Fam. Code § 2400). All amounts are periodically adjusted for inflation.

PART VII

ECONOMIC CONSEQUENCES OF DIVORCE

CHAPTER 25
ALIMONY

§ 25.1 The Burden of History—Who Owes Alimony to Whom and Why

Alimony dates back to the time when limited divorce from bed and board (*a mensa et thoro*) and annulment (*a vinculo matrimonii*) were the sole remedies for broken marriages. Traditional annulment, of course, did not permit alimony because, retroactively, there had never been a marriage (Ch. 21). Since limited divorce did not terminate the marriage (the parties could not remarry, the inheritance relationship remained in effect, etc.), alimony originally represented no more than the definition and continuation of the husband's marital support obligation past the termination of cohabitation. Since the support obligation was solely the husband's, the impoverished husband of a rich wife could not be awarded alimony and, conversely, even a poor husband would owe alimony to his rich wife. Many states began allowing alimony to be awarded to the husband some time ago, often with the qualification that he be "in need." In 1979, the gender limitation on alimony was removed when a husband's constitutional attack on his disparate obligation succeeded in the U.S. Supreme Court (*Orr*).

When *full* divorce (with the right to remarry) became available, the concept of alimony was taken over from limited divorce without much thought. Commentators have used this history to attack alimony as illogical and unjust.

Courts and legislatures have mixed futuristic ideas with historical notions. Antipathy to the very idea of alimony is widespread among men as well as feminists. Courts have attacked alimony as a "free bread ticket for life", inconsistent with married women's property acts (§ 8.6), the divisibility of marital property on divorce (§ 26.3), and improved employment opportunities for women. Invoking "women's equality" as a *fait accompli,* some courts have denied alimony altogether, except in cases of actual need and for a limited time, often termed a "retraining" or "rehabilitation" allowance. A basic change in attitudes toward alimony has occurred and traditional judicial chivalry vis-à-vis at least the "innocent" divorcing wife is being replaced with attitudes that, in some cases, are not quite free of vindictiveness. And it does seem anomalous that a support obligation would continue after the marriage is over. Long before the reform debate began in earnest, Texas, a community property state, did not allow alimony under any circumstances, and Indiana granted alimony only "when the court finds the spouse to be physically or mentally incapacitated to the extent that the ability of such incapacitated spouse to support himself or herself is materially affected" (*Ind. Code* § 31–1–11.5–9(c) 1983–84 Supp.). These are not good models. It is not difficult to find a satisfactory modern rationale upon which to uphold, in appropriate cases, continued payments after marriage by the economically stronger ex-spouse to the economically weaker, and not all such payments need to be labelled "property" or "child support" (§ 25.15).

§ 25.2　Factors Determining Amount

As a practical matter, alimony is *not* a common incident of divorce. The Census Bureau reports that of all 20.6 million ever-divorced or separated women in 1990, only 15.5% were awarded alimony. And many spouses awarded alimony do not collect the full amount or anything at all. Too often the media report the ex-chorus girl's million dollar alimony and too rarely the more typical case where there is inadequate money to pay appropriate or any alimony. Typically unreported go the cases of the more affluent who usually negotiate alimony, along with the rest of the economics of divorce, in a separation agreement (Ch. 29), thus taking this troublesome issue out of the hands of the courts. Of course, such negotiations are heavily influenced by the underlying law (§ 24.8).

Traditional alimony statutes allowed the judge to award alimony as he or she "deems equitable and just". Usually no specific guidelines fettered judicial discretion. The role of marital fault has declined, but the "wife's needs" and the "husband's ability to pay" were and remain the common denominators, even while there is little agreement as to the meaning of this in specific circumstances.

§ 25.3 The UMDA

UMDA § 308 provides the following radically new view of alimony:

"(a) * * * [T]he court may grant a maintenance order for either spouse, *only* if it finds that the spouse seeking maintenance: (1) *lacks sufficient property* to provide for his reasonable needs; and (2) *is unable to support himself* through appropriate employment or *is the custodian of a child* whose condition or circumstances make it appropriate that the custodian not be required to seek employment outside the home." (Emphasis added).

Only after this threshold for awarding alimony is crossed, the following factors apply:

"(b) The maintenance order shall be in amounts and for periods of time the court deems just, *without regard to marital misconduct,* and after considering all relevant factors including: (1) the financial resources of the party seeking maintenance, including marital property apportioned to him, his ability to meet his needs independently, and the extent to which a provision for support of a child living with the party includes a sum for that party as custodian; (2) the time necessary to acquire sufficient education or training to enable the party seeking maintenance to find appropriate employment; (3) the standard of living established during the marriage; (4) the duration of the marriage; (5) the age and the physical and emotional condition of the spouse seeking maintenance; and (6) the ability of the spouse from whom maintenance is sought to meet his needs while meeting those of the spouse seeking maintenance."

The UMDA's radical move away from life-term or even long-term alimony and its mandate that alimony, except where young children need to be cared for, should be available only after the property and job thresholds are crossed has turned out to be too radical and the harsh results achieved in some early cases illustrate why (*Otis*). The UMDA, however, has left a broad trail and the law of alimony may or may not be the better for it. For instance, the concept of "imputed income" has been applied to both parties, *i.e.*, a spouse with unrealized earning capacity will be assessed at that level rather than at his or her actual income. The notion that the dependent spouse is entitled to be maintained at the level he or she lived during the marriage remains alive but not popular. Obviously, that standard always was an illusion. Assuming a finite amount of dollars, two households cannot be maintained at the same level as one.

Away from the harshness of the UMDA ideal, recent cases show a trend toward allowing permanent or long term alimony where the marriage was of substantial duration and the ex-spouses' earning powers are unequal (*Gardner*), and even where the "dependent" spouse has received a very large marital property settlement (*Hamlet*). By 1995, the American Law Institute's project on "Family Dissolution" was thinking in terms of reconstituting alimony in the form of "compensatory payments", to fairly allocate between divorcing parties the economic losses caused by divorce.

§ 25.4 The Traditional Relevance of Fault

Even if clearer definitions had evolved of the husband's ability to pay, the needs of the wife or the marital standard of living, the tradition that alimony depends on fault would still have raised havoc. Our jurisprudence abounds with homilies such as "the wrongdoer shall not profit from his own wrong" and other variants of equity's "clean hands" doctrine. It thus may be easily seen how, in a fault-based system of divorce, the notion developed that the "rewards" of divorce should likewise be apportioned by fault, so that a "guilty" wife should not receive alimony and that a wife's right to alimony should depend on her husband's "fault" (*e.g., Bender, Dyer*). Indeed, the husband's egregious marital fault may still result in an award to his wife that resembles punishment (*Magruder*). An Iowa marriage was dissolved in 1994 because of the husband's extraordinary and, as the wife claimed, "retaliatory" flatulence, and even though the marriage had lasted only 16 weeks, the wife was awarded alimony for 15 months. The dissenting judge complained that "the price of gas is going up in Sioux City" (*Osman*).

"Fault" traditionally was (and where divorce for fault survives, still is) found in the divorce judgment itself, *i.e.,* in the ground on which the divorce decree is based. This, perhaps as much as old-fashioned chivalry, explains the traditional practice of having the wife sue for divorce so that the husband, as the "guilty" party, may be obligated to pay. "Fault" may be found in another statutory ground for divorce, even where that ground is not the basis for the judgment. There may be consideration of the relative merits or faults of the parties in regard to their marriage and divorce, whether or not such "fault" qualifies as a ground for divorce. In 1978 Justice Neely of the West Virginia Supreme Court still said that even in a no-fault divorce, "a spouse seeking alimony must show the other spouse guilty of inequitable conduct" and "a totally blameless party can never be charged with alimony" (*Dyer*).

Statutory direction and judicial reaction have varied. The traditional range ran from absolute prohibition of alimony to any "guilty" spouse, to a more limited bar applicable, for instance, only in the case of adultery, or as in Florida today, the consideration of "fault" as merely one *factor* in setting the amount of alimony. An ingenious defense succeeded in 1994 in Kentucky where a wife showed that only one of her thirteen "alter personalities", and not her "host personality," committed adultery (*Tenner*).

§ 25.5 No–Fault Divorce and Alimony

Divorce without fault raises the question whether the "no-fault" concept should carry over to alimony. Early in the no-fault era, the Minnesota Supreme Court decided that even in a divorce for "irretrievable breakdown", "evidence of marital misconduct should, upon a showing of proper circumstances, be considered by the court for purposes of property division and award of alimony" (*Peterson*). That decision was subsequently overruled by the legislature. The UMDA and numerous states unreservedly embrace "no-fault" with respect to financial consequences. Thus, after Mrs. Popeil had served 19 months in a California prison for trying to hire a "hit man" to kill her husband, her lawyers obtained for her a $250,000 property agreement, plus $14,250 in past due temporary alimony plus $73,750 in legal fees for themselves (*Popeil*). The lawyers' fee was well-deserved, but in these circumstances awarding the fee against the husband added injury to insult. In *D'Arc*, a psychiatrist-husband had tried unsuccessfully to hire a "hit-man" to murder his Johnson & Johnson-heiress wife. In the ensuing divorce, he brazenly invoked New Jersey's no-fault statute and sought $120,000 a year, tax-paid alimony. He did *not* get it. Neither did the wife in Wisconsin, after her attempt to hire a "hit-man" to kill her husband was foiled.

The court's logic was that if she had succeeded she would have received no alimony because her husband would have been dead, and that the misconduct at issue was not marital and thus not comparable to, say, adultery which is the kind of marital misconduct that may *not* be considered (*Brabec*).

§ 25.6　Fault Reemerges In the Guise of Tort Claims

Are not the risks of marriage increased and is marriage not diminished as a legal status and as an economic good, if "good" or "bad" behavior does not matter? Is it not intuitive—at least to the general public—that "fault" and "merit" *are* relevant to achieving "fairness?" Fault and merit are relevant in all other areas of the law, so why are they not relevant to the fair distribution of the financial burdens (and benefits) of divorce? Of course they are! The true question is *what* is fair, and *how* should (or can) "merit" and "blame" be judged. While the standard, preferred answer "we can't tell, we don't want to know, and there's no such thing as a nice husband or a nice wife anyway" is not wholly satisfactory, it is not easy to define a workable standard of marital merit and blame.

In several U.S. states, an extreme return to marital fault through an unexpected side door is now creating havoc with no-fault divorce. *Tort* law has become the vehicle, alongside or after a divorce action, to compensate one spouse financially for torts inflicted during the marriage by the other spouse. This became possible only with the recent wholesale abolition of traditional tort immunities prohibiting tort litigation between spouses (§ 9.2, 4). And in law, what is possible, usually becomes real. Leaving to one side the legitimacy of litigating *physical* torts inflicted on one spouse by the other intentionally or negligently, "emotional distress" is most deserving of concern and caution. Here is the case that fired the starting shot: In 1988, a jury in Houston awarded a divorcing wife $1.4 million, for "severe emotional distress" caused by her husband's marital misconduct. Not the lurid National Enquirer, but the staid Wall Street Journal reported that "on a visit to her husband's office in 1986, she found him sprawled nude with a former company secretary" (W.S.J. 2/2/88). The Texas appellate court reversed this award (*Chiles*), but in a worse case involving "*deviate* sexual acts", the Texas Supreme Court later allowed at least the possibility of recovery of damages for outrageous marital conduct in a divorce (*Twyman*). Similar cases are reaching the appellate level elsewhere *(e.g., Hakkila)*. Many other claims are settled for fear of litigation, and the risk of fundamental incursion into post-divorce financial arrangements is considerable.

This is not an issue of defending family lawyers' "turf" and their sources of income. It gives reason for concern when tort lawyers argue:

"Nationwide, marital tort recoveries are high. * * * When considering the more common torts—such as intentional or negligent infliction of emotional distress, assault, defamation, false imprisonment, and interference with child custody—counsel must give careful thought to asserting as an element of damages post-traumatic stress disorder (PTSD). * * * State no-fault statutes often do not do enough to redress wrongs. With no-fault, one spouse may abuse the other without legal consequence—even though the conduct would be deemed tortious if committed by a non-spouse" (Conlin, Trial, 10/92).

But even today, some rational romantics are still convinced that it is the very essence of marriage that it is *not* a relationship between strangers.

Of course, many arguments militate against the traditional mechanical application of the old marital fault grounds for divorce, from adultery to desertion. The discussion need not stop there. Could a *new*, modernized notion of "fault" be factored into the decision how to apportion the financial burdens or benefits of divorce? Fuzzy concepts such as "blame" and "merit," "unjust enrichment" or "quantum meruit" may furnish a start.

Actually, courts in separate property states are adapting jurisprudence that originated in community property states, concerning the "dissipation" of marital assets, imposing what amounts to a duty on the owner of separate (but, on a future divorce, marital) property to deal with such property in good faith even during the ongoing marriage. (See § 26.6). Along with and beyond economic misconduct, there is a way to deal responsibly with cases of misconduct that overstep the proper bounds of even an "unhappy" marital relationship. Consider the following statute that was enacted in Germany after years of pure no-fault divorce:

"A claim for support must be denied, reduced or limited in duration, if the imposition of the obligation * * * would be grossly inequitable because * * * (2) The recipient is guilty of a crime or of a severe intentional offense against the obligor or against a near relative of the obligor; (3) The recipient has caused his or her own need intentionally or recklessly; (4) The recipient has intentionally or recklessly disregarded significant financial interests of the obligor; (5) For a considerable period of time before the separation, the recipient has grossly violated his or her duty to contribute to the support of the family; (6) The recipient is responsible for obviously serious, clearly unilateral misconduct against the obligor; * * *" (BGB § 1579).

Does this statute signal a "reactionary" return to a past that would best be forgotten, or can it be improved upon? Probably the latter. For instance, it may not be altogether fair that this provision paves only a one-way street. For some time, the abolished marital fault law was used almost exclusively to allow the escape from, or reduction of, an obligation, whereas it is arguable that some fault should weigh in by increasing the obligation (*cf.* § 25.4). That is one answer tort law provides clearly.

In any event, if the idea of right and wrong is one whose time has never gone, its return to the financial aftermath of marriage through *tort* law will reintroduce to the divorce process more and worse acrimony than no-fault divorce ever eliminated. Existing tort law is the worst-case alternative. The appropriate answer should be developed in the context of divorce law. Regrettably, the Tentative Draft of the ALI's "Principles" approved in May 1995, maintains the disregard of non-economic fault in divorce and defers to tort law remedies without at least bringing them into the divorce picture.

§ 25.7　Modification

If a divorce decree has awarded alimony, the court usually retains jurisdiction to modify the award on either party's application, if a "change in circumstances" has occurred. Such change may involve the payor's reduced or increased ability to pay or the dependent ex-spouse's reduced or increased need. If the divorce decree is silent as to alimony, the states are not in agreement as to whether an award may be imposed later. The answer may depend on specific statutory wording. However, a decree that expressly bars modification or a subsequent award usually is honored, even in the face of changed circumstances. A decree awarding token alimony, such as $1 per year, preserves the opportunity to modify, if and when needed.

Courts have wide discretion as to what may warrant a change in alimony. The basic standard remains the ex-spouses' needs and ability to pay. So far, no consensus has emerged on what that means. Should an extraordinary work-regime be held against an obligor? Where the husband had worked 16 hours a day at $18 per hour during the marriage, and upon divorce, had switched to an 8–hour a day job paying $13 per hour, the California Supreme Court required use of the lower income figure (*Simpson*). Should the creation of a new family be deemed a relevant change in circumstances? If the payor's new spouse is rich or has good earnings, should that be considered in assessing ability to pay? If, on the other hand, remarriage further strains the ex-spouse's limited resources, should there be relief? Traditional views of alimony have insisted that the earlier family has priority over the later, but that may not always hold today (§ 15.5). Another question arises when the *dependent* ex-spouse improves *his or her* financial position by employment (*Carter*). The simple answer is that in such a situation alimony should be reduced, but should it not be considered that such a disincentive may overwhelm the dependent ex-spouse's willingness to work? Similar considerations are discussed in connection with child support (§ 15.5), but one difference should be noted: Where the obligor-spouse's fortunes improve after divorce, children continue to share in a parent's improved circumstances, whereas the ex-spouse does not (unless an inadequate obligation was imposed at the time of divorce).

§ 25.8 Retirement and "Ability to Pay"

As in the case of child support, not only the *actual* earnings of the obligor, but also *potential* earning capability, now control the definition of "ability to pay" and often the recipient's "need" (*cf.* § 15.5). For instance, a fifty-five year old ex-husband left his job in relatively good health and his retirement had reduced his income from $265 per week to $295 per month. He was not granted any reduction in alimony. The court held that if inability to pay support is "self-inflicted or voluntary, it will not constitute a ground for reduction of future payments" (*Tydings*). On the other hand, an appellate court allowed a sixty-one-year-old man relief after the lower court had refused to consider that the man had been employed for forty-five consecutive years and suffered from duodenal ulcers, hypertension, kidney stones, depression, obesity, nephrolithiasis, prostatism, rectal polyps, diverticulosis, emphysema and gastro-intestinal problems (*Burns*). As a rule of thumb, courts usually allow relief at age 65, even to one in good health and still capable of earning a good income (*Mangino*).

§ 25.9 Death

As do other support obligations, alimony usually terminates at the death of either the payor or the payee. However, if the separation agreement is phrased appropriately or even ambiguously (*Cohen*), an award may extend beyond death (Ch. 29). Some courts insist that the intent to provide past death be "unmistakably clear" (*Kendall, cf. Kuhns*). Even if alimony may not be awarded past the spouse's death, an order that the obligor maintain life insurance, payable to the ex-spouse, has been employed as a means of providing continued support. Note, however, that some courts will *not* allow life insurance, not even if the recipient pays for it. To illustrate, in 1993 the Mississippi Supreme Court reversed a trial court's order that an ex-husband submit to a physical examination so that the ex-wife might obtain life insurance on him to secure her continued support. The Court reasoned that since the alimony obligation is maximally for life, no further act, however minimal, could be required of the obligor to extend support beyond his death (*Hardin*). On the opposite extreme, where life insurance was legitimately used to provide support after the obligor's death, an obligor's estate was held liable to the ex-spouse when, after the obligor's intentional suicide, the life insurance company refused to pay *(Tintocalis)*. Manipulation of the "death-ends-alimony" rule may also be possible by labelling a periodic payment as a division of property by installments, not alimony. Tax and other legal consequences must be weighed (Ch. 28).

§ 25.10 The Alimony Recipient's Remarriage

When the recipient remarries, termination of alimony is automatic, or the remarriage is a "changed circumstance" that ensures success upon application to the court. In the latter context, the Tennessee Supreme Court has held that an alimony recipient who remarried is under no obligation to notify the payor whose obligation continues until the court order is modified (*Butcher*). Specific wording in the separation agreement controls, especially when it is incorporated into the decree (Ch. 29). More recently, "rehabilitative alimony" has been held *not* terminated by the recipient's remarriage or cohabitation, because these events did not affect the need for "rehabilitation" (*Isbell, Musgrove*).

§ 25.11 *Attempted* Remarriage

Substantial litigation has involved the question of whether a prior alimony obligation ends when the alimony recipient enters into either a void or voidable new marriage. Alimony normally is at least "suspended" during the continuation of the new relationship, and arrears may not be collected after annulment. Some courts have reinstated prior alimony in the case of later annulment or declaration of nullity of a *void* marriage. In the case of an annulment of a *voidable* marriage, on the other hand, alimony typically is not reinstated. More recently, courts have not distinguished between void and voidable marriages and usually do not reinstate alimony in either case (§§ 21.5, 6). It is significant that the putative spouse doctrine and other devices, including the UMDA's non-retroactive annulment, have sprung to the rescue of some dependent "ex-spouses" in terms of allowing a remedy against the partner to an annulled void or voidable marriage (§ 21.7). Questions of "revival" of rights relating to a former spouse also arise in connection with eligibility for social security benefits and other rights. In that context the courts are more generous: Annulment of even a void marriage has resulted in reinstatement of social security benefits (*Holland*).

§ 25.12 The Ex–Spouse's "Cohabitation"

Short of formal remarriage, many courts have *not* terminated alimony when the ex-spouse opted for cohabitation, instead of remarriage, some even where alimony payments helped support the new lover (*e.g., Sturgis*). Other courts have strained to reach a different result, some by modifying alimony to assure that no portion of it would go to the paramour (*Hall*) and others by eliminating alimony for the duration of the cohabitation (*Taake*). An Ohio case terminated a cohabiting ex-spouse's alimony on the ingenious theory that the parties' separation agreement contemplated the Ohio definition of (re)marriage which includes common law marriage, even though the cohabitation took place in a state not recognizing common law marriage (*Fahrer*).

As less social stigma attaches to informal relationships, the attorney drafting separation agreements must be increasingly careful in dealing with this problem. Marlon Brando's separation agreement with Movita contained the following language: " 'Remarriage' shall include, without limitation, (Movita's) appearing to maintain a marital relationship with any person * * * ". The Court held that Movita and James Ford had "enjoyed a relationship of substantial duration, which bore the objective indicia of marriage", and found further that, as Movita had paid for many of Ford's expenses, their "living together" fell under the phrase used in the agreement. The Court rejected Movita's argument to the effect that she and Ford were not giving the appearance that they were married, and that they were just living together (*O'Connor*). In 1994, however, a New Jersey court refused to enforce a detailed and seemingly well-drafted cohabitation clause in a decree-incorporated separation agreement when the cohabitation did not have an economic impact. The court held such an "*in terrorem* clause" to inappropriately "control the social activities of the payee" (*Melletz*).

A number of states have enacted statutes that allow a court to modify alimony upon proof that the ex-wife is "habitually living with another man and holding herself out as his wife, although not married to such man" (*New York,* Dom. Rel. Law § 248), or if the ex-spouse "cohabits" "on a resident, continuing conjugal basis" (*Illinois,* 750 ILCS 5/510(c)). Interestingly, Illinois' Supreme Court has ruled that "conjugal basis" need not involve sexual contact to invoke the statute (*Sappington*). California has abandoned its former "holding-out-as-a-spouse" requirement, and now imposes a rebuttable presumption of reduced need if the recipient of alimony cohabits with a person of the opposite sex (*Cal.Fam.Code* § 4323(a)).

An additional complication arises where the ex-spouse is gay and lives with a lover of the same sex. In that situation a Minnesota court held that "defendant's post-decree lesbianism is a material change in circumstances which justifies the termi-

nation of alimony" (*Anonymous MN*), whereas the
Georgia Supreme Court held that Georgia's "live-in
lover" statute does not allow modification of alimony if the lover is of the same sex (*Van Dyck*).
When a former wife became a nun (thereby materially reducing her opportunity to remarry), her ex-
husband was denied termination of his $250 a
month alimony payment. His argument that paying the money to the convent converted his payment to a religious purpose in violation of his
constitutional rights persuaded neither the Illinois
nor the U.S. supreme courts even to hear his appeal
(*Lane*).

§ 25.13 Social Security

A spouse's eligibility for Social Security is entirely
derivative and terminates with divorce, unless the
marriage has continued for at least 10 years. Insupportable inequities remain in our social security
system, unless each spouse has had his or her own
adequate earnings. Similar problems are being
remedied, albeit haphazardly and often poorly, under private and public pension schemes (Ch. 27).

§ 25.14 Conflicts Problems

Due to the understandable desire and tendency of
divorced ex-partners to put distance between themselves and their past, conflict of laws questions
often arise in this area. Care and caution will avoid
unpleasant surprises. An early question is whether
the divorce decree's attitude on alimony remains
governed by the law of the rendering state, if it is to

be enforced elsewhere. Where the decree expressly bars alimony or imposes a final, one-time lump sum payment in lieu of alimony or where it expressly bars modification, Full Faith and Credit is due the decree in accordance with its terms (*Yarborough*). Even if Full Faith and Credit technically is not due as in the case of future obligations under a *modifiable* sister state judgment, a sister state judgment with jurisdictional defects or any foreign judgment, estoppel may apply. If the decree is modifiable in the rendering state, it also will be modifiable where it is sought to be enforced, but probably in accordance with the criteria for modification that prevail at the new forum. The answer is less clear where the decree is silent. Many other questions and answers are substantially analogous to the case of child support (Chs. 15, 16).

§ 25.15 Should Spousal Maintenance Obligations Survive the Modern Marriage?

When "divorce from bed and board" (that left the marriage relationship legally intact) was the only "way out," it was entirely sensible to continue the husband's *support* obligation, especially when women had extremely limited employment opportunities. With full divorce, continued application of the support concept made substantially less sense. Some reasoned that the original marriage contract included the husband's promise to support his wife for life, and that divorce, except for her fault, should not affect that "contractual" obligation.

Today, however, we like to think that divorce *ends* marriage. The availability of property division— relatively new in the forty-plus separate property jurisdictions—has encouraged the belief that the accrual of rights and obligations should end on divorce. Men have become increasingly unwilling to accept alimony as an open-ended obligation, and many women see it as a "demeaning" continuation of their dependence. Reacting to this, some legislatures and some courts have switched to equally unsupportable extremes at opposite ends of the scale. Some judges apply traditional notions of alimony, others jump into a future where there is to be no alimony. The concept of "rehabilitative alimony" for a limited period, designed to make a dependent spouse self-sufficient, falls somewhere in between.

The important questions are what economic interests (1) were accrued during marriage *or* (2) continue to accrue past the living marriage? At the extremes, the equities obviously differ between the childless, still young former truck driver who has been married for a few years to an aging millionaire actress, and the older wife who, after financing her husband's education and bearing and raising their five children, now finds herself without an appropriate entry into the job market. In the days of divorce-for-fault-only, it was not just vindictiveness that persuaded many an older wife to oppose her husband's divorce even while she agreed that their marriage was dead. The loss of the dependent spouse's derivative entitlements relating to the working spouse often cannot be compensated adequately in settlements incident to divorce. So long as marriage continues to involve role division and the consequent creation of reliance interests on the part of the economically dependent spouse, the law must give adequate legal protection to these interests. Unfortunately, no law can freely allow unilateral divorce *and* give such protection—except to the well-off.

Perplexingly, much of what has been hailed as reform has reduced the role of "enforced loyalty" on the part of "providers" and has depreciated reasonable reliance interests in the most confidential legal human relationship—at the very time when other areas of our law have moved from *caveat emptor* to an extraordinary, unprecedented concern for the economic underdog. Without fair regard for economic reliance interests, role-divided marriage is an economically unacceptable proposition for the stay-at-home partner, be that man or woman. With divorce predictions in the 50 per cent range, no *reasonable* person should forego career development by accepting the stay-at-home role with a good chance of being on welfare or in a beginning level job in middle age or later. While reasonableness is rarely the main ingredient in the decision to marry, the law should not make the choice to marry unreasonable *per se*. There is the further question of whether it makes sense (or indeed is not unfair) to apply current ideas concerning the meaning and durability of the marital relationship to marriages that were contracted in a wholly different socio-legal climate (*Walton, Gleason*). To protect legitimate expectations and justified reliance interests, thoughtful divorce reform might well have differentiated between new marriages (based on *present* law and social circumstances) and those entered into a generation or two ago that had a very different basis in law and culture.

Whatever the law on alimony and separate or community property, in many or most divorces, especially where there are children, there is neither enough property nor sufficient support-paying capability to satisfy all legitimate needs. No law can remedy that. Where there *is* money, however, a more satisfactory consensus regarding post-marital transfer payments could be achieved if we differentiated consciously and expressly between various types of marriage that have quite different internal equities and call for corresponding differentiation in economic settlements (§ 2.5). At one extreme, the now unpersuasive tradition of an open-ended, lifetime support obligation based on careless words in wedding ceremonies should be abandoned. At the other extreme, blind abrogation of support obligations or equal division of property should not be the substitute. Instead, *marital settlements should be proportionate to the specific relationship,* and "equities" should be identified and "monetized". These "equities" should have accrued *during* marriage, *or* arise from marriage-related services that are performed *for the obligor* after marriage.

To illustrate, the custodial parent after divorce should be paid for services rendered in raising the children. The custodial parent of small children after the divorce should be compensated for loss of earnings and loss of opportunity to develop a career while taking care of the children. The custodial parent should receive a measure of support for herself/himself while taking care of the children. More speculatively, by entering into marriage, staying at home, forsaking advanced training, and raising children, the home-maker spouse may have created a reliance interest that should be compensated if divorce occurs. Still more speculatively, the long-term home-maker spouse may be seen as an "equitable partner" in the earning spouse's business or career, so that, on divorce, a part interest in the earning spouse's business or career should be subject to "distribution". Finally, perhaps depending on the circumstances of the divorce (fault?), an allowance (or deduction) might be made for frustration of the earning spouse's reliance interest in housekeeping services and "cohabitation" which must now be sought elsewhere.

In short, there is no lack of contemporary ideas supporting post-marital transfer payments from one spouse to the other that are not alimony, not property, nor child support in the traditional sense. This points to an important particular in which the law has failed: We remain bound by a rigid, three track classification of post-marital payments as "property", "alimony", or "child support". Each has immutable legal consequences (§ 28.1) that may not be well suited to a specific case or, more accurately, to the specific *reason* why a payment is ordered. We must take a new look at the legal attributes (terminability, modifiability, tax deductibility, enforceability, etc.) of post-marital equalization payments and custom-tailor consequences to each occasion (§ 28.2).

CHAPTER 26

DIVISION OF PROPERTY ON DIVORCE

§ 26.1 Traditional Common Law Jurisdictions

Knowledge of the operation of marital property regimes during marriage and upon death (§§ 8.5–11), is indispensable background for this Chapter. As in the ongoing marriage, the basic dividing line is between systems of "separate (common law) property" and "community property." Divorce, however, puts marital property regimes to a further test from which we learn more about their natures and the differences between them.

Traditionally, all but eight states adhered to the separate property principle in marriage. In 1984, Wisconsin joined Arizona, California, Idaho, Nevada, New Mexico, Louisiana, Texas, and Washington in the community property club by adopting the Uniform Marital Property Act (§§ 8.11, 26.5). As discussed in Chapter 8, the traditional separate property system allocates to each marital partner that which he or she owned before marriage and what comes to him or her during marriage through personal earnings, gift and inheritance, as well as earnings on or appreciation of such separate proper-

427

ty. A spouse acquires an interest in the other's property by way of gift (including, importantly, *presumptive* gifts, § 8.7) or through a business relationship. Considerable interpretative problems may arise: For instance, what is the status of the family home paid for with only one spouse's earnings, when title was taken jointly by both spouses, as mortgage lenders require routinely? What is the status of investments resulting from the non-employed spouse's savings out of a household allowance provided by the earning spouse? Indeed, does the recipient spouse really own expensive personal property (*e.g.*, jewelry) given him or her during marriage, the second car (would it matter if title were in the non-earning spouse's name?), household appliances or furniture? The traditional answer lies in the parties' intent at the time of the transaction (§§ 8.5–8), but that intent may be difficult to reconstruct when a relationship of intimate trust has become vindictively adversary. In the past, rigid, gender-based presumptions "of gift" and "of advancement" helped resolve disputes, but now are themselves in dispute (§ 8.7).

Subverting these rules, many common law jurisdictions have long allowed their courts to transfer property between *divorcing* parties. Generally, courts may "make such direction, between the parties, concerning the possession of property, as in the court's discretion justice requires having regard to the circumstances of the case and of the respective parties" (N.Y. Dom. Rel. Law § 234). Before the concept of "marital property" was introduced in

1977, Illinois held that "the court may order the husband or wife, as the case may be, to pay to the other party such sum of money or convey to the party such real or personal property, payable or to be conveyed either in gross or by installments as settlement in lieu of alimony, as the court deems equitable" (*Sahagian*).

Traditionally, property settlements rested on (1) the court's (clear) power to disengage the possibly quite tangled (jointly held or equitably traceable) assets of the parties, *i.e.,* to define which assets are whose separate property, including consideration of interspousal and other gifts, (2) the court's (usually not at all clear) power to apportion "marital assets" between the ex-partners, (3) the court's (usually not very clear) power to dip into either party's separate property to achieve a "fair" settlement and (4) the court's (typically clear) power to allow alimony, which would justify the transfer of property "in lieu of alimony" or the award of property as "lump-sum alimony". Often it was not clear what—if any— property was properly before the court. The consequence was confusion, and that resulted in unpredictability and arbitrariness in awards.

A 1971 New York case illustrates the operation of the pure, traditional common law property regime at its worst. In a marriage of several decades, the husband had carried on a crash savings program, telling his wife that it was "for our latter days." For many years, all of the wife's earnings and some of the husband's were employed to defray family expenses, whereas the bulk of the husband's earnings went into savings and investments. Title was taken in his name. When the wife claimed half of that property upon divorce, the Court held that she had no claim at all since title to the invested funds had always remained in the husband. The Court pontificated that "there may be a moral judgment that can be made on the basis of [the husband's] conduct and the imperfectly expressed intention of some possible future benefit to [the wife], but that is not enough to set the court in motion" (*Wirth*).

It should not be supposed, however, that the title rule invariably worked to the disadvantage of the wife. When the Kansas Supreme Court dealt in 1975 with a marriage of 29 years and farm property the wife had brought into the marriage, the dissenting judge complained:

"It occurs to me that the defendant has received scant consideration from a bad tempered old lady who met him at the door with a shotgun upon his return from a sojourn in the hospital. She now emerges from the twenty-nine year old marriage with a farm worth at least $62,000, plus one-half in value of the personal property acquired over the years, while Mr. LaRue comes out at the short end of the horn with the other half of the value of the personalty, or $10,000. The equities of the situation escape me" (*LaRue*).

Today, all separate property jurisdictions have switched to a more liberal and literal conception of marriage as a partnership. In 1970 the Wisconsin Supreme Court presaged this trend:

"The division of the property of the divorced parties rests upon the concept of marriage as a shared enterprise or joint undertaking. It is literally a partnership, although a partnership in which contributions and equities of the partners may and do differ from individual case to individual case. In a brief marriage, particularly as to property which the husband brought to the marriage, one third to the wife may be too liberal an allowance. In a long marriage, particularly as to property acquired by the parties during the marriage, fifty-fifty division may well represent the mutuality of the enterprise. * * * The contribution of a full-time homemaker-housewife to the marriage may well be greater or at least as great as those of the wife required by circumstances or electing by preference to seek and secure outside employment. The formula for division derives from the facts of the individual case" (*Lacey,* as reaffirmed in *Parsons*).

In 1994, Mississippi was the last state to write the title theory's "obituary" when it recognized "that marital partners can be equal contributors whether or not they both are at work in the marketplace" (*Helmsley, Ferguson*).

No-fault divorce has made it more necessary than ever that the dependent spouse's economic interest in marriage be defined clearly. So long as fault was the sole basis for divorce, the "innocent" spouse (or if the other spouse also was "guilty", even the "guilty" spouse, § 19.9), was at least able to prevent a divorce outright (§ 19.14). That power enabled the dependent spouse to insist on a fair economic settlement that compensated for economic interests in marriage. Abuses of this power—wives using the threat of preventing divorce to coerce their husbands into unduly oppressive property settlements—received far more publicity than did the salutary effects of the old rule. Today, with unilateral, no-fault divorce the rule, no bargaining tool remains in the hands of the economically weaker spouse, and the dependent spouse's financial fate depends entirely upon specific marital property law.

These factors and the belated realization—after a century!—that the formal equality provided by the Married Women's Property Acts had not in fact achieved economic equality of the spouses, contributed to disenchantment with the common law property regime. Increasingly, law reformers in separate property jurisdictions looked to the community property systems for ideas and solutions.

§ 26.2   Community Property States

We have seen that some community property systems hedge on crucial points of community ownership, especially on the question of management of the "marital capital" (§§ 8.8, 10). Further inconsistencies with the logic of community property appear in divorce. In a "pure" community property system, divorce should involve the return to each spouse of his or her separate property and the division of community property by halves (*cf. Eastis*). This, however, is not necessarily what happens. More typically, while separate property (however defined) *is* assigned to the respective owners, the court has discretion to distribute the community property (however defined) "equitably" (*but cf. Hatch*, constitutionally interpreting "equitably" to mean "evenly"). In several states this is done with, and in others without, regard to marital misconduct. At the extreme end of the spectrum of disregard for the logic of community property, Washington takes *all* property (community and separate) before the court for possible distribution and requires property to be distributed "as shall appear just and equitable" taking into account the duration of the marriage and the economic circumstances of each spouse (RCWA § 26.09.080). Elsewhere, even if *direct* apportionment of separate property is not allowed, the very existence of separate property importantly affects a discretionary distribution of community property, as well as the alimony award. Indeed, ripples of the property situation may extend as far as child support. To illustrate, a "property" award of the family residence to the custodial parent may be partially in the nature of child support.

Why have so many community property jurisdictions abandoned the certainty and predictability potentially offered by their regime? The answer lies in reality. Too many divorces involve inadequate assets to provide for all legitimate needs and take the parties to or over the brink of economic disaster. Accordingly, "pure" community property offers no significant help, except for the quite well-off. Applied there, the rigidity of equal division may produce no more "justice" than it denies—at least in the absence of the parties' full freedom to contract out of the system.

§ 26.3 Equitable Distribution, the UMDA, and "Marital Property"

All separate property states now allow their divorce courts varying measures of power to divide property. Considerable differences remain in the states' views as to whether the court may "divide" only "marital" property or both "marital" and "separate" property. Divergence also persists in the definition of what is marital and what is separate property, and whether "equitable" means "50/50", or "even", or "fair".

In making their break with tradition, most separate property states adopted what has been aptly called "deferred community property". Some did this in a non-technical sense, others highly technically. The non-technical (equitable distribution) approach is exemplified in UMDA § 307, Alternative A:

"In a proceeding for dissolution of a marriage, legal separation, or disposition of property following a decree * * * the court, *without regard to marital misconduct,* shall, and in a proceeding for legal separation may, finally equitably apportion between the parties the property and assets belonging to either or both however and whenever acquired, and whether the title thereto is in the name of the husband or wife or both. In making apportionment the court shall consider the duration of the marriage, any prior marriage of either party, *any antenuptial agreement of the parties,* the age, health, station, occupation, amount and sources of income, vocational skills, employability, estate, liabilities, and needs of each of the parties, custodial provisions, whether the apportionment is in lieu of or in addition to maintenance, and the opportunity of each for future acquisition of capital assets and income. The court shall also *consider the contribution or dissipation of each party in the acquisition, preservation, deprecia- tion, or appreciation in value of the respective estates,* and as the contribution of a spouse as a homemaker or to the family unit.'' (Emphasis added).

For use in community property states, UMDA § 307 suggests the following ''Alternative B'':

''In a proceeding for dissolution of the marriage, legal separation, or disposition of property follow- ing a decree * * * the court shall assign each spouse's separate property to that spouse. It also shall divide community property, without regard to marital misconduct in just proportions after considering all relevant factors including: (1) con- tribution of each spouse to acquisition of the marital property, including contribution of a spouse as homemaker; (2) value of the property set apart to each spouse; (3) duration of the marriage; and (4) economic circumstance of each spouse when the division of property is to become effective, including the desirability of awarding the family home or the right to live therein for a reasonable period to the spouse having custody of any children."

An earlier draft of UMDA § 307 for use in separate property states had been discarded by the Commissioners on Uniform State Laws. That draft had contained substantially the language of current "Alternative B" with a reference, however, to *marital* (instead of *community*) property. The draft provided detailed definitions of separate and marital property (such as would already exist in community property states), as follows:

"(b) For purposes of this Act, 'marital property' means all property acquired by either spouse subsequent to the marriage except: (1) property acquired by gift, bequest, devise, or descent; (2) property acquired in exchange for property acquired before the marriage or in exchange for property acquired by gift, bequest, devise, or descent; (3) property acquired by a spouse after a decree of legal separation; (4) property excluded by valid agreement of the parties; and (5) the increase in value of property acquired before the marriage. (c) All property acquired by either spouse after the marriage and before a decree of legal separation is presumed to be marital property, regardless of whether title is held individually or by the spouses in some form of co-ownership such as joint tenancy, tenancy in common, tenancy by the entirety, and community property. The presumption of marital property is overcome by a showing that the property was acquired by a method listed in subsection (b)."

Alas, when the Uniform Law Commissioners rejected that draft, not all copies were shredded. For whatever reason, perhaps just plain bad luck, several separate property states adopted this rather technical, retrospective if not retroactive, marital property regime. Making a bad thing worse, these states often further "refined" the technical "marital property" approach (*e.g.,* Illinois, 750 ILCS 5/503) and reaped an inordinate harvest of highly technical litigation, for very little benefit, except to lawyers. With sincere effort and at great expense, dozens of appellate cases struggled with careful definition of separate and marital property and the question of whether and how separate property "transmutes" into marital property through "commingling" (*e.g., Rogers*) or when title is taken jointly (*Bonnell*), leaning on the older custom of presuming a gift in such cases.

Another fine point has been answered differently in different jurisdictions and sometimes in the same. This is whether *appreciation of,* or *income on*, separate property during the marriage is to be classified as marital or separate property. Numerous states have specific provisions, and the literal language of the statute has controlled. There are obvious and perhaps nearly equal merits to answering this question either one way or the other. The worst answer is the statute that provides different treatment for the two types of gain, given that modern financial instruments often resist classification as one or the other, and the relative ease with which earnings may be manipulated into appreciation and *vice-versa* (interest vs. capital gains). UMPA, remarkably, fell into that trap. Another layer of complexity comes in where appreciation of or earnings on separate property was produced by the active management by the non-owning spouse.

The ultimate irony is that courts quite frequently have fallen back on provisions that (1) allow a disproportionate allocation of marital property where one spouse owns substantial property, (2) make alimony and property awards interdependent in the sense that the more property is awarded, the less need there is for alimony, or (3) even allow a spouse's mere expectancy of an inheritance to be considered. These "loopholes" may reduce a highly technical analysis to an expensive but often pointless exercise.

§ 26.4 Disability Pay, Accrued Leave and What Else Is There?

Laboring the property-approach toward the breaking point, some courts have, though others have not (*Thompson*), divided personal injury awards, disability payments or workers' compensation as marital property. Courts divided into two camps: Some insist on a strict reading of statutory language that all property acquired during marriage is marital (*Marsh*); others use the "analytical approach" that seeks to characterize the award by looking at the loss that is being compensated (*Waggoner*). In the latter camp, compensation for pain and suffering and future earning capacity usually is viewed as *non*-marital. Straddling, the Massachusetts Supreme Court has classified pain as personal and future earnings as marital (*Dalessio*). The trouble is that both types of award resist classification as "property", marital *or* separate, but both may logically be the source of alimony. It is worth noting that the Uniformed Services Former Spouses Protection Act does *not* apply to military disability benefits (*Mansell*). Nevertheless, some courts have taken account of such pay (*Clauson, Kraft*). IRA's, tax-shelters and a wide variety of "fringe benefits", such as executive incentive plans, stock options, a "golden parachute" offered five years after the divorce (*Stouffer*), medical insurance, and even frequent flyer miles have come under scrutiny as marital property. A state trooper's 400 hours of unused personal leave were counted as divisible marital property (*Schober*).

§ 26.5 The Uniform Marital Property Act

Other chapters discuss diverse aspects of UMPA (§§ 7.13, 8.11, 29.8). That Act purports only to regulate the property status of spouses *during* their marriage and "takes the parties to the door of the divorce court only" and "leaves to existing dissolution procedures * * * the selection of the appropriate procedures for dividing property." As also acknowledged in the Prefatory Note to the Act, however, "the sharing mode during marriage is an ownership right already in existence at the end of a marriage" (*cf. Hatch, Fournier, Kujawinski*). Protestations in the Prefatory Note notwithstanding—"though drafted with an awareness of various community property statutes and cases, the Uniform Marital Property Act is not an image of any of them"—the Act *does* impose community property, prospectively.

§ 26.6 No–Fault, Marital Fault, Economic Fault and "Dissipation"

The advent of no-fault legislation brought to many states a specific legislated mandate that "marital misconduct" (as the UMDA puts it) is *not* to be considered in the distribution of property. With respect to property accumulated during the marriage, of course, that makes more sense than when a prospective, future support obligation (alimony) is at issue (§§ 25.5, 6). However, numerous *separate* property states continue to weigh (and not all *community* property states disregard) fault in the allocation of marital or community property upon divorce (*Sparks, Chamblee*). In "mixed" fault and no-fault jurisdictions, the relevance of fault may depend on whether a fault ground is used for the divorce.

UMDA § 307(1)(a) introduces the notion of "economic" fault in the very same section in which it excises "marital" fault (§ 26.3). Specifically, "the court shall also consider the contribution or *dissipation* of each party in the acquisition, preservation, depreciation, or appreciation in value of the respective estates." The idea stems from the community property states (*Martin, Beltran*), and has been adopted in many separate property states. A new jurisprudence concerning the "dissipation" of marital assets imposes what amounts to a duty on the owner of separate (but, on a future divorce, marital) property, to deal with such property in good faith even during the ongoing marriage. This has been carried to the extreme where a professional football player upon divorce was held liable to his wife for breaking and thus "dissipating" a sports contract for games not yet played (*Gastineau*). "Dissipation" disputes tend to get as bitter as old-line fault divorce, as illustrated in a wife's racketeering (RICO) claim against her husband's lover for diversion of marital millions (*Farkas*). In some states, "dissipation" can occur only *after* a marriage is "undergoing an irreconcilable breakdown" (*Hazel*). The close relationship of the concept of dissipation to *fault*, though not old line moral "marital fault," but a pragmatic notion of "economic fault," is worth at least another thought. Note also that its positive mirror image, "economic *merit*," has not had nearly the same impact, although the UMDA mentions "contribution" in direct conjunction with "dissipation". The marital estate typically is defined and divided without or with little regard to whose *economic* effort produced it, with the curious exception of some professional license cases (§ 27.9).

§ 26.7 Deprivation of Separate Property Without Due Process of Law?

When separate property states first took to dividing "marital" property on divorce, some husbands claimed that the imposition of the new regime un-

constitutionally deprived them of their separate
property without due process of law—as was held
some forty years ago regarding the retroactive imposition of community property in Pennsylvania
(*Willcox*). The near-unanimous (if somewhat disin-
genuous) judicial response has been that these new
laws impose no *property* regime at all and only
provide a formula for the distribution of assets upon
divorce and that, being remedial in nature, they do
not offend constitutional principles (*Fournier, Kujawinski*). If this reasoning is inconsistent with
earlier cases that did *not* allow a wife to be deprived
of *community* property on divorce, the courts did
not notice (*Arnett, Pfaff*). If nothing else, the new
holdings *are* consistent with the cases that denied
wives' claims for "deprivation of property" inherent
in marital status when no-fault divorce laws were
enacted (*Gleason, Walton*, §§ 7.1, 20.1, 24.4).

§ 26.8 Conflicts Problems

A variety of conflicts of laws problems may arise
in connection with the division of property on divorce. Typically these will involve couples who, in
the course of their marriages, have lived, earned,
consumed, saved and invested in both separate and
community property states. Problems may range
from the classification of certain property as joint or
separate, to the court's power to touch the property.
The classification by several community property
states of certain separate property acquired in a
separate property state as "quasi-community property" has already been touched upon (§ 8.12).

Lack of space does not permit further discussion, but the reader may consider that in most jurisdictions the courts' broad powers to transfer property incident to divorce makes the classification of property upon divorce less of a problem than it is upon death (§ 8.9), although the same rules of classification generally apply. It remains the rule that a court may not *directly* effect the transfer of realty located in another state, although the same result is achieved by ordering the owner to make the appropriate transfer here and now, on threat of holding the owner in contempt (*Kane, cf. Mack*).

CHAPTER 27

DIVISIBILITY OF PENSIONS AND PROFESSIONAL LICENSES

§ 27.1 Pension Rights as "Marital Assets"

The divisibility of pension rights on divorce is an old issue that has resurfaced in another guise. In contrast to the community property states, traditional separate property states did not ask the question whether pensions are divisible *marital* property, simply because there was no marital property. In the day of permanent alimony, the question was whether the reduction in income caused by the husband's voluntary or compulsory retirement was a circumstance justifying a reduction in his alimony obligation (*Ellis*). However, when nationwide publicity was given in 1975 to a California (community property) lawyer's loss of a $100,000 malpractice suit because he had neglected to consider the wife's possible interest in her husband's military pension (*Lewis*), the bell tolled. Lawyers in separate property states—by then moving toward equitable distribution or marital property approaches—hurried to introduce the pension issue into their cases. Today, common law as well as community property jurisdictions look to the principal earner's (still typically the husband's) pension rights as "marital property" subject to division.

If *both* marital partners have held jobs and earned pensions during their marriage, logic dictates that, in the absence of a specific and enforceable marital property agreement, both pensions should be "equalized", and each partner should be allocated one-half of the combined pension rights earned during the marriage (*Welder, Murff, Haun*). Alternatively, the fact that both pursued their separate careers and other circumstances may indicate the spouses' intent to keep their earnings and pensions separate and may amount to an implied marital property arrangement. With luck, that may be given effect on divorce.

§ 27.2   Federal Pensions

Too late for lawyer *Lewis* (whose liability had been predicated on his failure to research the issue), the U.S. Supreme Court held in 1981 that military pensions were just as indivisible (*McCarty*) as it previously had held railroad retirement pensions to be (*Hisquierdo*). Completing the circle, Congress overturned *McCarty* in 1982 and *Hisquierdo* in 1983. The Uniformed Services Former Spouses Protection Act now provides for the division of military retirement, though not disability, pensions on divorce. Congress has opened a variety of other pensions to division, such as foreign service pensions, and shown broad interest in the pension issue with the "Retirement Equity Act" of 1984. Important provisions benefit divorced homemakers under "ERISA", originally the Employee Retirement Income Security Act of 1974.

The ex-spouse's independent interest in social security benefits that arises after ten years of marriage (twenty before 1979) has furnished the basis for decisions holding that an earner's social security benefits may *not* be divided upon divorce (*Umber, dicta* in *Hisquierdo*). However, there is nothing to stop a court from *considering* the value of future social security benefits when deciding on the distribution of a couple's assets or when fixing alimony (*cf. Stumpf*). From that point of view, it may make sense to compensate a non-earner-spouse on divorce for the loss of her *contingent* expectancy of social security entitlement, if the divorce occurs after, say, nine years of marriage. Insupportable inequities remain in our social security system, unless each spouse has had his or her own separate and adequate earnings. One fair answer may lie in a fundamental redefinition of eligibility standards to be based on the mother's "contribution" of her children, by bearing and raising them, to the pool of social security providers for the "working" population (§ 25.13). A second-best solution would be an actuarially sound apportionment between husband and wife of social security "credits" on the basis of the duration of the marriage, to be added to and subtracted from credits carried in each individual spouse's account.

§ 27.3 Are Pensions Property or Income "Insurance"?

Today, a spouse's pension is usually allocated on the basis of the proportion earned during the marriage. In principle, that approach can hardly be faulted. In execution, many cases have left a lot to be desired. Is a pension really a *saving* of marital property, comparable to earnings "put away" during the marriage and as such divisible upon divorce as property, or should it be viewed as income insurance, to replace earnings lost after retirement and, as such, more properly a basis for continued alimony? *The uncomfortable fact is that most pension rights fall somewhere in between.*

Problems that are difficult to resolve include (1) the valuation of pension rights, especially when the pension is not vested (*Axtell*, *Robert C.S.*) or is subject to contingencies such as death or early retirement options, (2) the timing of the distribution of the pension interest to the non-earner spouse, and (3) the relationship between an award now of pension rights as property and a long-term award of alimony. The following two cases convincingly raise but do not convincingly answer typical valuation questions that several states now try to deal with by statute (*Blazis*).

Kis follows the "annuity purchase approach". The earner-husband had contributed $14,000 to his retirement plan and the court, looking to the benefits ultimately to be received, "accepted evidence establishing the cost of an annuity, purchased for a 51–year-old male, yielding $10,000 per year from and after his 55th birthday." The pension was valued at $118,833 and counted toward the husband's share in the distribution of the parties' other property.

In *Boyd,* the court made an actuarial computation of benefits that would be received if the employee lived to and past retirement, a division of that amount by the percentage accrued during the marriage, and a reduction of that to "present value":

"Since * * * plaintiff was 55 years old at the time of the divorce and was not eligible to receive any pension benefits until at least age 59, the following * * * calculation would be necessary. First, the lower court would have to ascertain the likelihood of a 55–year-old man dying before he becomes 59. If, for instance, five 55–year-old males out of each 100 die by the age of 59, the value of the pension benefits would have to be reduced by 5%. Second, the life expectancy of plaintiff at retirement age would have to be calculated. By MCL 500.834; MSA 24.1834, a 59–year-old person has a life expectancy of 16.81 years. Third, the life expectancy of Plaintiff would have to be multiplied by the yearly pension benefits the plan provides. Fourth, this figure must be reduced by the percentage of possibility that plaintiff would die before he is eligible for retirement. (In this example, we have used 5% for purposes of illustration only.) Fifth, this figure must be reduced to present value. This sum will constitute a reasonably ascertainable present value for the pension."

§ 27.4 When to Pay?

The timing of the pay-out, whether in a lump sum or in installments, offers five options: The non-earner's share may be ordered paid (1) at the time of the divorce, (2) upon the earliest possible retirement date of the earner whether or not he or she actually retires, (3) beginning at a mutually agreed time, (4) upon a court-defined "normal" retirement age, or (5) when the earner actually retires. Many courts prefer a complete "pay-out" at the time of divorce, if possible by offset against other marital property (*Kis*), because a final settlement of the ex-partners' accounts is deemed a virtue in itself (*Braderman*). Some courts strongly prefer the cash value of a vested pension to be paid out in a lump sum on divorce, and a deferred pay-out is ordered only when a lump sum pay-out is not possible:

> "Another advantage mentioned for the reserved jurisdiction method is that it avoids the often difficult problems encountered in calculating the present value, at the time of dissolution, of the spouses' community interest in a defined-benefit pension plan. It *is* true that various assumptions must be made in arriving at the present value of a non-employee spouse's community interest in a retirement plan. There *are* various contingencies that may affect that present value, the effect of which must be quantified, in many cases through the use of expert testimony. However, we do not believe that an expert's informed making of assumptions and evaluation

of them based on accepted actuarial and statistical techniques render the outcome any more unacceptably 'speculative' than, say, the computation of earning capacity to establish damages in a personal injury case. In some cases, a trial court may have little choice but to defer distribution and enter a 'pay as it comes in' order. In many other cases, however, an immediate, outright distribution will better serve the parties' and the court's interests" (*Ruggles*).

In the case of a substantial amount at issue, however, many good arguments favor a court, at the time of divorce, limiting itself to assigning a specific percentage share of the earner's pension to the nonearner, to be payable when the earner retires and actually draws benefits. That solution raises a problem in the case where the earner has an early retirement opportunity at, say 55 years of age, but wants to go on working. The Supreme Court of California held:

"Earl cannot time his retirement to deprive Vera of an equal share of the community's interest in his pension. It is a settled principle that one spouse cannot, by invoking a condition wholly within his control, defeat the community interest of the other spouse. * * * Earl's claim that he is being forced to retire misses the point. He is free to continue working. However, if he does so, he must reimburse Vera for the share of the community property that she loses as a result of that decision" (*Gillmore*).

In a worse scenario, a divorce decree had ordered the husband to pay his ex-wife $600 per month whether or not he actually retired, as of the time he reached age 55, then the early retirement age under his pension plan. When his retirement plan subsequently reduced his retirement benefit significantly and changed his eligibility age to 65, the court refused to change her entitlement. The court held that modification was not appropriate just because a predicted value as of the time of divorce did not match subsequent events (*Barnes*). What to do? Some courts have required a pay-out to begin, or a pension to be valued, *not* as of the earliest possible retirement date, but as of the time of a *normal* retirement, such as age 65.

Both *Gillmore* and *Barnes* involved a *deferred* pay-out of pension rights accrued during the marriage. There the possible relationship to spousal support was obvious. What, however, is to be the stance on alimony if a wife's interests in her husband's pension was paid to her as property on divorce and, by the time she and her ex-husband reach retirement age, she has nothing left? If, in such a case, the ex-wife's *need* and the ex-husband's *ability to pay* continue to be the controlling criteria for alimony (and they remain just that in many jurisdictions), alimony may well end up being "double dipped" after the husband's retirement, out of his other assets or, worse, out of his remaining pension.

A deferred pay-out may not survive the earner's death, as the earner would never collect the pension. This problem may be dealt with in discounting a pay-out at the time of divorce (*Boyd*, above), or by appropriate provision in a separation agreement. The next question is whether a deferred pay-out should survive the obligee's death? Consider the following case:

"Phyllis Berling [ex-wife] died, leaving no will. She was survived by their two children. As part of the distribution [of the estate], the decedent's interest in the retirement benefits [was] assigned in equal shares to Farver [the daughter] and her brother. John Berling [ex-husband] retired from the State Patrol in June of 1979, with retirement benefits of $1,340.59 per month. * * * The property to which [Phyllis] was entitled is the stated interest in whatever income Mr. Berling actually received from retirement benefits. Her property right to the judicially specified percentage of John's income from retirement benefits was subject to the State's statutes governing the descent and distribution of property" (*Farver*).

Nice kids he had, poor John!

§ 27.5 Tax Consequences

The transfer upon divorce of pension rights may have tax consequences, depending on the specific facts, type of plan (especially whether the plan is tax-deferred) and method of pay-out. In any case, tax consequences must be weighed intelligently when putting a value on a pension or other retirement benefit. Federal legislation alleviates problems, especially by *not* treating certain distributions as taxable events. Space limitations forbid analysis at a level that would avoid flagrant inaccuracy, but any lawyer must know that the key is the Qualified Domestic Relations Order (QDRO) (*e.g.*, *Metropolitan Life*). A QDRO gives an alternate payee the right to receive benefits from a qualified pension plan. The order must *very* carefully follow precise statutory requirements. (See 29 U.S.C.A. § 1056(d)). One expert asserts that more than 70% of all QDRO's that are initially submitted fail to qualify (Shulman, QDRO Handbook, 1993).

§ 27.6 Business, Good Will and "Division" of Professional Licenses

Problems still more perplexing than those encountered in the pension area have become commonplace when a professional license is classified as marital *property*. A little less persuasively than in the case of the pension debate, the argument of those who, upon divorce, would divide such a license has a certain plausibility. After all, business *good will* long has been recognized as an asset. Its value is ascertainable by accepted accounting principles and practice—primitively, what would a willing buyer pay for the going business over and above the market value of its physical assets? And if a *business* that was developed by one of the parties during marriage is a marital asset (as it now typically is), all its constituents, including good will, constitute divisible marital property. Where it is not practical to *pay out* the value of a business, because that might wreck it or force a sale, periodic installments will bridge that problem. If the business does not produce an adequate cash flow to handle installment payments, the answer may lie in incorporation and the issuance of stock, depending on the case. In short, "good will" is a recognized asset and, if classified as marital property, "divisible" in some appropriate way. No problem.

Moving over to *service* businesses, such as professional practices, conceptual and practical problems become more pronounced. Aside from *physical* assets, the market value of a professional practice is much more inextricably bound up with the professional's *personal* service than is the case with the typical hamburger franchise. No doubt, in the typical established practice, especially a prominent multi-partner law practice such as Cravath, Swaine & Moore (*Anonymous NY*), there is a "good will" factor approaching the nature of property that must not be confused with the value of real estate, office furniture, equipment, or accounts receivable. The smaller the operation in question, however, the more pronounced the difficulty, and the more reluctant courts are (and should be) to assign good will as a marital asset (*Zells, Trull, Sorensen, Eslami*). Of course, no sale actually takes place on divorce. The chief concern thus is whether it is possible (or sensible) to distinguish between a professional's license as representing *earning capacity* (as such, potentially the basis for alimony) and a professional's license as *property* (as such, subject to division) (*Travis*). The conceptual difficulty is compounded further by the fact that, *whatever* is paid out must ultimately come out of the professional's *income* from *working* at his or her profession. So far, so good.

Some courts have carelessly confused a professional *practice* with a professional *license*. Overly motivated by antipathy to alimony, they have divided the "value" of a professional *license* as marital property (an early case is *Weinstein*). In contrast to commercial "good will" or to the *established* professional practice, however, professional licenses are unsalable abstractions. The license represents the professional's enhanced future *earning* capacity, as does a high school diploma or a mechanic's skill. What has caught many courts' attention is that a professional license represents an *increase* in earning power that, if acquired during the marriage and through the other spouse's financial contribution, should be reflected in the divorce settlement. But should that be done by capitalizing this increased earning capacity as *property*?

Cases have fallen into several categories: One group of cases (*not* neatly classifiable in terms of community or separate property jurisdictions) has denied outright that professional licenses can be subject to "division" (*Graham, DeLa Rosa, Olah*). Since there is no market value, these courts do not classify the degree or license as property at all, whether separate, marital, or community (*Sullivan*). A second group has focused on special circumstances, especially the support of the other while he or she studied for a degree. In these cases, consideration of the value of the license has been

based on restitution or unjust enrichment reasoning
(yes: *Postema*; no: *Martinez, cf. Washburn*). A
third category has not seriously concerned itself
with the conceptual difficulties inherent in any such
division and the "value" (however speculatively ascertained) of the license was ordered divided (*Wood-
worth, O'Brien*). In *Morongiello*, marriage to a law
student after the first year of study was held to
merit 50% of 2/3rd of the astonishingly precisely
calculated $568,420 "value" of the degree. In a
thoughtful opinion, the Kentucky Supreme Court
refused to go the property route, but recognized the
"diploma dilemma" and held that a professional
degree and license are factors to be considered in
setting an alimony award even though specific statutory (UMDA-similar) criteria for alimony were not
met (*Lovett*).

Some states, such as Illinois, enacted statutes
requiring, in the determination of *alimony*, consideration of "any impairment of the present and
future earning capacity of the party seeking maintenance due to that party devoting time to domestic
duties or having foregone or delayed education,
training, employment, or career opportunities due
to the marriage" and "contributions and services by
the party seeking maintenance to the education,
training, career or career potential, or license of the
other spouse" (750 ILCS 5/504(a)(4), (10)). By
contrast, California enacted, in a framework of numerous factors affecting the end-result, that in the
context of *property* division, "the community shall
be reimbursed for community contributions to edu-

cation or training of a party that substantially en-
hances the earning capacity of the party. The
amount reimbursed shall be with interest at the
legal rate, accruing from the end of the calendar
year in which the contributions were made" (Cal.
Civ. Code § 4800.3).

At the extremes of this subject, an attorney-wife
was earning $28,200 and her physician-husband,
still in training, earned $22,100. At the time of
divorce she claimed that her expected long-term
earnings and those of her husband should be equalized—she expected to earn about two million and
alleged his expectation to be triple that. This fresh
idea was rejected in *Sattler,* although the court gave
her alimony of $100 per month for three years, plus
substantial attorneys fees. Furthest afield are New
York cases that, after the path was lit by *O'Brien,*
went on to divide as *marital property*, for instance,
an uncertified emergency room practitioner's experience, although he had acquired his medical license
prior to marriage (*Madori*), an attorney's 12–year
political career as a Congressman (*Martin* N.Y.),
and the very careers of a variety of "celebrities"
with special "innate, ineffable talents" whose fame
increased during the marriage (*e.g.,* Stan *Getz*, Mar-
isa *Berenson* (*Golub*) Joe *Piscopo*, Frederica von
Stade (*Elkus*). If the question is whether on divorce the less successful partner should share in the
success of the more successful, the answer may well
be "yes", but to speak in terms of the *current*
divisibility of the partner's *future* earnings in terms
of a *property* award that will not be modifiable (as

alimony would be, if circumstances changed (*Travis*)) seems unnecessarily rigid.

§ 27.7 Conclusion

The pension and license division cases have been encouraged by the recipients' widespread disdain for alimony, not only emotionally, but because alimony may be modifiable by change of circumstances or terminable by cohabitation, remarriage, and death—as well as difficult to collect over the long term. Similarly, many obligors dislike the potential open-endedness of alimony. All this has coalesced with the general movement toward making divorce a more final event. As should by now be obvious, the pension and license cases are hybrids. They represent on the one hand something in the nature of an asset that was acquired during the marriage, but in the typical case they do not lend themselves to accurate valuation at the time of divorce and therefore not to "division". A satisfactory solution must recognize that these items share attributes both of assets and of future income, and any payout and its legal consequences should be tailored to the specific situation.

In *theory*, it is doubtful whether the highly controversial and technical question of valuing pension interests and professional licenses, only to "divide" them, is worth resolving when, in most states, the judge may consider *everything,* whether income source or property, when dividing marital property and when fixing alimony. Costly litigation regarding the proper classification of these items may often be, at best, a waste of time and expense and, at worst, productive of unfairness often quite unforeseeable at the time of divorce. In *practice,* much of the trouble we are in is due to the fact that we remain bound to a rigid, two track classification of post-marital payments as either "property" or "alimony", each with a long list of specific legal consequences (See §§ 28.1, 2).

CHAPTER 28

TAXATION, ENFORCEMENT, DURATION AND OTHER LEGAL ATTRIBUTES OF ALIMONY, PROPERTY DIVISION AND CHILD SUPPORT

§ 28.1 Post–Marital Payments—Enforcement, Taxation, Duration, Bankruptcy

For the sake of brevity, but even more to highlight crucially important similarities and distinctions between the three categories of post-marital payments (alimony, property distribution, and child support), their principal legal attributes are now discussed side-by-side:

(1) Alimony and child support may be enforced by the civil or criminal contempt power of the court, and other (*e.g.*, criminal or wage garnishment) nonsupport remedies may apply, whereas a property settlement must rely on regular civil means of enforcement.

(2) Alimony is deductible by the payor from his or her gross income and must be included by the recipient in her or his taxable income, whereas a property settlement or child support is neither deductible to one nor income to the other.

(3) Alimony (usually) and property distributions (always) may be compromised, settled or waived, whereas a compromise concerning the parental obligation to render child support does not bind the child and thus cannot bar a court from reopening the question of child support (§ 15.4, Ch. 29).

(4) Alimony usually, unless otherwise agreed in the separation agreement or provided in the divorce decree (§ 25.7, Ch. 29), and child support always (§ 15.4) remain modifiable if circumstances change, whereas a property settlement is final and not modifiable.

(5) Alimony usually terminates upon the recipient's remarriage or possibly, cohabitation, whereas obligations relating to a property settlement remain due until paid. Child support usually terminates when the child reaches majority (§ 15.6, 7).

(6) Alimony and child support generally terminate upon the death of either the recipient or the payor, whereas obligations relating to property settlements remain enforceable by and against an estate.

(7) Alimony and child support are not dischargeable in bankruptcy, whereas obligations under a property settlement traditionally could be discharged (*Harrell, Farrey*). The Bankruptcy Reform Act of 1994 (P.L. No. 103–394) provides new protections for children and spouses, by improving procedures and ending dischargeability for certain debts arising out of a division of property incident to divorce. The House Judiciary Committee ex-

plained that debts related to martial property would no longer be dischargeable "where the debtor has the ability to pay them and the detriment to the nondebtor spouse outweighs the benefit to the debtor of discharging such debts". However, even when the bankruptcy laws show no mercy regarding alimony and child support, the bankruptcy itself and the payor's change in ability to pay that led to the bankruptcy may be sufficiently serious to justify a modification of future alimony support payments, possibly even extending to accrued arrears (*Goldin*).

(8) Until 1984, the transfer to one spouse of the other spouse's separate property was a "taxable event." If the property had appreciated, the transfer produced capital gains tax liability, or if the property was worth less than its basis, a capital loss (*U.S. v. Davis*). Today, the recipient of a property distribution incident to divorce takes over the transferor's adjusted basis in the property. Property distributions from pension funds that qualify as "QDROs" (§ 27.5) are exempt from immediate tax consequences.

(9) Federal gift taxes do not apply in the case of a transfer to a spouse of property incident to divorce nor to transfers in the ongoing marriage, but gift taxes do apply to transfers to children in excess of the tax-free exemption. An estate tax deduction is available for all property transfers to a surviving spouse as well as for property transfers relating to divorce.

§ 28.2 The Tyranny of Labels

So far, so good! We are barely into this Chapter and know most of the law as well as many practical considerations. Before we consider some of the complexities of alimony, property settlements and child support, the basic simplicity of *all* these transactions must be highlighted: One spouse (still typically the husband) transfers or promises to transfer value (typically money or property) to the other spouse (still typically the wife). *A pays or promises to pay money to B.* That is all!

Given this fact, it seems foolish (and may fool us), to look separately at the several classifications of "post marital transfers," *i.e.*, alimony, property settlements and, in many cases, child support. Indeed, in the usual case, no sensible evaluation can be made of the adequacy or appropriateness of any one item without considering the other(s). Why then belabor the distinctions? A simple but unhelpful answer is that the label of the payment indicates the reason why it is to be paid. A worse but very real answer is that quite different legal consequences attend each of the three types of post-marital transfer payments. Even more to the taste of lawyers, some variation in legal consequences may be evoked by intelligent manipulation of labels.

The wild card is the classification of any one item as alimony, as child support or as a property distribution. What makes this area difficult is that what we think we see is not necessarily what there is. For instance, alimony and child support may be paid out in lump sums, and property may be distributed in short- or long-term installments. Nor would that be unusual. For tax and business reasons, property settlements often are paid in installments and, to avoid enforcement hassles, the recipient of alimony and child support may prefer a lump sum.

Worse, what bears one label in one context may be labelled something else in another. Depending on the label that is attached to the payment ("alimony," "property," "child support" or "pension distribution"), and whether the label sticks under different tests applicable under different laws, a considerable variety of legal consequences may be evoked—with each label typically carrying not just one specific and largely immutable attribute, but a *combination* of attributes. These attributes typically include a payment's enforceability, taxability, dischargeability in bankruptcy, modifiability, duration and terminability. For instance, what qualifies as alimony for federal income tax purposes is not necessarily enforceable by contempt, nor dischargeable in bankruptcy, nor modifiable or terminable on remarriage.

§ 28.3 Tax Consequences of Divorce–Related Payments

The Domestic Relations Tax Reform Act of 1984 and later tax reforms considerably reduced the room for manipulation of tax consequences of divorce settlements. Most significantly, legislation now provides clear(er) distinctions between child support and alimony, and gain on transferred property is not taxed on divorce. Moreover, lower rates and increased bracket sizes have reduced the weight of pure tax considerations in deciding on financial arrangements upon divorce.

§ 28.4   Tax Treatment of Alimony

Alimony paid under a decree or separation agreement is deductible by the payor from his or her gross income and is includable by the recipient in her or his taxable income, thus carrying past divorce some of the tax advantage of the income-splitting joint return available during marriage. The alimony deduction is taken from gross income; prior to 1976 it was an itemized deduction. Since a greatly increased number of taxpayers do not itemize and, for high income taxpayers itemized deductions now are substantially reduced, this technical detail is valuable to many divorced taxpayers.

In contrast to alimony, property settlements or child support payments are *not* deductible by the payor, nor includable as income by the payee. Prior legislation imposed pronounced differentials in progressive marginal tax rates that had made the alimony deduction into a valuable tax-saving device. To illustrate, the higher-income payor would deduct the alimony payment at, say, a 70% marginal rate which meant that alimony cost 30 cents on the dollar. Taxed to the recipient at, say, a 40% marginal rate, alimony would be realized at 60 cents on the dollar. This "subsidy from Washington" created a considerable incentive to classify post-divorce payments as alimony. That incentive—though not so much the opportunity—is returning with the reappearance of federal income tax rates ranging up to 39.6%.

As of 1985 (further changes were made in 1986), alimony was redefined for federal income tax purposes. The alimony changes developed out of the thoroughly frightening proposal to abolish the alimony deduction altogether. Their most significant impact is the substantial reduction in opportunity to package as deductible alimony what in substance is child support or a property transfer, neither of which would otherwise be deductible. For alimony to be deductible by the payor and includable in income by the payee: (1) Payment must be in money, not in property or by use of property or services; (2) Payments otherwise qualifying as alimony may be designated by the parties *not* to be alimony, but not the reverse; (3) Payor and payee may not be members of the same household, with a narrow exception concerning payments pursuant to a written separation agreement or decree *other* than a divorce or separate maintenance decree; (4) Payments must end at the death of the recipient without liability for substitute payments or transfers; (5) Payments must not be described as child support, or treated as child support by being contingent on events relating to the child, including the child's attaining a specified age or income level, dying, marrying, leaving school, leaving the household, or gaining employment; (6) If payments are to be more than $10,000 per year, they must be made for at least three years (six under the original legislation), unless either ex-spouse dies or the recipient remarries. If during this period, annual payments decrease by more than $10,000 (increased in 1986 to $15,000), there generally will be a "recapture" of "excess" alimony, by "reversing" the tax advantage previously obtained. Exceptions to "recapture" include payments received under temporary support orders, as well as payments made under a continuing liability over the post-separation years to pay a fixed part of income from a business or property or from compensation for employment or self-employment.

As parenthetically indicated above, the 1986 tax changes replaced the six-year term with a three-year recomputation formula, and the amount of reduction that brings on "recapture" was increased from $10,000 to $15,000. Moreover, the specific calculation now operates differently. One practical effect of this change was to reintroduce an improved though still quite imperfect opportunity to package as deductible alimony what may in substance be a property settlement that otherwise would not be deductible.

Alimony payments required under pre–1985 court orders or agreements incident to divorce or separation, are and remain deductible under the *old* rules. Under these, payments must be based on the marital or family relationship, paid after the decree, and be "periodic." The payment period must be in excess of 10 years or subject to specific contingencies such as the death of either spouse, the remarriage of the alimony recipient, or a change in the economic status of either spouse. Pre–1985 alimony obligations may be brought under the new rules by specific election.

§ 28.5 Tax Treatment of Child Support

Whether paid in the ongoing family, pursuant to a paternity adjudication, or after divorce, child support is not deductible. Under earlier tax law, highly different marginal income tax rates were applicable to the spouses' disparate incomes. Accordingly, if post-divorce payments were so packaged that the Internal Revenue Service accepted them as alimony, the federal government had materially contributed to child support (or to a property settlement). Indeed, unless child support payments were expressly identified, or a "sum certain or percentage of the payment" was fixed as child support, the whole payment qualified as alimony, and became deductible as such by the payor and includable by the recipient (*Lester*). The current rules make it much more difficult to package child support payments as alimony in order to make them deductible to the payor and includable to the custodial parent. At the same time, the advantage of so doing has been reduced substantially by lower and more uniform rates. The current trend toward careful court scrutiny of the adequacy of child support awards poses a real risk, if child support awards and payments to an ex-spouse are not separated explicitly. Last, not least, it must be kept in mind that any packaging for tax purposes may pose risks in terms of non-tax consequences.

Varied tax considerations relate to the specific manner in which child support is rendered. For instance, the obligated parent may undertake to render child support by retaining title to, and making deductible mortgage and real estate tax payments on the children's shelter. These income tax deductions will be worth more in tax savings to a high income obligor than to a lower income recipient. Such an arrangement also saves for the obligor potential appreciation in value upon a later sale.

The tax reform adjusted the dependency exemption for inflation ($2,450 in 1994). Unless otherwise agreed by the parties, the exemption is taken by the custodial parent. Since the dependency exemption is phased out for high income parents, the most effective allocation of the exemption depends on the specific case.

Various trust arrangements have in the past offered interesting possibilities of shifting the obligated parent's high-bracket income to the recipient child's lower bracket income—assuming, of course, that the trust income was not imputed to the payor as being in satisfaction of a legal support obligation. The 1986 tax reform ended most of that. In 1995, the rate for trusts was 39.6% after the first $7,500 of trust income. Moreover, trust income is taxed to the grantor at the grantor's rate if the capital of the trust will revert to the grantor and the value of the reversionary interest exceeds five percent of the initial value. Turning to children under fourteen years of age, only the first $1,000 of unearned income are now taxed at the child's own rate, and the rest is taxed at the custodial parent's marginal rate. 1984 saw another loophole closed. The income earned on interest-free loans from parents to their children and invested by the children had previously been taxed at the children's lower rate (*Crown*). The first blow to such arrangements was the U.S. Supreme Court ruling that federal *gift* tax applies to the interest foregone by the parents, if the annual exemption of $10,000 per parent and child is exceeded (*Dickman*). Even more significantly, the 1984 amendments impute the value of interest foregone as taxable income to the parents.

§ 28.6 Property Transfers on Divorce

Traditionally, the transfer to one spouse of the other spouse's appreciated separate property had produced federal capital gains tax liability (*U.S. v. Davis*). In many separate property states, however, court holdings and state legislation had eroded that rule by following the example of community property states and by viewing divorcing partners as "constructive co-owners" of their *marital* property, thereby avoiding tax consequences on divorce. In 1984, Congress overturned the worn-out *Davis* rule. The recipient of a property distribution incident to divorce now takes over the transferor's adjusted basis in the property. This means, of course, that a later sale of *appreciated* community property by the transferee will cost her or him income (capital gains) taxes at the time of sale. Conversely, if property has *decreased* in value below its basis, a later sale will give rise to a deductible loss.

If, incident to the divorce (or at any other time) the family home is to be sold, consideration should be given to the $125,000 lifetime appreciation exclusion that is available to persons over 55 years of age—and to the quirky rule that limits married owners to one such exclusion whereas as single persons, they would *each* be entitled to a $125,000 exclusion. In short, a home transferred to one party at the time of divorce should not be sold until *after* the divorce. Note also that the use of the exclusion, whether as a married or as a single person, not only follows the user into a new marriage but "taints" even the partner to the new marriage, making the latter ineligible to claim the exclusion—a potentially expensive surprise to someone whose lawyer did not anticipate this.

As has already been said, property transfers, or payments made as property transfers, are not deductible by the payor and do not constitute income to the recipient. The 1984 alimony rules made it considerably more difficult (and riskier, as either party's death would end the obligation) to "package" a property transfer as deductible alimony. This situation is aggravated by the growing preference courts have for labelling distributions as property, instead of alimony, as well as the tax authorities' tendency to take the state court at its word. As also remarked above, the 1986 shift to a (higher) $15,000 trigger amount and a (shorter) three-year recomputation formula somewhat alleviated the impact of the 1984 rules. Incidentally, the three-year period provided by the 1986 reform accommodated the movement toward granting substantial "rehabilitative" alimony for rather short periods after the divorce. Many had feared that the greater after tax cost carried by high short-term alimony under the 1984 (six-year) rule had negatively affected this trend.

The divisibility of pension rights on divorce has added a new dimension to the concept of "marital property." For the careless, the financial consequences under the normal rules of taxation can be severe. For the careful, the invention of the Qualified Domestic Relations Order (QDRO) has alleviated many potential problems (§ 27.5).

§ 28.7 Legal Fees Incident to Divorce

Legal fees incident to obtaining taxable alimony or related to other tax issues are deductible. In current practice, however, the utility of this deduction is severely restricted as such fees now fall into the category of "miscellaneous" itemized deductions, which may be deducted only if, in the aggregate, they exceed 2% of the taxpayer's adjusted gross income.

§ 28.8 The Revival of the "Marriage Penalty" and a Thought on Tax Policy

President Clinton's 1993 income tax reform resurrected the "marriage tax" problem that had been alleviated, though not laid to rest first by the enact-

ment of a "two-earner bonus" under the Economic
Recovery Tax Act of 1981 (long since repealed),
then by the substantial flattening of the federal
income tax rate schedule in the 1980's. Prior to
the 1993 reform, where each partner earned $115,-
000, an unmarried couple paid twice $31,304.50,
i.e., $62,609, whereas a married couple paid $64,-
051. In that example, the "marriage tax" was
$1,442. Where each partner earned $250,000, an
unmarried couple paid twice $73,154.50, *i.e.*, $146,-
309, whereas a married couple paid $147,751, re-
sulting in the same amount of "marriage tax," *i.e.*,
$1442.

Under the Clinton reform, the 36% tax rate
"kicks in" at taxable incomes of $115,000 for *single*
unmarried earners, but at *combined* incomes of
$140,000 for dual earner *married* couples. As a
result, the *additional* "marriage tax" on a married
couple, *each* of whom has a taxable income of $115,-
000, is $4,500. (Calculation: The marginal tax rate
of the *un*married couple remains at 31%, whereas
the marginal tax rate of the married couple jumps
to 36% for their *combined* income above $140,000,
i.e., an additional 5% tax is imposed on $90,000).
Because the top 39.6% tax rate applies to *all* incomes over $250,000 *without regard to marital sta-
tus*, where each partner earns $250,000, the *addi-
tional* marriage tax is $13,500. (Calculation: 5% on
the married couple's combined income over $140,-
000 and under $230,000, *i.e.*, the $4,500 calculated
above, *plus* 8.6% (5% *and* 3.6%, the latter being
10% of the 36% rate) on $250,000, *i.e.*, $9,000).
More than even at the height of the previous mar-

riage penalty debate, this makes divorce an interesting, if not appealing tax planning tool for some maritally happy (but tax weary) high dual income couples. For high income *one*-earner couples, on the other hand, the income splitting feature still provided by the joint income tax return continues a solid "marriage *bonus*,"—a probably unintended strike for traditional role division and stay-at-home spouses.

It should be emphasized that for the sake of brevity, the simplistic calculations above ignore manifold variations that may be induced by manipulation of special filing status (such as head of household), the *specific* deduction network provided by the Internal Revenue Code and the now *general* "phase-out" of exemptions and itemized deductions for high and higher income taxpayers. Also ignored in the simplified discussion above are (1) complex and potentially very expensive, marriage-based tax consequences for many *low* income *working* couples, due to the sometimes nefarious workings of the "earned income tax credit," and (2) marriage-based higher taxes for social security recipients above a certain income level, in that a single recipient's "tax trigger" is set at $25,000 of income and a married couple's at $32,000. Some may be amused to recall that the 1980s' tax reforms were marketed under the banner of "tax simplification."

The complaint of married persons who are *dis*favored by reason of their marital status has been dealt with summarily:

"The taxpayers feelingly and forcefully assert that the rate schedules of the Internal Revenue Code violate the due process clause of the Fifth Amendment, the free exercise clause of the First Amendment, and the right to associate in marriage protected by the First, Fourth, Fifth, Ninth and Tenth Amendments to the Constitution, in that higher tax rates are imposed on the taxable income of a married person whose spouse has significant income than on the same taxable income of an unmarried person. * * * We agree with the district court that the inequities asserted to inhere in the 'marriage penalty,' whatever may be their persuasiveness as arguments for legislative change, do not rise to the level of constitutional violations of appellants' rights. * * * [I]t has not been demonstrated to us that perfect equality or absolute logical consistency between persons subject to the Internal Revenue Code has been, at least since the adoption of the Sixteenth Amendment, a constitutional *sine qua non* " (*Barter*).

In *Druker*, pending the outcome of the litigation and to be certain to obtain the tax benefit, the couple had obtained a divorce, but had continued to live together. Circuit Judge Friendly, responding to Druker and his ex-wife, flatly rejected the constitutional arguments, refused to allow the Drukers to amend their return to take advantage of the (lower) joint return rates (compared with the rates for a married couple filing separately) and, to boot, imposed a five percent penalty on them.

The troublesome principle has been and remains: Tax law uses marriage, not children, as the "tax-significant" event. Driven originally by state law definitions of community income, "family" tax relief has come indirectly through income splitting by way of the joint return. This approach has always been in conflict with the underlying justification of income taxation—ability to pay. Many modern forms of marriage (especially childless marriage, see §§ 2.5, 6) have no bearing on ability to pay—or, indeed, mere marriage, just like unwed cohabitation, reduces expense through "economy of scale" and *increases* ability to pay.

For years, the marriage tax debate has focused on married dual earners who complain about the marriage penalty, while *unmarried* cohabitants complain about the unavailability to them of the joint return. Both situations raise the reasonable question why, for tax purposes, the *married*, two-earner, equal career partnership established for emotional and sexual satisfaction should not be equated with the *un*married, two-earner, equal career partnership established for exactly the same purpose. Seen from that perspective, both complaints have obvious merit, even if the Internal Revenue Service and the courts do not agree. But the deeper problem is that this has been the wrong question all along.

Properly put, the question should be why our tax law, based as it is on ability to pay, does not make a distinction between (1) the two-earner, equal career partnership, *married or unmarried*, and (2) the wholly or partially role-divided family structure, married or unmarried, with children?

To both the "wrong" and the "right" questions, the appropriate answer seems clear: Married and unmarried "DINKS" (double incomes, no kids) should indeed be treated alike. We should discontinue or at least thoroughly reevaluate the tax preference (or penalty) triggered by the *technicality* of legal marriage. Instead, tax recognition and relief should be focused on the *actuality* of ability to pay as reduced by children, where they *are* (affecting ability to pay), and where they *were* (affecting the "former" caregiving parent's ability to earn in step with her or his childless sibling). That would recognize expenses for child rearing as being on a higher level of social utility than, say, love-boat cruises—and that seems a socially sensible value judgment. In short, Congress should focus tax preferences on dependent children, instead of joint returns triggered by a marriage certificate.

§ 28.9 Conclusion

To emphasize and recapitulate, tax consequences are important, but they are not everything. *Non*-tax considerations include the following: A large, installment-type property settlement from a spouse in a high-risk (of bankruptcy) business may be worth less than a much more modest (but not dischargeable) alimony obligation. (Note, however, that what may seem to be an installment property transfer or a mere contractual obligation may not be dischargeable under the bankruptcy laws). If a divorcing dependent spouse is thinking of early remarriage, or if the payor-spouse is near death, a small, but final and indefeasible, property settlement may be much better than generous alimony that would terminate on either party's death or the recipient's remarriage. Where the ex-spouse is antagonistic and bitter, an alimony judgment, with its threat of jail for contempt, may be preferable to a larger installment property settlement.

While these examples do *not* exhaust the list of nontax considerations, the flattened rate schedules have reduced the incidence of significant differences in marginal rates applicable to the ex-spouses (even the new 36% and 39.6% brackets are historically low, at least in terms of the last half century), and thus have reduced the value of maneuvers that the old, steeply progressive rate schedules (once up to 91%) invited.

Even now opportunities remain to save money on divorce by "playing" the different tax consequences of alimony, property and child support by repackaging them in accordance with the tax laws depending on the specific couple's circumstances. Even now the intelligent lawyer—on both sides—looks at a divorce settlement in *after*-tax terms. At the minimum, *all* tax consequences of a financial settlement on divorce must be fully understood, even if or especially when the financial apportionment between the parties is not optimal between the parties and the IRS. With competent lawyers on both sides, negotiations must play the decisive role. Both lawyers must carefully and precisely assess the client's full situation when deciding what form of economic settlement should be sought. The area continues to offer opportunity for good service and remains a minefield of potential mistakes.

It is noteworthy that some courses of action may not turn out to be mistaken until the tax law is changed again! In working out a longer term settlement, it would seem reasonable even now to contemplate and plan for a possible return to higher and more progressive rates, a reinstitution of capital gains tax treatment, and, if Congressional tax posturing is any guide, radical tax reform by way of a flat tax, or a consumption tax, or an abolition of the deduction for alimony.

Traditionally, many judges were unresponsive or even hostile to counsel who objected to unnecessarily expensive (or urged arrangements producing more favorable) tax consequences of divorce settlements. Appellate courts are now known to reverse cases that fail to consider tax consequences, and many states have *legislated* that tax consequences should or must be considered on divorce.

CHAPTER 29

SEPARATION AGREEMENTS

§ 29.1 Traditional Policies

For the third time we reach the question of the validity of a contract between spouses (Ch. 7). Now we are considering the contract made during marriage that looks to its termination, involves the settlement of the parties' economic affairs and may extend to questions relating to custody, visitation and support of children.

Many traps stood in the way of separation agreements and limited the parties' freedom to contract concerning their own affairs. Traditional law governing separation agreements was the illogical—or too logical—product of the conflict of two policies. The older policy held void as "conducive to divorce" any contract that assured the consequences of divorce (§§ 7.4, 6). The newer policy encourages parties to settle their own affairs without unnecessary recourse to the judiciary. If the older policy were to be taken at face value, a valid separation agreement could not be. Worse, even while such an agreement would be void, traditional fault doctrine might have held the agreement to evidence "collusion" and, if so, the divorce itself would have had to be denied (§ 19.13). To illustrate, if the agreement had one or both parties promising to seek a divorce or not to defend a divorce, it would fail under the "collusion" bar. This was true even if actual grounds for divorce existed and where there were no other defenses or bars to divorce. Fortunately, for quite some time the courts have been willing to close at least one eye. Separation agreements have generally been upheld when separation was about to take place or had already taken place, and the parties did not express their "collusion". Valid agreements had to take pains how they referred to divorce to be insulated from the objection that they encouraged divorce. Thus, an agreement expressly conditioned on a divorce being obtained was in trouble. If the parties had not yet separated and were not about to separate, their agreement concerned *eventual* divorce and might well have been held invalid. Agreements in which either spouse promised to appear in a divorce action brought by the other fell somewhere in between. (In the heyday of "migratory divorce," of course, the promise to appear was of substantial value in view of the "*Sherrer* Rule" (§ 23.2)). Curiously, a husband's express promise to pay the wife's counsel fees was sometimes held to invalidate separation agreements, although such an agreement did no more than what courts would typically order in a divorce action. Long standing exceptions relate to "reconciliation agreements" (§ 7.9).

As late as 1981, the Restatement (Second) of Contracts, § 190, illustrated the difference between invalid and valid separation agreements as follows (*cf.* § 7.4):

"A, who is married to B, promises to pay B $50,000 in return for B's promise to obtain a divorce. The promises of A and B tend unreasonably to encourage divorce and are unenforceable on grounds of public policy. The result does not depend on whether or not there are grounds for divorce or on whether or not B has performed."

"A, who has begun divorce proceedings against B, promises B that if divorce is granted, alimony shall be fixed at a stated sum, in return for B's agreement to relinquish all other claims to alimony. A court *may* decide that in view of the disintegration of the marriage relationship, the promises of A and B do not tend unreasonably to encourage divorce and their enforcement is not precluded on grounds of public policy." (Emphasis added).

§ 29.2   The Consideration Requirement

The question of consideration plagues *any* agreement between spouses during marriage, particularly when the agreement deals with duties imposed by the marital bond (§ 7.8). Such duties extend to one spouse's promise to take custody of the children, another's promise to support the spouse and children, or to the release by a spouse of property rights which he or she may not even have. This made it difficult to find effective consideration that would withstand serious scrutiny. Worse, if the true consideration, the parties' mutual agreement to get a divorce, had been stated expressly, the "collusion" bar would have rendered the agreement void and divorce impossible (§ 19.13). Serious scrutiny on this issue was rare, however, and the consideration requirement found its role primarily in providing courts with a ready device to invalidate separation agreements of which they did not approve. Today, the UPAA renders consideration unnecessary for *pre*marital agreements, including postmarital modifications, in nearly half the states, and UMPA would extend that rule to all postmarital agreements (§ 7.13).

§ 29.3 "Fairness" and Full Disclosure

The circumstances and formalities of execution of the separation agreement are governed by rules similar to those applying to antenuptial agreements. There must at least be full disclosure *or* fair provision for the wife (§ 7.3). Preferably, there should be full disclosure *and* fair provision, because the courts, when dealing with separation agreements have been very intent on satisfying themselves that no undue influence was exercised, or "unconscionable" advantage taken.

§ 29.4 Contract or Proposal?

Under the traditional rules, it was difficult to draft a separation agreement that could not be upset. In practice, most separation agreements are adhered to by both parties and are accepted by the court without question. Even today, however, a very one-sided separation agreement is less a contract than a proposal to the court. Since scrutiny still runs heavily in favor of a dependent wife, a separation agreement resembles an irrevocable offer by the husband to the wife which, if she has changed her mind or sometimes even if she has not, may be accepted or rejected by the court. The Illinois Court of Appeals has held that "reviewing courts not only focus on whether such contracts are free of actual fraud and coercion, but emphasis is also placed on whether they are reasonably fair and sufficient in light of the station in life and circumstances of the parties" (*Crawford*). The Supreme Court of Iowa accepted a wife's argument that she agreed to a settlement under duress and emotional stress induced by *the trial judge,* even though she had had independent counsel and the advice of her brother (*Hitchcock*).

A 1976 illustration of the "double standard" favoring wives, but holding husbands to their deals, involved a $40,000 per year physician who was very eager to marry his paramour. So eager that he "bought" a no-contest divorce from his wife for open-ended monthly alimony of $1,430 out of his first $2,400, plus 50% of any amounts he earned in excess of $2,400, tax free, plus provision for medical expenses and their children's college educations. When the ex-husband woke up in the arms of his new wife, he attacked the agreement as "unconscionable". The South Dakota Supreme Court agreed that the agreement was "harsh", but held that the husband got "exactly what he bargained for" (*Jameson*). Another physician was so depressed about his impending divorce that he refused to obtain counsel and signed everything that his wife's attorney took to him. When he later attacked the settlement, the Michigan Court of Appeals told him that, absent fraud, he could have no relief (*Firnschild*). Even in 1994, an Oregon man who had "sat on his rights" while his wife obtained a default divorce that gave her nearly $750,000 and him only $57,000, was held to the decree. The court would have allowed relief only if there had been misconduct in the procurement of the decree but not where, as here, the unfairness was in the substance of the agreement (*Gilbert*). And when a desperate husband committed suicide (perhaps to invoke the clause calling for support payments to his ex-wife only *until his death*), it took an appellate court to overrule the trial court's holding that his suicide constituted a compensable tort upon his ex-wife (*Wilmington*). In *Tintocalis*, an ex-husband's suicide was held to breach his court-imposed obligation to maintain life insurance in favor of his ex-wife. Other husbands *have* been given relief short of suicide. According to a New York court, where the agreement "literally permitted (the husband) to leave with his debts and the clothes on his back" and imposed very burdensome and long-run support obligations, in circumstances in which the husband thought of the separation as temporary and had had no counsel (and the wife's lawyer represented only her), it "should not be enforced in equity", even though it was not a "classic case of fraud or duress" (*Schauer*). Times are changing: In 1993 in Maine, a *wife* did *not* obtain relief from her divorce judgment, in the absence of concealment or misrepresentation, even though the bar grievance committee had found the property settlement was substantially unequal in the husband's favor, and that the husband's attorney had acted improperly when he represented both spouses (*Kolmosky*).

§ 29.5 Reconciliation

The parties' reconciliation generally terminates a separation agreement. This rule finds modern support in the parties' probable intent and is consistent with the traditional rule that an agreement looking to separation and divorce may not burden an ongoing marriage. It is not always clear, however, just what constitutes a reconciliation or what the parties intended. Executed property transfers will be unaffected and, if such transfers were in lieu of inheritance rights, a stipulation regarding the latter may survive the reconciliation as well. A separation *decree,* of course, is *not* terminated by the parties' reconciliation, but must be dealt with by the court. When a *divorced* couple reconciles and remarries, property rights conferred under the divorce decree remain separate property in the new marriage and are dealt with as such upon a second divorce (*Nordberg*).

§ 29.6 Relationship of Separation Agreement to the Divorce Decree

It is common practice to incorporate separation agreements into divorce decrees, either by reference or by setting forth their terms expressly. The latter, when clothed in mandatory language, gives separation agreements the status and enforceability of judgments. In most jurisdictions, the contract then ceases to exist as a contract (*Pauling*). Among other things, this means that the parties' agreement now may be modified only in accordance with the rules for modifying judgments (or in accordance with its terms, if the court has chosen to adopt the terms of the agreement concerning modifiability). When an agreement is incorporated by reference only, the chief effect is that its *validity* is assured by *res judicata,* but the agreement does not gain the status of a judgment, so that its provisions are not enforceable by an order for specific performance (*Eickhoff*). To facilitate enforcement abroad where a contract may fare better than a judgment, UMDA § 306(e) provides that even if the parties opt for merging their separation agreement into the divorce decree, their contract nevertheless continues to have independent existence alongside the divorce decree.

§ 29.7   Freedom to Contract: The Law of Yesterday and That of Today

While yesterday's law set up the strawmen of consideration, collusion, and "the policy against divorce," it actually *functioned* in most cases to bar agreements that were unfair to the economically weaker party, typically the wife. Is much greater (complete?) autonomy of the marital partners called for? Does the public interest in the *fair* economic settlement of marital affairs remain so great that no agreement should stand solely on the parties' own judgment? So long as, under traditional fault-divorce law, an "innocent" wife could not be divorced against her will, her power to prevent her husband's divorce typically persuaded him to pay to her exactly what freedom to remarry was worth to him (*Jameson*). Now that divorce is freely and unilaterally available, separation agreements can be measured against the clearer definition of the economic consequences of divorce that modern law provides and it may be argued that a court should not interfere with contracts of adults beyond situations in which other contracts may be upset. But a marital agreement is not just another contract, and "overreaching" is not so easily defined (*cf.* § 7.3). To illustrate, a husband who, when signing a separation agreement, was unaware of his wife's adultery which, had he known about it, would have seriously affected her rights, failed to persuade the Virginia Supreme Court that he should be allowed to rescind the agreement (*Barnes*). When a Jewish man refused his wife a religious divorce, unless she waived essentially all property and alimony rights and had *her* father agree to pay child support, a court found "duress" (*Segal*). And an ex-husband—by then in jail for tax offenses—obtained relief from a decree-incorporated property settlement that his ex-wife had obtained by threatening to inform the tax authorities that he had been evading income taxes for 15 years (*Gordon*).

§ 29.8 Separation Agreements Under Uniform Laws

UMDA § 306 provides that a separation agreement is "binding upon the court unless it finds, after considering the economic circumstances of the parties and any other relevant evidence produced by the parties * * * that the separation agreement is unconscionable." One difficulty is that "unconscionable", by and large, still means what a particular judge may think it means—and that may not offer as much predictability as the parties may want or should have. The UMDA's "official comments" refer to *commercial* law definitions of "unconscionable", but that may not be a useful reference in the peculiar circumstance of divorce. Moreover, the UMDA specifically provides that the parties' stipulations providing for child support, custody and visitation are *not* binding on the court. This raises the question whether *non-binding* stipulations regarding child support or custody are compatible with *binding* stipulations regarding the parties, when the agreement may be highly interdependent and concessions in one sector may have been made in response to advantages gained in the other (*cf. Kelley, Sullivan*). It should be noted that stipulations in favor of children that go beyond what the law would impose will generally be enforceable, where appropriate even by the child (*Morelli*).

Neither the U.M.P.A. nor the U.P.A.A. expressly address separation agreements. There seems to be no room for doubt, however, that the terms of both acts are potentially applicable in the context of separation agreements. After all, a separation agreement is one species of post-marital contract, or it may be the final modification of a previous marital or premarital contract. Given the breadth of subject matter both acts permit to be covered and, equally importantly, their provisions guaranteeing marital agreements relative immunity from attack (unless "unconscionable" *when made*), we may expect that both acts will play an important role in the future interpretation of separation agreements (§ 7.13).

§ 29.9 Caveat

Some rules governing separation agreements date back to the days of divorce-for-fault-only and automatic bars to divorce. In a few states, remnants of these antiquated rules continue to stand in the way of the parties' free decision regarding the consequences of the termination of their marriage. This remains so even though most of the old rules, such as the prohibition on "collusion", are rooted in policies that have no logical application in a no-fault context. Some courts still may not act on the reality that the long-standing state policy disfavoring divorce is negated by modern no-fault divorce that is obtainable essentially at the will of one party. On the other hand, long before the general move toward "no-fault", even the fault-only jurisdictions did not apply the old rules to separation agreements so long as they were drafted carefully— if hypocritically. Unless the jurisdiction has enacted, or the courts follow, clear guidelines, the practitioner should continue to watch carefully what he or she is doing and pay what lip service to the past may please a backward court, in the sometimes unfocused light of older and newer decisions.

INDEX

References are to Sections

491

COLLUSION (Divorce), 19.13, 19.14, 24.8, 29.1

COMMON LAW MARRIAGE, 4.3, 6.4

CONCILIATION, 22.6

CONDONATION, 19.11

CONFLICTS OF LAWS
See also specific topics
Alimony, 25.14
Annulment, 23.3
Child custody, 18.20—18.22
Child support, 16.3, 16.4
Comity, 23.2
Foreign divorce, 23.2
Full Faith and Credit, 23.2
    Alimony, 25.14
    Annulment, 23.3
    Custody, 18.21, 18.22
    Divorce, 23.2
    Support, 16.3
Marital agreements, 7.16
Marital property, 8.12, 26.8
Migratory divorce, 23.2
Property on divorce, 26.8
Residence requirements, 23.1
Sister state divorce, 23.2
Void and voidable marriages, 5.6

CONNIVANCE, 19.12

CONSANGUINITY
See also Incest
Marriage impediment, 3.5

CONSENT
Abortion, 9.5, 14.10
Adoptions, 11.17, 12.6—12.8
Divorce, 19.13, 19.14
Marriage, 4.1

CONSORTIUM, LOSS OF, 9.3

CONSTITUTIONAL LAW, 1.4, ch. 2
See also specific topics

†